Historical and International Comparison of Business Interest Associations

(19th-20th Centuries)

P.I.E. Peter Lang

Bruxelles · Bern · Berlin · Frankfurt am Main · New York · Oxford · Wien

Danièle FRABOULET, Andrea M. LOCATELLI
& Paolo TEDESCHI (eds.)

Historical and International Comparison of Business Interest Associations

(19th-20th Centuries)

« Enjeux internationaux »
n° 29

This book was funded by Università Cattolica del Sacro Cuore (research action D.3.1. 2012) among its programs of promotion and diffusion of scientific research.

The book was subject to a double blind refereeing process.

1 avenue Maurice, B-1050 Brussels, Belgium
www.peterlang.com; info@peterlang.com

Printed in Germany

ISSN 2030-3688
ISBN 978-2-87574-079-3

D/2013/5678/99

CIP available from the Library of Congress, USA, and the British Library, GB.

"Die Deutsche Nationalbibliothek" lists this publication in the "Deutsche Nationalbibliografie"; detailed bibliographic data is available on the Internet at <http://dnb.de>.

Contents

Preface

The role of social and economic organisations in contemporary society has been a fundamental issue in the studies promoted by the "Archivio per la storia del movimento sociale cattolico in Italia" since its establishment in 1961. During much the same period, the economic historians of the Department of Economic History, Society and Local Sciences "Mario Romani" at the Catholic University of Milan, focused their research on the development of organisations operating in the social and economic system.

Mario Romani was a professor of economic history at the Catholic University of Milan and his scientific studies are the cultural references for the work presented here. From the middle of the twentieth century, rather than following the dominant cultural ideologies concerning the Italian economic and social system, Romani in fact criticised the traditional interpretation of Italian economic development in the nineteenth and twentieth centuries. While the mainstream theories of Italian economic development, namely the neoclassical and the Marxist interpretations, were centered on the role of the state, Romani proposed a new theory based on the relationship between social structures and economic factors. So, the analysis of social and economic structures became the key to exploring and defining the relationships between forces in the market economy.

For this purpose, Romani identified some relevant research conditions: the existence of a relevant interdependence between the social and the economic factors concerned; the need to consider the social and economic system as a whole; the large amount of time and effort that the researchers have to spend analyzing direct sources which provide endless opportunities for historical studies. These research conditions represented a real legacy for all researchers inspired by Romani's studies and thought.

Furthermore, Romani suggested that social modernisation and social economic processes should be studied in league rather than being considered as mutually exclusive. He emphasised the need to make international and interdisciplinary comparisons. These techniques were realised through a collaboration between the Institute of Economic History and the Giulio Pastore Foundation in Rome (founded by Romani himself in 1971).

For over half a century, the researchers whose work has been inspired by Romani's studies and thought have analyzed the rules and behaviour in the economic system of collective subjects, in particular cooperatives, friendly societies and workers' trade unions. In more recent years, a new generation of researchers has started to analyze the experiences of the business associations: since 2011, in particular, Andrea M. Locatelli and Paolo Tedeschi have been working on the research project entitled "The Business Associations in Lombardy: Aims, Organisation, Strategies (19th-20th Centuries)" and involving researchers from the Catholic University of Milan and University of Milan-Bicocca DEMS.

All members of the Department "Mario Romani" and of the "Archivio per la storia del movimento sociale cattolico in Italia" hope that the significant heritage of the ideas collected in this volume will be further developed by Locatelli and Tedeschi (in particular in a volume concerning the Italian business associations). This obviously implies that they will be supported in their future research on the history of business associations and, moreover, that they will continue their collaboration with relevant colleagues such as Danièle Fraboulet and all the contributors of this volume.

Aldo Carera

INTRODUCTION

Historical and International Comparison of Business Interest Associations (19th-20th Centuries)

The papers published in this volume were presented at the session number 168 of the 16th World Economic History Congress (WEHC) which was held in July 2012 in Stellenbosch (South Africa). It was dedicated to the "Historical and international comparison of Business Interest Associations (19th-20th centuries)"[1]. It was also part of a five-year, large-scale research project on Business Interest Associations (hereafter BIAs) started in 2009 by French academics and supporting institutions[2]. The project involved historians from around Europe forming a dedicated scientific committee and collaborating on research of international and interdisciplinary significance. Developments concerning BIAs had previously been examined by political scientists and sociologists in isolation, and therefore did not present satisfactory historical and cross-border perspectives. It was utterly appropriate, then, that historians and social scientists conducted a mutually beneficial comparative inquiry into the history of BIAs in Europe.

At the time of writing, the project continues apace. Its goal remains the provision of comprehensive studies of BIAs as major components of the European social model and the democratic State in the nineteenth and twentieth centuries. The program is designed to clarify and elucidate, through historical approaches, the strategies adopted by unions, professional societies, chambers of commerce, trade organisations, clubs, and a variety of miscellaneous groups in their efforts to promote and defend business interests. It investigates the genesis of the BIAs, the historical context of their creation, their functions and the geographical scope of their activities (local, regional or national). It attempts to build

1 The session in Stellenbosch was organised by Danièle Fraboulet (University of Paris 13 - Sorbonne Paris Cité) in collaboration with Cédric Humair (University of Lausanne) and Pierre Vernus (University Lumière Lyon 2), chairmen of two thematic roundtables. Cédric Humair and Pierre Vernus also collaborated at the drawning up of this introduction.

2 The large scale research project is a Danièle Fraboulet's initiative and is financed by the following universities: Paris 13 - Sorbonne Paris Cité (Centre de recherche Espaces, Sociétés, Culture EA 2356), Paris 1 - Panthéon Sorbonne (Institutions et dynamiques historiques de l'économie, UMR 8533) and Lumière Lyon 2 (Laboratoire de recherches historiques de Rhône-Alpes).

a sociological profile of the members of the BIAs, and to chart the economic sectors in which their presence was most pronounced. This allows for an analysis of how evolving social, political and cultural contexts influenced the way business associations operated. A comparative chronological and geographic perspective has been adopted so as to reinvigorate the study of an area which hitherto received only piecemeal and inconsistent attention from scholars and lawyers and social scientists[3].

In order to facilitate this major undertaking, three international symposiums were held in Paris in June of each of 2010, 2011 and 2012; another one has just been held in Lyon in June 2013 and a further, and final, symposium will be organised for June 2014[4]. The proceedings of

---

3 See for instance, among others publications: Berger, S., *Organizing interests in Western Europe: pluralism, corporatism, and the transformation of politics*, Cambridge, CUP, 1981; Windmuller, J.P., Gladstone, A., *Employers associations and industrial relations: a comparative study*, Oxford, OUP, 1986; Lynn, L.H., McKeown, T.J., *Organizing Business. Trade Associations in America and Japan*, Washington, American Enterprise Institute for Public Policy Research, 1987; Ullmann, H.P., *Interessenverbände in Deutschland*, Frankfurt am Main Suhrkamp, 1988; Yamazaki, H., Miyamoto, M. (eds.), *Trade Associations in Business History*, Tokyo, Tokyo University Press, 1988; Lanzalaco, L., *Dall'impresa all'associazione: le organizzazioni degli imprenditori: la Confindustria in prospettiva comparata*, Milan, Angeli, 1990; Tolliday, S., Zeitlin, J. (eds.), *The Power to manage? Employers and industrial relations in comparative historical perspective*, London, Routledge, 1991; Schmitter, P.C., Streek, W., *The Organisation of Business Interest: studying the Associative Action of Business in Advanced Industrial Societies*, Max-Planck-Institut für Gesellschaftsforschung Discussion Papers, n. 1, Köln, Max-Planch-Institut, 1999; Garrigues, J., *Les patrons et la politique. De Schneider à Seillière*, Paris, Perrin, 2002; Vernus, P. (ed.), *Les organisations. Une approche locale (XIXe-XXe siècles)*, Lyon, Institut des sciences de l'homme, 2002; Lemercier, C., *Un si discret pouvoir. Aux origines de la chambre de commerce de Paris (1803-1853)*, Paris, La Découverte, 2003; Streeck, W., Grote, J., Schneider, V., Visser, J. (eds.), *Governing Interests: Business Associations Facing Internationalization*, Routledge, London/New York, 2006; Fraboulet, D., *Quand les patrons s'organisent. Stratégies et pratiques de l'Union des industries métallurgiques et minières 1901-1950*, Villeneuve-d'Asq, Presses du Septentrion, 2007; Offerlé, M., *Sociologie des organisations patronales*, Paris, La Découverte, 2009.

4 The first symposium concerned "Business organisations in Europe: meanings, translation, historiography and archives" and its aim was to clarify the scope of the project, establishing the state of the art and archival resources available in several countries: it laid the ground work for further research collaboration between historians and social scientists. The second symposium was about the "Genesis, Structures and Temporalities of European Business Organisations". Participants looked into the strategies adopted by BIAs for promoting and defending business interests. They discussed the historical context of the origins of BIAs, and tried to understand whether these organisations had been driven and/or curbed by ideological, social, political, or judicial actions. They also adopted a comparative perspective covering both time and space and analyzing failures as well as successes. The third symposium explored the "Ways and Means of the Trade and Business

the symposiums of 2011 and 2012 were published in French language: proceedings will be also published for symposiums of 2013 and 2014[5].

Given the particular context of session n. 168 of the WEHC and the need for the widest possible diffusion of the findings of the research project, an English edition was desirable. The session aimed to further extend the span of the comparative approach (which has been expanding since the first workshop of 2010) and to enlarge the network of the researchers involved in the program. Thus, a Swedish, two Dutch and two Russian colleagues joined some of the previous program's participants from France, Italy, Switzerland and the United Kingdom. It is evident that this expansion required an English edition with a relevant international publisher. So, two participants at the session 168 took on the task of preparing the proceedings for publication: the volume was financially supported by their respective institutions[6].

Organisations in the Public Sphere". Researchers analyzed business organisations as constrained by political, economic and institutional surroundings and how those conditions evolved over time and across space through the dynamics of competition, collaboration, and the working relationships between BIAs and public administrations, parliament houses, governmental institutions, judiciary systems, etc. The following issues were discussed: scales of policy interventions by BIAs (local, regional, national, European); ways and means of adapting business models (family and kinship, school and social networks, lobbying, financial support and funding, active groups, hiring experts and specialists, reports and documentation, expenditures and budget, etc.); and the capacity of business organizations for adaptation in response to the ebb and flow of economics and politics. The fourth symposium challenged the "Appraisal of the Relationships between Business Associations and other organizations". Participants tried to explain how BIAs established, developed, fostered and maintained different types of relationships with other organisations (domination, collaboration, competition, dispute etc.). They studied relationships built over time by the BIAs themselves with other Business and Trade Organisations or Chambers of Commerce, Employers' Organisations, Clubs and Think Tanks, Workers' Organisations, and Political Parties. They also focused on themes revolving around the exact nature of the relationships between BIAs and other kinds of organisations, the forms and manifestations of these relationships (financing, collective bargaining, collaborative, friendship and personnel relationships, and wider social networks).

5 See Fraboulet, D., Vernus, P. (eds.), *Genèse et morphologies originelles des organisations patronales en Europe (XIXe-XXe siècles)*, Rennes, PUR, 2012; Fraboulet, D., Druelle-Korn, C., Vernus, P. (eds.), *Les organisations patronales et la sphère publique. Europe XIXe et XXe siècles*, Rennes, PUR, 2013. The proceedings of the symposium in Lyon will be prepared by the same editors and published within the Spring 2014. Finally, the symposium of 2014 will deal with "Business Associations and Market Regulation" and will conclude the five-year research project.

6 Andrea M. Locatelli (Catholic University of Milan) and Paolo Tedeschi (University of Milan-Bicocca DEMS) edited the proceedings. The support of their universities was fundamental for the publication of this volume.

The following themes and questions were considered during the session in Stellenbosch and the contributions of this book try to give readers some answers and explanations:

a) "Roots, early stages and specific framework underlying BIAs". Why were BIAs founded? In what historical and legal context, for what reasons, and where (ie. were they local or nationwide)? Why did they survive or why did they fail to survive?

b) "BIAs at work". How were they managed? By elective leaders or by paid officials? What were their functions? What services did they offer to their members? What were the relations of these organisations with the members of the unions? How did the business organisations interact with each other?

c) "Finances". What were their sources of income and how much did they collect from their members and from other sources of assets? How did they use this money?

d) "Membership and representativeness". How many members joined the business associations? Was there a connection between the representativeness of these organisations and the number of affiliates? What were the dominant features of this representativeness? What was the sociological background of their members?

e) "Strategies". What strategies have been adopted for the promotion and defense of business interest? How did BIAs modify their strategies to adapt to changing political, social, economic and legal contexts? How did they contribute to the building of sectoral or overall identities? In which fields of the economy were they best organised?

In Stellenbosch two thematic roundtables were organised: this partition serves to structure this book too. The first roundtable dealt with "The Origins and Functions of BIAs" at regional and national levels. The period covered was the second of the four phases defined by Lanzalaco in his article on the evolution of BIAs[7], that is the "Diffusion and Integration Phase" which covered much of the nineteenth century and up to the First World War in some European countries and regions (Russia, Switzerland, France and Lombardy, the most relevant industrial region in Italy). According to Lanzalaco, this phase was bounded by the appearance of the first local associations on the one hand and the founding of the first national peak associations on the other.

An analysis of this period is extremely complex, since it has to incorporate both the decline of the old system of merchants and craft guilds, which was sometimes sudden and sometimes gradual, and the

[7] See Lanzalaco, L., "Business Interest Associations", in G. Jones, J. Zeitlin (eds.), *The Oxford Handbook of Business History*, Oxford, OUP, 2008, pp. 293-315.

emergence of a new system of economic organisation and representation. The rise of this new system was based on two relatively different features, one of which was the official system of representation, the best known form of which was the Chamber of Commerce in France, and the private associations independent of political power, the nature of which is still largely unexplored. A comparative analysis of the five contributions published, however, enables us to propose three fields of reflection.

Firstly, a more precise definition of the concept of BIAs should be set. Indeed, the incredible diversity of the associations taken into account in the papers poses the question of the criteria that permit the field of analysis to be delimited. Is any organisation involved in one way or another in the smooth running of the economy of a BIA? For example, can a scientific society intended to facilitate technology transfer be considered a BIA, even if its members are not predominantly employers, but scientists, technicians and prominent figures? In the case discussed by Kerov, can a religious community whose members develop ways of coordinating their economic activity be considered a BIA?

The second set of issues is about the chronologies of the process of organising the economy. On the basis of the five contributions, it is very difficult to carry out a comparative analysis on local and regional BIAs. However, it seems possible to compare the formative period of the different types of national-scale BIAs. We observe that in the countries being analysed the creation and densification of stable national associations took place in the period between 1865 and 1890. However, this common chronology did not lead to a simultaneous appearance of the first national peak associations. On the contrary, the creation of the latter was spaced between 1870 (in Switzerland) and 1919 (in France).

The third field consists of explanations of these chronological evolutions. Concerning the concurrence of the transition to national scale organisation, two main factors are stressed in several contributions. The first is the important role played by tariff and trade agreements policies in a context of economic crisis and rising protectionism in Europe. The second is the growth of state economic interventionism, which was not restricted to trade policy, compelling businessmen to organise themselves in order to provide an effective response in defense of their own interests. As far as the time lags between the appearance of the first national peak associations are concerned, two more issues require further exploration. What influence did the laws on associations have on the emergence of BIAs and peak associations in particular? What role was played by the presence or absence of an official system of representation of the economy similar to the French Chambers of Commerce?

The second roundtable dealt with "The Business Interest Associations in Europe during the Twentieth Century: Some Case Studies". The contributions presented during that session pondered the last three periods defined by Luca Lanzalaco, that is to say the diffusion and integration phase of the nineteenth century, the phase of penetration, centralisation and consolidation from the beginning of the twentieth century to the end of the First World War, and lastly the transitional phase since the end of the Second World War, characterised by a process of trans-nationalisation, especially in Europe. Papers focused on some national cases: the Netherlands, France, United Kingdom and Sweden. Furthermore, most of the contributions were at least partly concerned with peak associations as the Union des Industries Métallurgiques et Minières, the Federation of British Industries, the Employers Organisations, the Swedish Employers' Association (and, to a lesser extend, the Federation of Swedish industry and the Eurofederations) which seem to be peak associations or branch of peak associations.

Bouwens and Dankers' contribution was the only one that offered a more comprehensive account of the Dutch BIAs. Thus, local and regional BIAs still require further investigation. Only Neil Rollings encompassed a wider space and paid attention to a higher level, the European one. He focused on the relations between Eurofederations and European Integration and he showed how essential it is to be critical when setting up a statistical population and how this can lead to new conclusions. By criticizing the CONNECTS database and by elaborating a new dataset he challenged the old ideas that associational development of Euro-federations reacted or followed European political integration.

Of the numerous issues raised by the contributors to the second roundtable, only some will be highlighted here. One that immediately echoes the first roundtable deals with the elaboration of a statistical population of BIAs and consequently the definition of such associations. Bouwens and Dankers have defined a BIA as an "organisation of employers or companies working for the common interests of its members" that can fulfil five functions whose combination and importance change over time according to the economic, politic or social context. The paper also raises the question of the role of BIAs in defining the employers' interests. Schmitter and Streeck highlighted the diversity of interests among capitalists[8]: consequently, if we postulate that capitalists' interests are social constructions and, moreover, as shown by

8 See Schmitter, P.C., Streeck, W., *The organization of business interests. A research design to study the associative action of business in the advanced industrial societies of Western Europe*, in *IIM Discussion Papers IIM/LMP*, n. 31, Berlin, Wissenschaftszentrum, 1981.

Ollerenshaw or Stenlås, given that the usual distinction between trade and employers' association is sometimes fuzzy and results from negotiations among peak associations and between peak and regional or sectoral associations, we must reassess our understanding of how business interests are elaborated and by whom. We should also reevaluate how the distribution of functions among associations evolved over time.

These considerations involve questioning existing national models. Indeed, in the long run, these models seem only transitional configurations of more or less lasting equilibriums. It appears that some of the characteristics of the equilibrium developed after the Second World War were already emerging during the interwar period. Although the contributions favour national cases, it may be somewhat surprising that they pay little attention to the national legal systems describing the legal form of BIAs, proscribing the range of functions they are allowed to perform and, finally, influencing the way they act within each national space.

Lastly, another crucial issue raised by the authors needs further exploration: how to estimate or at least to guess the impact of the activity of BIAs, whether local, regional or national peak associations.

All the authors involved in the book would like to thank the personnel working in the archives and libraries visited, who have kindly assisted in the provision of the material and documents cited in the text. They are also deeply grateful to Michel Dumoulin (UCL, Louvain-la-Neuve) for publishing the book in the "Enjeux Internationaux" collection and obviously to the Catholic University of Milan and the University of Milan-Bicocca which supported the publication of this book. Finally, the editors and authors wish to thank the anonymous referees for their advice and suggestions, and Ilaria Suffia (University of Milan-Bicocca DEMS) and John O' Callaghan (University of Limerick) for their precious help concerning the editing of the volume.

Danièle Fraboulet

Old Believers' Communities of the Nineteenth Century as the First Business Interest Associations in Russia (1861-1914)

Valeriy KEROV

Peoples' Friendship University of Russia - Moscow

Introduction

It is considered that the active process of foundation of Business Interest Associations (hereafter BIAs) in European countries began in the last decade of the nineteenth century and the first decades of the twentieth century. According to the existing research, the creation of BIAs in significant numbers resulted from the reaction of businessmen to state pressure, the demands of free capitalism and the first workers' organisations. Facing common difficulties, entrepreneurs banded together to compensate for theit shortcomings[1].

The Russian situation was different, however. Merchants' self-management bodies in cities were class organs reduced to philanthropy and class economy. Manufactory and Commercial Councils were no more than state institutions drawing on poor entrepreneurs' assistance. Councils' private members were very respectable but deprived of any influence on state economic policy. Any social organisations were prohibited until the First Russian Revolution of 1905-1907. Without the possibility of consolidation or real corporatism, Russian entrepreneurs were unable to resolve their problems in the face of powerful traditional individual corruption. However, BIAs emerged and became highly effective. They carried out the specific functions defined by the religious character of the links between their members. The focus here is on Old Believers' communities.

---

1 See for example: Bouwens, B., Dankers, J. "Business interest associations: a service to the industry" in *Het Bedrijfsleven in Nederland in de twintigste eeuw (BINT). 2004. Sent.* (URL: http://www.bintproject.nl/textfiles/2004_bouwens-dankers.pdf).

1. The origin of the Old Believers' confessional BIAs

First of all, the confessional ethic and institutional factors played their part. Developing the ideas of seventeenth-century Eastern theology and interpreting anew the traditional Christian texts in the new sociopolitical and socioeconomic environment, the Old Believers created new confessional values and secured the emergence of a special type of religiosity. Ideas of the moral value of a man, of confessional and social activism, of personal responsibility, of religious Methodism, of a new work ethic, a new attitude to property and a perception of business as a worthy, "gracious" work for God, promoted the transformation of Old Believers' communities from purely confessional to confessional-economic ones and turned Old Believers into leaders in a number of branches of the economy in the first half of the nineteenth century[2].

In addition, there were other contributing factors such as the corporatism, solidarity and resistance of Old Believers' communities in the face of their repression by the authorities. The Old Believers' confessional-economic communities became the first BIA in Russia.

The Old Believers' BIA had peculiar features:

a) every association was composed of numerous local communities of the same Old Belief denomination;

b) in the first half of the nineteenth century there existed four enormous associations (with thousands of members) and two or three dozen which really coincided with Old Belief denominations (*soglasiye*);

c) it was a voluntary association as a religious community;

d) all three sectors of entrepreneurs, managers and workers formed this mixed association;

e) members of the association acted in industry and trade but also in agriculture;

f) operating securities and organising credit, they actively were engaged in financing themselves.

2. The functions of the Old Believers' BIA

In the specific form of increased personal activity and personal liability implication, the religious community remained an intermediary between God and man in the economic process. This idea was based on the traditional Orthodox Church teaching, of which the community was

2 See Kerov, V.V., *"Se chelovek I delo yego…": Konfessionalno-eticheskiye factori staroobriadcheskogo predprinimatelstva v Rossii* [*"Behold the Man and His Cause…" Confessional Ethic Factors of Old Believers` Entrepreneurship in Russia*], Moscow, Econ-Inform, 2004.

a prototype. During the first half of the nineteenth century the Old Belief community was the centerpiece of the corporation.

Being responsible for the main internal economic function of the community, the association coordinated and ensured its economic activities and specific business mechanisms. In this context, specific strategies were adopted to pursue commercial interests and increase profit. The confessional economic community – the community of the brothers in faith – provided economic solidarity to the denomination's members and this was a major factor and condition for the functioning of its entrepreneurial networks. The Old Believers "helped each other in every way, jointly conducting their trade and manufacturing affairs and supporting the members of their corporation. They would easily accept to their community, closed for even a wealthy stranger, any poor person who was" part of their denomination (the soglasiye)[3].

Opponents always noted the absolute solidarity of the Old Believer entrepreneurs. The head of one police mission complained that Old Believers were united "by code of silence, they help each other and defend each other [...] A merchant-Schismatic would always prefer a person of his own faith to a follower of the Russian Orthodox Church, and offer a better credit. He therefore would rarely be unsuccessful in his trade". Deputy Interior Minister Ivan Liprandy, after he reviewed all of the reports about Old Belief, did not doubt that the prosperity of Old Belief "merchants and industrialists [...] is far greater than that of the Orthodox merchants [followers of the Synodic Church] who often go bankrupt, while that never happens to the Old Believers since in difficult situations they do not let a follower of their faith down and undoubtedly support him"[4]. As evidenced by contemporaries, mutual assistance by the Old Believers who were running factories and mer-

---

3 See Melnikov, P.I., "Ocherki popovchini [Studies in Popovtsi` denomination]", in *Id.*, *Sochinenia* [*Works*], St Petersburg, Moscow, Wolf, 1989, vol. 13, p. 327.

4 See *Ibid.*, pp. 132, 327; "O chernigovskikh raskolnikakh. Polojenie raskolnikov s 1840 po 1846 god" [About Chernigov Dissenters. Position of Dissenters from 1840 to 1846], in *Sbornik prsvitelstvennikh svedeniy o raskolnikakh* [*Collection of Governmental Data on Dissenters*], London, Trübner & Co, 1861, issue 2, p. 33; Stenbok, [Y.I.], "Kratkiy vzgliad na prichini rasprostraneniya raskola. Iz zapiski o strannikakh" [Short View of the Reasons of Fast Distribution of Schism. From a Note about Wanderers], in *Ibid.*, 1862, issue 4, pp. 329, 332; Liprandi, [I.P.], "Kratkoye obozreniye sushestvuyuchikh v Rossii raskolov, yeresey I sekt, kak v religioznom, tak i v politicheskom znachenii; s nekotorimi po semu predmetu zamechaniyami" [Short Review of Splits, Heresies and Sects existing in Russia, both in Religious, and in their Political Value; with some Notes in this Subject], in *Ibid.*, 1862, issue 4, pp. 114, 156.

chants helped them "sell their products profitably as compared" to the followers of the official faith[5].

As again witnessed by contemporaries, the entire industrial branches, for example, of textile production in the Central Region surrounding Moscow was organised as a common network where businesses of the Old Believers had differentiation in their functions. Some of them purchased raw materials, others processed them, and still others engaged in retail and wholesale trade. All of the components of this network were under the control of the Old Believer merchants of the same soglasiye[6]. Coordination in supply of raw materials, manufacturing and sales was practiced in other industries as well.

The association, in other words the denominational community, also functioned as a marketing center. The confessional ties of Old Believers allowed the carrying out of marketing research unavailable to the officially Orthodox majority. "For example, for Moscow corn chandlers it was essential to have reliable agents to perform favourable grain purchases in fertile provinces. So, they got ones in Tula, Orel, Voronezh, Tambov, Penza, Simbirsk and Saratov provinces from among the local Old Belief communities". With the help of the adherents, corn chandlers "were constantly and accurately updated on grain prices and grain growing, potential output yields, landowner reserves and other". The same was true in the fish, livestock and food trades. The network of agents worked all over the country to gather information on the catch, unloading vessels, local prices and the business climate in general[7].

The creation and maintenance of an internal credit system was another important economic function of a community when the enterprise credit in Russia was practically non-existent. The arrangements allowed a long-term and low-interest (or even interest-free) unsecured loan which could be extended by the leaders of a community or on their recommendation. The Preobrazhenskaya community had special rules for delaying repayment deadlines in case loans could not be repaid on time, "twice for a year and then for a half-year". After that, a loan could

---

5 See Brianchaninov, [P.A.], Arnoldi [L.I.], "O raskole v Kostromskoy gubernii (Kratkaya zapiska o sosotoyanii raskola i nastoyachem chissel raskolnikov v Kostromskoy gubernii)" [About Split in the Kostroma Province (A Short Note about a Condition of Split and the Real Number of Dissenters in the Kostroma Province)], in *Ibid.* 1862, issue 4, pp. 311–312.

6 See Raskov, D.E., "Novie svedeniya o moskovskikh staroobriadtsakh-predprinimateliakh" [New data on the Moscow Old Believers businessmen], in *Staroobriadchestvo: istoriya, kultura, sovremennost. Materiali* [*Old Belief: History, Culture, Present. Materials*], Moscow, Muzey istorii y kulturi staroobriadchestva, 2002, pp. 88-89.

7 See Melnikov, P.I., *Ocherki popovchini, op. cit.*, vol. 13, pp. 334–335.

be written off. An Old Believer businessman "was a kind of an agent of the community in charge of effective use and augmentation of its capitals"[8]. In Rogozhskaya community, loans extended to community members were either interest-free or carried minor interest rates of some 4 per cent per annum in the first third of the nineteenth century[9].

Given the confessional purposes of the loans, they were interest-free or at times non-refundable and were not granted to only big businessmen. The Preobrazhenskaya community (as was the case with the Rogozhskaya comunity) "since its very establishment never declined to extend" a loan. As a contemporary describing the overall situation in Moscow's Fedoseevtsi community noted, for the members of the soglasiye "the treasure box [...] was always open"[10]. Old Believers newly arrived to reside in Moscow, lived in community houses formally registered under the name of one of the trustees. Later on, those who were willing could obtain interest-free community loans for purchasing the "means for independent living", i.e. for launching their own business[11].

Even the very first researchers of the Old Belief noted that many of the "main Moscow capitalists got the capitals which became the foundation of their growing wealth, from the funds of the dissenting communi-

---

8 See Startsev, A.V., "Khoziaystvennaya etika staroobriyadchestva"[Economic ethics of Old Believers], in *Staroobriadchestvo: istoriya i kultura* [*Old Belief: History and Culture*], Barnaul, Barnaul State Pedagogical University Publ., 2002, issue 1, p. 78.

9 See Cм. Barsukov, V.L., "Piotr III I predprinimatelstvo v Rossii" [Peter III and Entrepreneurship in Russia], in *Sibir в XVI–XX vekakh. Economica, obchestvenno-politicheskaya jizn I kultura* [*Siberia in Sixteenth – Twentieth Centuries. Economy, Social Political Life and Culture*], Novosibirsk, Siberian Branch of the Russian Academy of Sciences, 1997, p. 81. For comparison: even later, in the 1830-40s public banks in Russia gave out loans on the basis of little security at a rate of 6 per cent, and more often at an annual rate of 8-10 per cent. See Morozan, V.V., *Istoriya bankovskogo dela v Rossii* [*Banking History in Russia*], St Petersburg, St Petersburg State University, 2001, pp. 147–149).

10 See "Fedosseevtsy. Istoriya Preobrazhenskogo kladbisha" [Fedosseevtsy. History of Preobrazhenskoye Cemetery], in *Sbornik prsvitelstvennikh, op. cit.*, issue 1, p. 40.

11 See *Dnevnie dozornie zapissi o moskovskikh raskolonikakh. Soobsheno A.A. Titovim* [*Day Patrol Records about the Moscow Dissenters, reported by A.A. Titov*], Moscow, ChOIDR [Readings of Society of Ancient Russia History] at Moscow University, 1885, p. 101; Rustik, O., "Staroobryadcheskoye Preobrazhenskoye kladbiche (kak nakoplialis kapitali v Moskve)" [Old Believe Preobrazhenskoye Cemetery (as the Capitals in Moscow collected)], in *Borba klassov* [*Fight of classes*], 1934, n. 7-8, p. 70; Raskov, D.E., *Novie svedeniya, op. cit.*, p. 89. Illegal enterprises functioned along with the officially registered. See Stadnikov, A.V., *Moskovskoye staroobryadchestvo i gosudarstvennaya konfessionalnaya politika* [*Moscow Old Believers and State Confessional Policy of Nineteenth - early Twentieth Centuries*], Moscow, Mosgorarkhiv, 2002, pp. 100-102.

ties"[12]. Community loans helped advancement of many minor entrepreneurs as well as the well known merchant houses of Zenkov, Shelaputins and Grachev in Moscow, Kastsov in St Petersburg, Mokhovs and thousands of other business people in other Russian towns. Some Old Belivers started small businesses while others such as the trustees of Preobrazhenskoye cemetery, Alexei Nikiforov[13] and Nosov (who got 500,000 rubles for three years with no interest and with 4 per cent interest per annum for the subsequent years[14]) started by launching rather sizeable factories financed from the community funds which were not really repaid since they became the investment base of the soglasiye. Papulin, a merchant from Sudislavl and a trustee of the Fedoseevtsy community in Kostroma, according to the information of the authorities, was granted 80,000 rubles which were invested in trade and generated serious wealth[15].

Once an entrepreneur developed his business and the company started to actively operate, a credit line did not disappear. Those observing the situation in Vyatka province, where the Old Belief was widespread, noted that the association did not merely maintain orphans, ill and lonely people but also supported merchants "in case of entrepreneurial risks"[16]. A prominent researcher of the mid-nineteenth century, Shchapov, wrote that "almost everywhere in Russia" the Old Believers have better living standards and are more successful in business in case "community loans are well developed"[17].

12 See Andreev, V.V., *Raskol i yego znacheniye v Russkoy istorii* [*Split and its Value in a National Russian History*], St Petersburg, M. Khan, 1870. C. 163.

13 See *Fedosseevtsi. Istoriya, op. cit.*, p. 40.

14 See Rustik, O., *Staroobryadcheskoye Preobrazhenskoye*, *op. cit.*, p. 76.

15 See Pivovarova, N.A. "Ob odnom episode iz istorii 'borbi s raskolom' v seredine XIX veka: Sudislavlskiye molennie N.A. Papulina i ikh sudba po dokumentam Rossiyskogo gosudarstvennogo istoricheskogk arkhiva" [About one Episode from History of "the Fight against Split" in the Mid-Nineteenth Century: Sudislavl Worship Houses of N.A. Papulin and their Destiny according to Documents of the Russian State Historical Archive], in *Staroobriadchestvo v Rossii (XVII–XX veka)* [*Old Believers in Russia (Seventeenth – Twentieth Centuries)*], Moscow, Yaziki Slavianskoy Kulturi, 2004, issue 3, p. 359.

16 See Trushkova, I.Y., "Sistema prirodopolzovaniya y organizatsiya truda u staroobriadtsev Viatskogo kraya" [System of Environmental Management and the Work Organization at Old Believers of Vyatka Edge], in *Staroobriadchestvo: istoriya, kultura, sovremennost. Materiali* [*Old Belief: History, Culture, Present. Materials*], Moscow, Muzey istorii y kulturi staroobriadchestva, 2000, p. 483; *Id.*, "Staroobriadchestvo kak pozdnesrednevekovoye pravoslavie (etnokulturniy aspect [Old Belief as Late Medieval Orthodoxy (Ethnoculturological Aspect)]", in *Ibid.*, 2002, p. 442.

17 See Shiapov, A.P., *Russkiy raskol staroobriadchestva, rassmatrivaemiy v sviazy s vnutrennim sostoyaniem russkoy tserkvi I grajdanstvennosti v XVII veke I v pervoy*

Loans were not only granted via a community led by its trustees. The Old Believers who were in the process of starting a business or launching a new enterprise and/or were not yet especially successful, could obtain directky from their more successful fellows (and often former employers) a share of their profit as a form of financial assistance. As Liprandy noted, "the Old Believers hire employees, clerks [...] and assist them with setting up their own factories by supplying the raw materials they need, at the lowest prices and allowing installment plans"[18]. That helped the new entrepreneurs "to make profit, get wealthier and become manufacturers and millionaires"[19].

It was not about any altruism. In fact, it was seen as the best way to reproduce the economic foundations of the Old Belief. In line with the ideas of the Old Believers about property, such loans were treated not as assistance but as reinvestments. As a result, even though in the late eighteenth and early nineteenth centuries the Old Believer entrepreneurs who were not part of well established merchant families usually lacked accumulated resources (tax benefits, inheritance, etc.)[20], their businesses rapidly sprang around Old Believer communities.

Without such private and community loans and contributions, the major business associations of the Old Believers would not have emerged. An example is the Fedoseevtsy Preobrazhenskaya association which in the 1820s through 1840s combined over 3,000 enterprises, including thirty two large and 120 small cotton factories[21]. It is necessary to rank as an Association of the denomination the numerous enterprises of partners of Muscovites naionwide, in Kaluga, Kazan, Astrakhan, Arkhangelsk, etc., which were also parts of the denomination's loan mechanism.

An intra-communal lending and paper circulation system was also successfully implemented. Old Believers did not have to transport cash to distant areas since in the major denominations of the Old Believers their own mechanisms of notes were in place.

---

polovine XIX [*The Russian Split of Old Belivers considered in Connection with Internal State of the Russian Church and Civic Consciousness in the Seventeenth Century and in the First Half of the Nineteenth Century*], Kazan, Ivan Dubrovin, 1859, p. 292.

18 See Liprandi, [I.P.] "Kratkoye obozreniye", *op. cit.*, p. 114; see also *Fedosseevtsi. Istoriya*, *op. cit.*, p. 18.

19 See Melnikov, P.I., *Ocherki popovchini*, *op. cit.*, vol. 13, p. 328.

20 See Rustik, O., *Staroobryadcheskoye Preobrajenskoye*, *op. cit.*, p. 72

21 See *Dnevnie dozornie zapissi*, *op. cit.*, p. 101; Rustik, O., *Staroobryadcheskoye Preobrajenskoye*, *op. cit.*, p. 70; Raskov, D.E., *Novie svedeniya*, *op. cit.*, p. 89. Illegal enterprises functioned along with the officially registered: see Stadnikov, A.V., *Moskovskoye staroobryadchestvo*, *op. cit.*, pp. 100-102.

Old Believers' associations also carried out internal, non-economic functions. These were the main purpose of Old Believer communities and basic functions of Old Believers' entrepreneurship. The reallocation of the profits of Old Believers' enterprises through various forms of ownership supported local communities, ensuring their vital activity, increasing their number and consolidating their influence, as well as financing Old Belief schools and monasteries, Churches etc.

There were also external functions concerning relations with State authorities and official Orthodox Church authorities. Protection against persecutions was the main external function of the association. The community spent huge amounts of money to neutralise the effects of governmental anti-Old Belief purges by resorting to corrupt methods in their dealings with different authority levels from minor police officials up to the Governmental Senate[22]. There were cases in the first half of the nineteenth century when direct decrees of the Russian Emperor were not carried out, thanks to bribes paid by Old Believers.

3. The sources of Old Believer BIAs' income

The community ensured the exercise of basic functions of Old Believers' entrepreneurship. But support of local communities, protection against persecution by the authorities and credit organisation all demanded huge amounts of money. But the strategies of Old Believers' confessional business associations accumulated great funds.

Officially, but also illegally, the community possessed and used different property. They held buildings, factories and other enterprises such as printing houses and baths, as well as securities. Special representatives of a community operated this often hidden economy. All profit went directly to the community.

Furthermore, all community businessmen were obliged to make enormous contributions to a community cash box and cover community expenses directly in quite sizeable amounts (up to a thousand rubles). For example, in the 1830s and 1850s Fedoseevtsy merchants in Moscow made monthly contributions to their community treasury in enormous amounts of 500 to 1,000 rubles each, and some of them paid even more (a cow cost about three rubles)[23]. In case of "any significant expendi-

22 See in detail: Kerov, V.V., "'Vremia kupli nastupayet...': Mediativnie funktsii korruptsii v otnosheniakh stsroobriadchestva I vlasti v Rossii XVIII – pervoy polovini XIX v." ["Time of a Purchase comes...": Meditative Function of Corruption in the Old Belief and Power Relations in Russia in Eighteenth - the First Half of the Nineteenth Century], in *Vestnik of Peoples` Friendship University of Russia, series "Russian History"*, 2004, n. 3, pp. 7-17.

23 See *Fedosseevtsi. Istoriya, op. cit.*, p. 56.

ture" suffered by the community treasury "it was immediately replenished either by a subscription or by a direct shared contribution" by wealthy Old Believers[24].

Community members also made regular contributions on various other occasions. These numerous contributions are marked in police reports and the various account books of Old Believers communities[25]. Large and small businessmen did not make endowments but made personal contributions, which was unlawful from the authorities' viewpoint.

In the mid- and even late nineteenth century the communities maintained control over huge capital sums donated by entrepreneurs[26]. Still, the money accumulated by Old Believer businessmen and not contributed officially to the community became increasingly important for the denomination. Such "private" funds were used to cover most of the costs of the community and its members.

A strongly pronounced religious character was a very important feature of Old Believers' BIAs. The communities analyzed here were actually religious denominations. The preservation and revival of Old Belief and preparation for the rescue of the immortal soul of each believer was their main goal. The high performance function and business efficiency of the system in the late eighteenth century and through the nineteenth century were due to close ties among communities of the Old Belief denomination and close trade and production relationships. Confessional contacts and links with people of the same faith throughout Russia were used by the Old Belief merchants as a network to support the flow of goods[27].

Religious and economic aspects of the Old Belief were so closely interlaced that outcomes of confessional discussions were often influenced by economic interests. In Preobrazhenskaya community in Moscow, for example, when a discussion on a possible recognition of

---

24 See Melnikov, P.I. *Ocherki popovchini*, *op. cit.*, vol. 13, p. 375.

25 On police reports see: *Id.*, pp. 374-375; *Dnevnie dozornie zapissi*, *op. cit.* On account books see: *Russian State Library*, research department of manuscripts, fund 246, inventories 40, 41.

26 See *Central Historical Archive of Moscow*, fund 357, dossier 11, sheet 62; "Ustav Preobrazhenskogo bogadelennogo doma v Moskve. 9 Iyulia 1877 g." ["The Charter of Preobrazhenskiy Almshouse in Moscow. 9 July 1877"], in Marcov, V.S., *K istorii rascola-staroobriadchestva vtoroy polovini XIX stoletiya* [*To history of Old Believe Split of the Second Half of the Nineteenth Century*], Moscow, ChOIDR at Moscow University, 1914, pp. 771-772, 778-779.

27 See Klibanov, A.I., *Narodnaya sotsialnaya utopiya v Rossii: Period feodalisma* [*National Social Utopia in Russia: Feudalism Period*], Moscow, Nauka, 1977, p. 186; Shiapov, A.P., *Russkiy raskol staroobriadchestva*, *op. cit.*, pp. 256–258.

marriages was taking place in the 1830s and 1840s, one of its trustees openly stated that a rejection of celibacy could cause a breakaway by conservative Fedoseevtsy communities in other towns resulting in "ruined trade. There will be no trust [of the local communities toward the Moscow community] hence the [Moscow] factories will collapse" because they sold their goods throughout the country via Old Believers[28].

Conclusion

In the mid-nineteenth century the Interior Ministry concluded that Rogozhskaya and Preobrazhenskaya communities were in fact "trade and manufacturing unions"[29], while each of the denominations became "a vast industrial and commercial corporation with branches all over Russia" or "a corporation of owners"[30].

By its structure, a social and economic association of the Old Believers had the community as the centerpiece with a group of private businesses of the community members surrounding it and many big and small businesses linked to it. It was a community of a new type which transformed itself from a confessional into a religious and economic community.

In order to save and strengthen "the True faith", the community actively engaged in distributing the profits of its members and in the process of manufacturing and selling the products of their private businesses. At times of corporate entrepreneurship a community of the Old Believers and its Trustees Board in fact remained the "chief manager" by ensuring the development of infrastructure, the functioning of loan mechanisms, the expansion of sales networks expansion, the coordination of the supply of raw materials, etc.

From the 1850s and 1860s, while some elements of community businesses remained, private family enterprise became the main actor of the Old Belief business association. In the late nineteenth century the funds of a community were only used for confessional, non-commercial purposes (such as charity, maintenance of religious buildings, religious education and other social and religious programs). The functions of

28 See Rindzunskiy, P.G., "Staroobriadcheskaya organizatsiya v usloviyakh razvityiya promishlennogo kapitalizma (na primere istorii moscovskoy obshini fedoseevtsev v 40kh godakh XIX veka)" [The Old Believe Organization in the Conditions of Development of Industrial Capitalism (on the Example of History of the Moscow Fedosseevetsy Community in the 40s of Nineteenth Century)], in *Voprosi istorii relighii I ateisma* [*Questions of History of Religion and Atheism*], Moscow, Academy of Sciences of USSR, 1950, p. 221.

29 See Melnikov, P.I., *Ocherki popovchini, op. cit.*, vol. 13, pp. 335-336.

30 See Andreev, V.V., *Raskol i yego, op. cit.*, p. 18.

business coordination were gradually diminishing, as was the corporatism of the Old Believer entrepreneurs (of the biggest ones at least). Some of the functions of coordination of business activities were shifting to the level of personal relationships, which also involved representatives of different confessions. in addition, the growing exchange committees, especially in large cities, were playing an increasingly essential coordination role. It was at the Moscow Exchange Committee, for example, where industrial laws, pricing policies, employer-employee relations, etc. were discussed[31].

The legal rights of Old Belief communities were not recognised by Russian state until 1906. The corporative activities of associations and their members looked from the outside as the relationships of individuals though the police traced them. Without understanding the essence of communal communications, in 1840 the deputy minister of internal affairs drew the conclusion that the Old Believers' community was "an establishment simultaneously of socialism and capitalism"[32].

As a result of the activity of these confessional BIAs in the first half of the nineteenth century the first Moscow factory suburb, Lefortovo[33], was established in the Guslitsky industrial area[34]. More so, it was primarily due to the Old Believers that in the first half of the nineteenth century industrialisation in Russia advanced in a number of leading industries, including in the textile industry, the biggest industry of all. By 1870, according to census data and factory statistics, the proportion of Old Believers in the textitle industry in the provinces of Moscow was 32 per cent and 75 per cent in Moscow itself (amounting to 80 per cent of the workforce). In the wool industry, the figures were 63 per cent in Moscow, 42 per cent in the provinces and 40 per cent nationally. And it should be remembered that many Old Believers did not publicly acknowledge their faith or allegiance[35].

---

31 See *Central Historical Archive of Moscow*, fund 143, inventory 1.

32 See Liprandi, [I.P.] *Kratkoye obozreniye*, *op. cit.*, p. 156.

33 See *Dnevnie dozornie zapissi o moskovskikh raskolonikakh* [*Day Patrol Records about the Moscow Dissenters*], p. 101.

34 See Melnikov, P.I., *Ocherki popovchini*, *op. cit.*, vol. 13, p. 328.

35 See Stadnikov, A.V., "Rol moskovskogo staroobriadchestva v razvitii rossiyskoy tekstilnoy promishlennosty" [Role of the Moscow Old Believers in Development of the Russian Textile Industry], in *Staroobriadchestvo: istoriya, kultura, sovremennost. Materiali* [*Old Belief: History, Culture, Present. Materials*], Moscow, Muzey istorii y kulturi staroobriadchestva, 1998, pp. 91-92; *Id.*, "Spisok kupecheskikh staroobriadcheskikh familiy Moskvi (XIX – nachalo XX v.)" [List of Merchant Old Believe Surnames of Moscow (Nineteenth – early Twentieth Century)], in *Mir staroobriadchestva: istoriya i sovremennost* [*World of Old Belief: History and Present*], Moscow, 1999, issue 5, pp. 341–377; *Id.*, *Moskovskoye staroobryadchestvo*, *op. cit.*, pp. 141–144.

In the early stages of Russian industrialisation, the confessional business associations of the Old Believers played an important part in the organisational, economic and technical modernisation of the country's trade and industry sectors.

The Genesis of Swiss Business Interest Associations (1860-1914)

Cédric HUMAIR

Université de Lausanne

Introduction

On the eve of the First World War the Swiss economy was criss-crossed by a dense network of Business Interest Associations (henceforth BIAs), which were deployed at the local, cantonal and national level[1]. Guaranteeing the coordination of this set of heterogeneous constituent elements, five peak associations enabled the employers to effectively influence the actions of the central state, thereby responding to the main function of these associations. However, nothing presaged such a development in 1860. Among the agricultural, handicrafts and trading societies existing at that time, none had as yet acquired a national dimension. How and why did business circles manage to institute this extremely dense enmeshing of associations and societies, thus conferring a high level of organisation on Swiss companies? The aim of this contribution is to respond to this question by inscribing it within economic and political developments at the national and international scale, and by underlining the specificity of this shift to organised capitalism in Switzerland[2].

---

1 For an overview of Swiss BIAs, see Gruner, E., *Die Wirtschaftsverbände in der Demokratie. Vom Wachstum der Wirtschaftsorganisationen im schweizerischen Staat*, Erlenbach-Zürich/Stuttgart, Eugen Rentsch Verlag, 1956; Meynaud, J., *Les organisations professionnelles en Suisse*, Lausanne, Payot, 1963; Humair, C., Guex, S., Mach, A., Eichenberger, P., "Les organisations patronales suisses entre coordination économique et influence politique. Bilan historiographique et pistes de recherche", in *Vingtième Siècle. Revue d'histoire*, 2012, n. 115, juillet-septembre, pp. 115-127.

2 Please note that this contribution is an English reduced version of: Humair C., "Du libéralisme manchestérien au capitalisme organisé: genèse, structuration et spécificités de l'organisation patronale suisse (1860-1914)", in D. Fraboulet, P. Vernus (dir.),

1. The beginnings of the BIAs: heterogeneous regional associations

Created in 1848, the Swiss national state, commonly known as the Federal state, was not without consequences for the evolution of the economy[3]. With the unification of the customs system, the Confederation acquired the means to implement a more active trade policy, which intensified at the beginning of the 1860s, thus prompting the employers to organise in order to protect their interests. Passed by vote in 1852, the law on railways led to the expansion of the Swiss rail network. Subjected to the abuses of private companies benefiting from a monopoly, rail users called on the public authorities for protection in terms of fares and civil liability[4]. As for the second federal constitution of 1874, this extended the Confederation's scope for intervention to commercial law, the protection of workers in the factory, and control of the issuing of banknotes.

Wishing to stimulate and orientate public intervention, the employers increased the density of their organisation at the end of the 1850s, creating the first long-term associations on a cantonal scale[5]. It was necessary, however, to wait until 1870 and the birth of a peak association, the Union Suisse du Commerce et de l'Industrie (USCI)[6], for the setting up of cantonal associations to become systematic. By 1913 only a few agricultural cantons were lacking in an organisation comprising the commercial and industrial sectors of big business. In the handicrafts and small-scale industry sector, a few cantonal associations were also created during the 1850s and 1860s. As for the agricultural societies, often made up of local elites, they only assumed the defence of professional interests in a marginal way.

Genèse des organisations patronales en Europe (19e-20e siècles), Rennes, PUR, 2012, pp. 133-142.

3 See Humair, C., *Développement économique et État central 1815-1914. Un siècle de politique douanière suisse au service des élites*, Bern, Peter Lang, 2004.

4 See Duc, G., *Les tarifs marchandises des chemins de fer suisses (1850-1913). Stratégies des compagnies ferroviaires, nécessités de l'économie nationale et évolution du rôle régulateur de l'Etat*, Bern, Peter Lang, 2010.

5 See Hauser, B., *Wirtschaftsverbände im frühen schweizerischen Bundesstaat (1848-1874). Vom regionalen zum nationalen Einzugsgebiet*, Basel / Frankfurt am Main, Helbing und Lichtenhahn, 1985.

6 Please note that today the name is "Economiesuisse".

Table 1 - Swiss BIAs: chronological overview

	Before 1860	1860s	1870s	1880s	1890s	1900s	1910s
A	**SICVD** 1859 Vaud	**BVHI** 1860 Bern **ACIG** 1865 Geneva	**THIV** 1870 Thurgovie **KGZ** 1873 Zurich **AHIV** 1874 Argovie **KSHIV** 1874 Soleure **BHIV** 1876 Basel				
B	**SGV** 1843-49 trade + industry + handicrafts						
C			**SIIJ** 1876 watchmaking **SSZWV** 1877 cotton	**SGCI** 1882 chemicals **SSH** 1882 tourism **VSL** 1882 linen **VSW** 1882 wool **VSM** 1883 machines		Employers' associations **ASM** 1905 machines **AST** 1906 textile	
D	**SHGV** 1849-64 handicrafts		**USCI** 1870 trade + industry		**USP** 1897 agriculture	**UCAPS** 1908 industry (employers)	**ASB** 1912 banking

Source: Humair, C., *Développement économique*, *op. cit.*, pp. 859-861.
A = Regional Multi-Sectorial BIAs with a National Vocation; **B** = National Multi-Sectorial BIAs; **C** = National Sectorial BIAs; **D** = National Peak BIAs.

One feature of the cantonal BIAs was that they were extremely heterogeneous[7]. To begin with, their economic and political weight varied according to the number of members and the BIAs' financial and administrative capacity[8]. In 1900 the Canton of Geneva association, at that time the best endowed, had 1,140 members and received 21,000 Swiss francs in revenue, while the Thurgau association had 105 members and had to content itself with 644 francs. The first

7 See Richard, E., *Kaufmännische Gesellschaft Zürich und Zürcher Handelskammer*, Zurich, Selbstverlag der Zürcher Handelskammer, 1924; Henrici, H., *Die Basler Handelskammer 1876-1926*, Basel, Riehm, 1927; Jouvet, R., *Aperçu de l'activité de la Chambre de commerce de Genève 1865-1940*, Geneva, Atar, 1940.

8 See Maurer, E., *Die schweizerischen Handelskammern, ihr Wesen, ihre Entwicklung, Organisation und Tätigkeit*, Zurich, Aschmann & Scheller, 1924, pp. 45-68.

organisation to have a permanent secretary, from 1863 onward, was the very old merchants' guild of St. Gallen, followed by the cantonal associations of Zurich (1874), Geneva (1894), and Basel (1896)[9]. Secondly, the strong geographical segmentation of the Swiss economy resulted in large variations in the composition of the associations: while in Geneva and Basel it was the milieus of trade and private banking that set the tone, the industrial employers were much more influential in Zurich and Glarus, whereas in Lucerne tourist interests were preponderant. Due to this diversity of interests, but also to the linguistic and religious segmentation of the territory, joint undertakings at the federal scale were made difficult.

2. Strength from unity: the creation of the USCI, the first national peak association

At the end of the 1860s the trade and industry employers' organisation was still a patchwork of extremely heterogeneous official organisms, stock exchange societies, and local and cantonal private associations, the efficiency of which left much to be desired. When the federal administration consulted the employers, it was confronted with a veritable cacophony of contradictory interests, which gave it the opportunity to divide and rule. Moreover, the federal departments (ministries) were the sole judges of the usefulness of consultation, something the employers could no longer be content with when state intervention intensified.

In 1869 the impetus for a national organisation was given by the Handels Commission in the Canton of Glarus[10]. Its president, the prominent textile manufacturer Peter Jenny-Blumer, proposed the setting up of a strong peak association that would act in unison[11]. His plan turned the USCI into an essential intermediary between the Federal state and the regional BIAs. Apart from the Delegates' Assembly, convened once a year, and the Board (Vorort), occupied by another section every two years, the purpose of a more stable central committee would be to reconcile conflicting interests and to elaborate a common

---

9 See Wehrli, B., *Le Vorort, mythe ou réalité. Histoire de l'Union suisse du commerce et de l'industrie 1870-1970*, Neuchâtel, La Baconnière, 1972, pp. 94-95.

10 About the creation of the USCI, see Hulftegger, O., *Der Schweizerische Handels- und Industrie-Verein, 1870-1882*, Zurich, Berichthaus, 1920.

11 See Archiv für Zeitgeschichte, Fonds USCI (henceforth Archives USCI), minutes of the USCI delegates' meeting, Protokoll über die Verhandlungen der für Gründung eines Schweizerischen Handels- und Industrie-Vereines am 15. November in Bern stattgefundenen Delegierten-Versammlung, 1869, pp. 5-7. See also Hulftegger, O., *Der Schweizerische*, *op. cit.*, pp. 93-94.

strategy that could be coherently defended within the state field (the "champ étatique").

The centralizing tendencies of the plan met with opposition from other regional BIAs, however, some of which feared that they would no longer be able to defend their particular interests. The statutes voted through on 12 March 1870 proved to be a Pyrrhic victory for the promoters of the USCI. Admittedly, contrary to the opinion of the federalists (a word that denotes the anti-centralisers in Switzerland), a central committee was established of eleven members, regrouping the Swiss economic elite. Nevertheless, by upholding the right to make requests directly to the authorities, Article 6 deprived the committee of much of its legitimacy, since its pronouncements could be repudiated by the sections[12]. The latter, twenty-one in number, formed a heterogeneous assembly of official organisms (5), stock exchange societies (4), and local and cantonal private associations (12). The only two sectorial associations were of a regional kind.

In creating a peak association that was national in scope, the trade and industry employers stole a march on other economic sectors. During the first phase of its activity, though, the USCI suffered from a low level of representativeness and a lack of cohesion that limited its political effectiveness. The influence it was able to exert on legislation still depended on the good will of the Federal counsellors (members of the government).

3. The Long Depression and sectorial organisations: towards an organised capitalism

Triggered by the stock market crash of 1873 in Vienna, the "Long Depression" was characterised by an extended period of deflation that called the profitability of investments into question. Alongside this, the first move towards trade globalisation intensified international competition, fueling the trend of prices to fall. As a result the free competition advocated by Manchester liberalism was rendered suspect, to the benefit of an organisation of capitalism according to the logic of professional and national solidarity[13]. Cornerstone of this organised capitalism, the BIAs increased in number. Their main function was to stimulate and orientate the intervention of the public authorities. Indeed, the latter were called upon to support national companies in their competitive

---

12 The statutes are in Hulftegger O., *Der Schweizerische Handels*, *op. cit.*, pp. 109-111.

13 On the concept of "organized capitalism" see Winkler, H.A. (ed.), *Organisierter Kapitalismus. Voraussetzungen und Anfänge*, Göttingen, Vandenhoeck & Ruprecht, 1974.

struggle by improving the appropriate frameworks of economic activity (access to markets, infrastructures, credit, training, and so forth).

Affected as early as 1876 by the effects of the Long Depression, Switzerland was not spared by the phenomenon of organised capitalism, which took on a particular form and rhythm[14]. Due to its strong dependency on external markets, industry was shaken by the rise of protectionism in Europe. Tariff reforms and trade agreements therefore played a leading role in the constitution of sectorial BIAs that were nationwide in scope. The first to be affected by the crisis, the employers in watch making (1876) and cotton manufacture (1877), quickly went beyond the bounds of their cantonal self-interest (see figure: third line). Stimulated, too, by the first national exposition held in Zurich in 1883, sectorial organisation quickened during the 1880s. In turn the chemicals (1882), linen (1882), wool (1882) and machine industries (1883) set up national associations. The movement gradually extended to handicrafts, agriculture, banking, tourism and other services, albeit with differing intensities and chronologies[15].

The purpose of the BIAs created was not just to influence the economic intervention of the Federal state. They rendered many different services to companies and took on a series of tasks to do with organisation and coordination aimed at improving their competitiveness: quality controls, joint purchases, advertising campaigns,

14 See Jost, H.U., "Aperçus théoriques des relations entre l'Etat, l'économie et le capital entre 1870 et 1913. Le cas de la Suisse", in *Bulletin du département d'histoire économique de l'Université de Genève*, 1979/80, n. 10, pp. 21-28; Gruner, E., "Werden und Wachsen der schweizerischen Wirtschaftsverbände im 19. Jahrhundert", in *Revue suisse d'histoire*, 1956, n. 6, pp. 33-101 (here 62-86); Humair, C., *Développement économique*, *op. cit.*, pp. 313-471.

15 About handicrafts see Gutersohn, A., *Les arts et métiers dans la vie économique de la Suisse. USAM 1879-1954*, Lausanne, Imprimeries Réunies, 1954. On the agriculture see Brugger, H., *Landwirtschaftliche Vereinigungen der Schweiz 1910 bis 1980*, Frauenfeld, Huber, 1989; Jörin, R., *Parastaatliche Organisationen im Agrarsektor*, Bern-Stuttgart, Haupt, 1985; Antenen, A., *Die Agrarpolitik der landwirtschaftlichen Verbände in der schweizerischen Milchwirtschaft und ihre Stellung in Staat und Wirtschaft*, Winterthur, Schellenberg, 1959. About banking see Guex, S., *La politique monétaire et financière de la Confédération suisse 1900-1920*, Lausanne, Payot, 1993, pp. 35-39. Finally about the tourism see Dasen, H., *Entstehung und Entwicklung der gesamtwirtschaftlichen Zusammenschlüsse im schweizerischen Fremdenverkehr*, Bern, Stämpfli, 1948; Humair, C., "The Long Depression and its impact on Swiss tourism: from Manchester Liberalism to the beginnings of 'organized capitalism' (1873-1913)", EBHA 2011, (http://www.ebha.org/ebha2011/files/Papers/Athens-Tourism-Humair.pdf); *Id.*, "Les organisations du tourisme suisse et leurs relations à l'Etat central: analyse d'une montée en puissance (1882-1939)", in D. Fraboulet, C. Druelle-Korn, P. Vernus (eds.), *Les organisations patronales et la sphère publique. Europe XIXe et XXe siècles*, Rennes, PUR, 2013, pp. 183-194.

information gathering, and the like. Some BIAs also assumed the function of limiting competition, while others delegated this task to veritable cartels. Nevertheless, compared internationally, the regulating of markets was not very intensive in Switzerland before 1914[16]. As for the employers' associations specializing in the class struggle, they only appeared with the massive strike waves of the beginning of the twentieth century[17].

A vital cog in the machinery of organised capitalism, the sectorial organisations yielded the predominant role of business interest representation to the national peak associations.

4. Getting the state to listen: the USCI at the heart of the Swiss model of business interest representation

As early as 1875 the inadequacy of the collaboration between business circles and the Federal state was denounced by the more interventionist branches of industry. The cotton industry in particular complained of the passivity of the federal authorities and of the impotency of the USCI in relaying its wishes. Between 1876 and 1882 the Zurich and Aargau representatives of financial capital, stemming from large-scale industry and the big banks, emerged as the main protagonists of the adoption of organised capitalism, seeking to improve the BIAs and their weight within the state field. During the course of this crucial period the mode of representation of the employers' circles was totally redefined[18].

Unlike certain European countries of the time, France for example, Switzerland did not possess a representative body for the interests of the economy within the central state. In 1877 and 1882 interventionist business circles twice saw the parliament reject their plan for the setting up of an official chamber of commerce. An alternative and original solution was then found: to turn the USCI into a state-recognised

---

16 See Jaccard, R., *Les syndicats industriels en Suisse. Contribution à l'étude des coalitions d'industriels*, Lausanne, Vaney-Burnier, 1925; Cortat, A. (ed.), *Contribution à une histoire des cartels en Suisse*, Neuchâtel, Alphil, 2010.

17 See Gerster, H., *Die Arbeitgeberorganisationen der Schweiz*, Binningen/Basel, Wirz, 1921.

18 On this crucial period, see Zimmermann, B.R., *Verbands- und Wirtschaftspolitik am Übergang zum Staatsinterventionismus: dargestellt anhand der Mitwirkung des Schweizerischen Handels- und Industrie-Vereins und der Kaufmännischen Gesellschaft Zürich bei der Ausgestaltung der schweizerischen Aussenhandelspolitik im ausgehenden 19. Jahrhundert*, Bern, Peter Lang, 1980, pp. 56-69, 77-92; Hulftegger O., *Der Schweizerische Handels*, *op. cit.*, pp. 26-82; Humair C., *Développement économique*, *op. cit.*, pp. 389-394.

chamber of commerce, while preserving its private character[19]. In 1878 a permanent secretariat was set up with the objective of making the federal authorities dependent on the economic information of the USCI, thus obtaining systematic consultation of the association[20]. That same year the Aargau section called for the recasting of the association on the German model of the Zentralverband deutscher Industrieller, which organised the employers on a sectorial basis[21].

Although the reform was rejected, the affiliation of sectorial associations was promoted and soon gained in importance, making the USCI a hybrid peak association: its members belonged at one and the same time to regional and to sectorial BIAs. As a result its representativeness rapidly improved, the number of affiliated BIAs ascending from 19 in 1882 to 62 in 1913. The peak association completed its reform with its statutes of 11 November 1882, which added to the effectiveness of its governance by reinforcing its decision-making bodies. The central committee was renamed the Swiss Chamber of Commerce, which gave it a semi-official status and reinforced its legitimacy among the employers. Moreover, the statutes made provision for the presence of civil servants at meetings of the Chamber, with consultative rights. In agreeing to assign an annual subsidy of 10,000 francs (starting in 1882), then of 20,000 francs (from 1898), the federal authorities ratified this official recognition, thus contributing to the association's rapid increase in influence[22].

How may we explain the help given by the state field to reinforcing the USCI? Founded in 1848, the Federal state was dominated by the trade and industrial elites that ran the peak association. Favoured by the political militia system, a genuine osmosis was established between the state and the export industry employers, whose interests were identified with the common good. Recently superimposed on these structural affinities was a more cyclical political configuration. After the 1874 revision of the constitution and the introduction of the legislative referendum, a law contested by 30,000 signatures had to be ratified by popular vote. As it was, between 1874 and 1884 this political tool was used successfully by the conservative forces that were blocking the

19 This strategy was clearly expressed in a speech by the Zurich industrialist Julius Maggi. See Archives USCI, minutes of the delegates' meeting, "Referat über die Reorganisation des SHIV. Gehalten im Auftrage des Vororts in der Delegiertenversammlung vom 9. Mai 1880 von Herrn Julius Maggi."

20 See Archives USCI, central committee minutes (Ausschuss), meeting of 6 June 1878.

21 See Hulftegger O., *Der Schweizerische Handels*, *op. cit.*, pp. 52-59.

22 See Wehrli B., *Le Vorort, mythe ou réalité*, *op. cit.*, p. 53.

legislative process of the Liberal-Radical state[23]. In this context of sociopolitical destabilisation, the USCI became a valued partner capable of getting business circles to give their backing to different legislative solutions. The stronger the USCI, the more effective was its political support. Finally, the Federal state found itself in a situation of dependency regarding economic knowhow. Confronted with the Long Depression, the political authorities were incapable of formulating a coherent crisis strategy on their own. On top of that, the endemic weakness of the federal administration did not permit a renewed economic intervention to be envisaged without the expertise and information provided by the BIAs[24]. The federal authorities had need, then, of the USCI in order to design and implant an organised capitalism adapted to the more dynamic sectors of the Swiss economy[25].

After 1882 the consultation process of trade and industry circles was systematised and intensified. The USCI gradually assumed a parastatal function, both during the legislative process and in the phase of applying the laws[26]. Its influence was exerted thanks to the setting up of extraparliamentary expert committees[27]. Attention must be drawn to the circulation of personnel between the USCI and the federal administration, which facilitated the intensity of the exchanges. This collaboration did not prevent the two partners from sometimes coming into conflict. Having to assure its legitimacy with the general run of Swiss citizens, the state field sometimes departed from the line dictated by the peak association. To restrict the room for manoeuvre of the authorities with regard to it, the USCI came up with two strategies: perpetuating the

23 See Neidhart, L., *Plebiszit und pluralitäre Demokratie. Eine Analyse der Funktion des schweizerischen Gesetzreferendums*, Bern, Francke, 1970.

24 This dependency was clearly expressed during a meeting of the USCI central committee. See Archives USCI, central committee minutes (Ausschuss), meeting of 9 September 1882.

25 See Siegenthaler, H., "Konsens, Erwartungen und Entschlusskraft: Erfahrungen der Schweiz in der Überwindung der Grossen Depression vor hundert Jahren", in *Schweizerische Zeitschrift für Volkswirtschaft und Statistik*, 1983, n. 119, pp. 213-235.

26 See Humair C., *Développement économique*, *op. cit.*, pp. 656-714.

27 For a theoretical approach to these relationships, see Schmid, H.P., *Wirtschaft, Staat und Macht. Die Politik der schweizerischen Exportindustrie im Zeichen von Staats- und Wirtschaftskrise (1918-1929)*, Zurich, Limmat Verlag, 1983, pp. 63-133; David, T., Ginalski, S., Mach, A., Rebmann, F., "Networks of Coordination. Swiss Business Associations as an Intermediary between Business, Politics and Administration during the 20th Century", in *Business and Politics*, 2009, n. 4, pp. 1-38; Eichenberger, P., Mach, A., "Organized Capital and Coordinated Market Economy: Swiss Business Associations between Socio-Economic Regulation and Political Influence", in C. Trampusch, A. Mach (eds.), *Continuity and Change in the Swiss Political Economy*, London, Routledge, 2011, pp. 63-81.

informational dependency of the state by limiting its financial and administrative capacity; and imposing its views by using the threat of the referendum. In 1897 the USCI thus managed to impose its semiprivate model of a central bank after causing a highly statist project to fail through a referendum vote[28]. Having demonstrated its clout in this way, the USCI would only rarely have to take advantage of the referendum in order to be understood.

5. Sharing power: the birth of other peak associations

The USCI did not remain the only nationwide peak association for very long. In 1879 the handicraft and small-scale industries founded the Union Suisse des Arts et Métiers (USAM), the organisation of which was modelled on the USCI[29]. In 1886 the association also obtained a federal subsidy of 10,000 francs, which enabled it to set up a permanent secretariat. However, due to the inadequacy of its political connections within the Federal state, the USAM came nowhere near to overshadowing its predecessor. Incapable of organising its base on a grand scale (108 sections for 20,344 members in 1897)[30] the association proved incapable of exploiting the referendum.

To start with, the organisation of the farming world was no more successful. Respectively founded in 1863 and 1881, the peak associations of German-speaking Switzerland (the Schweizerischer Landwirtschaftlicher Verein) and French-speaking Switzerland (the Fédération des Sociétés d'Agriculture de la Suisse Romande) continued to be highly elitist and had little influence on the federal authorities. In 1897 the situation changed with the founding of the Union Suisse des Paysans (USP)[31]. Representing 78,000 farmers in 1900 (and they became 164,000 in 1912)[32], this peak association was a particularly formidable referendum force due to being run in a highly authoritarian

---

[28] See Zimmermann, R., *Volksbank oder Aktienbank? Parlamentsdebatten, Referendum und zunehmende Verbandsmacht beim Streit um die Nationalbankgründung, 1891-1905*, Zurich, Chronos, 1987.

[29] See Tschumi, H., Jaccard R., *L'Union Suisse des Arts et Métiers. Histoire et activité, 1879 à 1929*, Lausanne, USAM, 1929; Humair, C., *Développement économique*, *op. cit.*, pp. 443-448.

[30] See *Denkschrift des Schweizerischen Gewerbevereins zur Feier seines 25jährigen Bestehens*, 1879-1904, Bern, Büchler, 1904, p. 32.

[31] See Brugger, H., *Schweizerischer landwirtschaftlicher Verein 1863-1963. Festschrift*, Zurich, SLV, 1963; Baumann, W., *Bauernstand und Bürgerblock. Ernst Laur und der Schweizerische Bauernverband 1897-1918*, Zurich, Orell Füssli, 1993; Humair C., *Développement économique*, *op. cit.*, pp. 640-656.

[32] See Humair C., *Développement économique*, *op. cit.*, pp. 644-645; this figure is an optimum one since it does not take account of the fact that a farmer could be a member of several sections of the USP.

and effective manner by its secretary, Ernst Laur, nicknamed "the king of the farmers".

The political configuration of the end of the nineteenth century obliged the "state field" and the USCI to make significant concessions to the USP: it was a matter of avoiding a Red-Green alliance that would bring the workers' and the farmers' movements, radicalised by the violent agricultural crisis of the 1880s and 90s, together under the banner of an anti-capitalist opposition programme. Although subject to extremely strong conflicts of interests, an alliance between the USCI and the USP, known as the Bloc bourgeois (Bürgerblock), was established in 1902 on the basis of a tariff policy reached by consensus[33]. To be sure, thereafter the USCI retained poll position in terms of the representation of the employers within the state field, but all the same the leaders of the USP were integrated into certain extraparliamentary expert committees.

During the years immediately prior the First World War, the hegemonic position of the USCI was further weakened by a differentiation of the big business BIAs. In 1908 the employers' associations specializing in labour relations founded a peak association, the Union Centrale des Associations Patronales Suisses (UCAPS), which sought primacy in this domain. As for the bankers, whose influence remained limited within an USCI dominated by large-scale industry, they created the Association Suisse des Banquiers (ASB) in 1912. Consisting of individual members, this sectorial association rapidly assumed the leading role in terms of the representation of banking interests, thus achieving the political status of a peak association[34].

Conclusion: the BIAs, the state and democracy

Between 1860 and 1914 the Swiss BIAs became both denser and more structured at the national scale. Pursuing their main objective, which was to stimulate and orientate the intervention of the state, the BIAs became the key players in the Swiss political system, thus driving change within the legislative process. By intervening in extraparliamentary expert committees, the peak associations acquired a parastatal status and the financial support of the state, without being subject to

---

33 See Baumann, W., *Bauernstand und Bürgerblock*, *op. cit.*, pp. 147-196; Müller, R., *Volk, Parlament und Schweizerische Zollpolitik um 1900*, Bern, Fritz Marti, 1966.

34 See Eichenberger, P., "L'Union centrale des associations patronales suisses: genèse d'une association faîtière du patronat (1908-1922)", in D. Fraboulet, P. Vernus (eds.), *Genèse des organisations patronales*, *op. cit.*, pp. 143-152; Guex, S., Mazbouri, M., "De l'Association des représentants de la banque en Suisse (1912) à l'Association suisse des banquiers (1919). Genèse et fonctions de l'organisation faîtière du secteur bancaire suisse", in *Ibid.*, pp. 205-226.

public control. Without the benefit of democratic legitimacy of any kind, the leaders of the economy gradually exerted an influence on legislation superior to that of the elected representatives in parliament. We can therefore legitimately pose the question of the compatibility of this "seizure of power" on the part of the BIAs with the democratic ideals that presided over the founding of the Federal state in 1848.

The Russian Business Interest Associations

Economic and Socio-Cultural Aspects of Maturation (1861-1917)

Irina POTKINA

Institute of Russian History, RAS, Moscow

1. The starting point and maturation process

Industrialisation and modernisation in all spheres of public life caused by the Emancipation act of 1861 launched the process of coordination of efforts by several social groups in order to achieve economic prosperity of the Russian Empire. Entrepreneurs, engineers and technologists constituted the most active group who created an acceptable form of union – voluntary associations for the development of industry and commerce.

The second half of the nineteenth century was the time of creation of numerous organisations of such a kind. The Society for Assistance to Russian Industry and Commerce was founded in 1867 in Saint Petersburg. It was the first voluntary association in the country created by entrepreneurs from Saint Petersburg and some provincial towns. The total number of founders was 34. The Society had established its branches in 20 Russian provincial towns by the end of the nineteenth century[1].

The next stage of the organisation process was marked by diversification of the voluntary associations. In the 1870s a number of branch unions appeared. They included, for example, the Society for

1 See *Polnoe sobranie zakonov Rossiiskoi imperii. 2 sobranie.* [*The Complete Collection of Laws of the Russian Empire. 2nd Collection*], Vol. XLII, part 2., n. 45169; *Otchet o deyatel'nosti vysochaische utverzhdennogo Obshchestva dlya sodejstviya russkoi promyschlennosti i torgovle s 1867 po 1892* [*Report on Activity of the Society for Assistance to Russian Industry and Commerce Affirmed by His Imperial Majesty from 1867 until 1892]*, Sankt Petersburg, Tipografiya A.S. Suvorina, 1892, pp. 4, 10.

Assistance to Commercial Navigation (founded in Moscow, 1873), the Convention of Representatives of the Mining Industry of South Russia (1873), the Convention of Representatives of Joint-stock Commercial Banks (1873). Later on, its Committee began to represent the interests of the metropolitan and provincial private banks of Russia[2].

From this point, the self-organisation process gained momentum. At the end of the nineteenth century the following influential bodies were organised: the Convention of Oil Manufacturers (1884), the Society for Assistance and Development of the Textile Industry (Moscow, 1889), the Convention of Flour Millers (1896), the Society for Assistance and Development of Factory Industry (Saint Petersburg, 1897), the Convention of Mining Industrialists of the Urals (1898) and some others. By the end of the nineteenth century, the creation of new associations had sped up noticeably. At that time, the so-called "convention of representatives" became the most popular form for territorial and branch business organisations.

According to the chronology of establishment of the Business Interest Associations (hereafter BIAs) in the second half of the nineteenth century, Russian entrepreneurs were united by branch or territorial principles. Narrow economic and even egotistical purposes pursued by several disunited groups of businessmen did not enable them to create a real all-Russian organisation. Nevertheless, it was a period of obtaining experience of interaction in solving common economic problems, decision-making, and the formulisation of consolidated, workable plans.

At the start of the twentieth century, the self-organisational process and unifying tendency spread widely among the entrepreneurial class. Committees of the Commodity Exchange Societies appeared in provincial towns where local entrepreneurs tried to get rid of the influence of the same committees in the capitals and large commercial cities and to conduct their own policy as deemed more suitable to regional needs. The consolidation of forces and co-operation of entrepreneurs from all over Russia became a pressing necessity.

The new wave of foundation activity coincided with the years of the Russian revolution of 1905-1907. In March 1906, the Russian Government adopted a new law introducing a registration system without prior permission for non-profit public associations and unions. In the context of longstanding economic and political crises, and

---

2 See Salomatina, S.A., *Kommercheskie banki v Rossii: dinamika i struktura operatsi 1864-1917* [*Commercial Banks in Russia: Dynamics and Structure of Operations, 1864–1917*], Moskva, ROSSPEN, 2004, pp. 71-78, 80-90.

widespread strikes, it gave momentum to the movement for unification on a national scale.

The amalgamation process started in Moscow in March 1905 and finished in Saint Petersburg where a constituent assembly took place in April 1906. Thus, the all-Russian Convention of Representatives of Industry and Trade was established. Famous Russian entrepreneurs and engineers Nikolai Avdakov, Alexander Konovalov, Grigorii Krestovnikov, Savva Morozov, Adolph Vol'ski, Vladislav Zhukovski, and Ignatius Yasyukovich were among the initiators and founders of that voluntary association. The main distinctive feature of the new entrepreneurial organisation became its strongly pronounced federative character. Due to that principle, it united large firms and companies, as well as entrepreneurial associations from the important Russian economic regions. There were two types of membership in the organisation, namely full and advisory, and they depended on the contribution made. The regional Stock-breeder Committees and the BIAs constituted a group of full members while joint-stock companies, partnerships limited by shares and railway companies were advisory members. In 1906, the Organising bureau of the organisation incorporated 19 Stock-breeder Committees, 7 regional and branch Convention Councils, 5 business representative associations and 2 permanent Consultative Offices[3]. By 1917, the Convention united 70 full and 350 advisory members. The leaders and ideologists Nikolai Avdakov and Vladislav Zhukovski considered the Convention of Representatives as a "business" organisation but not a political one, but it had political influence based on the enormous economic significance of industry[4].

At the beginning of the twentieth century, the Russian political system and Russian society changed significantly under the pressure of the revolution. Those events influenced greatly the creation of a new type of BIAs which grouped employers. Approximately 20 associations had been organised by 1917; however, the Moscow and the Saint

---

3 See *Zhurnaly zasedaniya organizatsionnogo byuro soyuza promyschlennykh i torgovykh predpriyati Rossiiskoi imperii, sostoyavshegosya 1 fevralya 1906 g. [The Minutes of the Organising Bureau of the Union of industrial and Commercial enterprises of the Russian Empire held on February 1, 1906]*, Sankt-Peterburg, no publisher indicated (hereafter [npi]), 1906, pp. 17-19; *Zhurnaly zasedani vtorogo ocherednogo s'ezda predstavitelei promyschlennosti i torgovli, sostoyavshegosya 22, 23 i 24 maya 1907 goda v Moskve [The Minutes of the Second Ordinary Congress of Representatives of Industry and Trade held on May 22, 23 and 24 1907 in Moscow]*, Sankt-Peterburg, [npi], 1907, pp. 19-26.

4 See Shepelev, L.E., *Tsarism i burzhuaziya v 1904-1914 gg. Problemy torgovo-promyshlennoi politiki [Tsarism and Bourgeoisie in 1904-1914. Problems of Trade-industry Policy]*, Leningrad, Nauka, 1987, pp. 74, 99-101.

Petersburg societies of factory and mill owners were the largest and most influential. The process of political liberalisation called into being one more nationwide BIA: the Convention of Representatives of Exchange Trade and Agriculture (1905). By 1917, there were three all-Russian organisations of more than 30 Conventions of representatives[5].

2. Number of BIAs: their goals and tasks

According to the official data reported by the Ministry of Trade and Industry, there were approximately 150 entrepreneurial associations in Russia at the beginning of the twentieth century. With the exception of 18 semi-Governmental institutions, the rest were voluntary public organisations. The majority of them were Stockbreeder Committees that took on a function of representing the interests of businessmen. The semi-Governmental organisations consisted of the Councils of Commerce and Manufacturing Industry and the Merchant Boards[6]. Those institutions were initiated by the Government to provide advice and analysis on the most important questions of home economic policy.

In 1910, the Imperial Russian Technical Society (hereafter RTS), which had been founded in 1866, counted 161 unions of various types. Its preliminary list consisted of the above-mentioned 18 semi-Governmental organisations, 70 Stockbreeder Committees of Universal Exchange Societies, 35 Councils and Offices of the Conventions of representatives, 34 Societies and Unions, and 1 Chamber of Commerce[7]. Adolph Vol'ski, a mining engineer and an active member of the Council of the Convention of Representatives of Industry and Trade, stated that the Russian entrepreneurial organisations drew in only one-third of all industrial enterprises in the country at the start of the twentieth century[8].

To clarify the reality of the situation with the entrepreneurial representative organisations, the RTS undertook cross-examination of existing associations by offering them a special questionnaire in 1910. It

5 See *Sovetskaya istoricheskaya entsiklopediya [Soviet Historical Encyclopedia]*, Moskva, Sovetskaya entsiklopediya, 1971, vol. 13, pp. 207-209.

6 Shepelev, L.E., *Tsarism i burzhuaziy., op. cit.*, p. 108.

7 See Gushka, A.O., *Predstavitel'nye organizatsii torgovo-promyschlennogo klassa Rossii. Po dannym ankety, provedennoi XI /Promyschlenno-ekonomicheskim/ otdelom Imperatorskogo Russkogo Tehnicheskogo obshchestva* [*Representative Organisations by Trade-Industry Class in Russia]*, Sankt-Peterburg, Tipo-litografiya Schrödera,1912, pp. 19-24.

8 See Vol'ski, A.A., *Predstavitel'stvo russkoi promyschlennosti i torgovli v nastoyashchee vremya i osnovy predstavitel'stva, neobkhodimogo v blizhaischem budushchem.* [*Representation of Russian Industry and Trade in Present Time and Representation Fundamentals Necessary in Nearest Future*], Sankt-Peterburg, [npi], 1906, p. 14.

included 49 questions requiring extended answers. The Society leaders addressed a circular letter to chairpersons requesting them to support strictly scientific observation of public entrepreneurial associations. Eventually, the preliminary list was reduced to 143 active organisations, and only 62 of them sent answers to the RTS[9].

The net result was that pre-revolutionary Russian historiography enriched itself with valuable, comprehensive and fundamental research that was unsurpassed in some aspects until recently. Today, the research undertaken by Osip Ermanski (pseudonym Gushka) may be regarded as a unique document reflecting an instant picture of that time.

In accordance with Russian legislation, each society was obliged to submit its charter for the highest confirmation. A charter signed by the Tsar was considered as a separate law that determined legal conditions of activities. The majority of active associations were organised in such a way; a general law of 1906 simplified the foundation procedure. Henceforth, newly founded organisations detailed their goals and activities independently and without state interference. Nevertheless, a common set of steady regulations and rules remained in the constituent documents bearing private character.

As the RTS examination witnesses, all the active Russian BIAs had representative and developmental functions. The meaning of representative function was reduced to an influence or even pressure on the Government[10]. We can present the evidence for this overall conclusion by analyzing charters, authorised before and after adoption of the law of 1906.

As the first paragraph of the Charter of the Society for Assistance to Russian Industry and Commerce postulated in 1867, it had "the purpose to promote development of domestic industry branches and expansion of internal and foreign trade". The third paragraph said that the Society was granted a right to petition the Government "on all questions concerning Russian industry and trade"[11]. Some years later, the Charter of the Society for Assistance to Commercial Navigation expanded its remit into shipbuilding and navigation[12].

The situation was reproduced with some variations in the following years. In 1889, one of the most prominent Moscow textile manufacturers organised the Society to undertake the accomplishment of another important task, the promotion of the introduction of new scientific

9 See Gushka A.O., *Predstavitel'nye organizatsii*, *op. cit.*, pp. 32-36, 38.

10 See *Ibid.*, pp. 69-70.

11 See *Polnoe sobranie*, *op. cit.*, 2, Vol. XLII, part 2, n. 45169.

12 See *Ibid.*, Vol. XLVIII, part 2, n. 52659.

discoveries and technical improvements into Russian industry[13]. Its activities acquired a distinctly applied character. In the end, that Society played a great role in the development of the textile industry and attendant branches in the region. In 1897, the Society for Assistance and Development of Factory Industry appeared in St. Petersburg. It united almost all owners of large firms situated not only in the capital, but also in Saint Petersburg's industrial hinterland. The majority of the Charter's paragraphs coincided with that of the Moscow organisation[14]. Both societies pursued the same goals and tasks with only one difference: each operated within its own economic jurisdiction.

It should be mentioned that almost all constituent documents of that time were based on the so-called "sample charter" that was elaborated by ministry officials.

As already mentioned, at the beginning of the twentieth century a new type of union emerged in Russia, the Society of Factory and Mill Owners of the Moscow Industrial Region being one example. The societies of employers corrected its goals and tasks to some extent, but they did not abandon the purposes of development and protection of the industry. In other words, representative and developmental functions remained fundamental in their activity. The first part of the charter was enlarged by inclusion of an extensive paragraph concerning the relationship between employers and hired workers. According to it, all conflicts would be solved by means of peaceful agreement and arbitration. To fulfil this task conciliator chambers had to be organised[15].

The rallying process that was the mainstream of the self-contradictory social evolution of the entrepreneurial class at the beginning of the twentieth century revealed itself in the simultaneous creation of two nationwide organisations. The years 1905 and 1906 were a time of rapid evolution of the intrinsic all-Russian BIAs. The first one came into being as a result of work of the Special Meeting on the Needs of Agricultural Industry organised by the Government in 1903. The issues related to the grain trade and other agricultural products were the sphere of interests of the Convention of Representatives of Exchange

---

13 See *Sobranie uzakoneni i rasporjazheni pravitel'stva [Collection of Laws and Orders of the Government]*, Sankt-Peterburg, Senatskaya tipografiya, 1890, n. 908.

14 See *Ustav S.-Peterburgskogo Obshchestva dlya sodejstviya uluchsheniyu i razvitiyu fabrichno-zavodskoi promyschlennosti* [*The Charter of the Saint Petersburg Society for Assistance and Development of Factory Industry]*, Sankt-Peterburg, [npi], 1905.

15 See *Ustav Obshchestva zavodchikov i fabrikantov Moskovskogo promyschlennogo raiona* [*The Charter of the Society of Factory and Mill Owners of the Moscow Industrial Region.* Moscow], Moskva, [npi], 1913, p. 3.

Trade and Agriculture[16]. That organisation united large-scale trading companies and mid-sized provincial enterprises.

The latter organisation generally represented the interests of Russian industrialists and traders in manufactured goods. According to the General Rules adopted on 14 April 1906, the main purposes of the Convention of Representatives of Industry and Trade were the following: a) "finding out and elaboration of questions which were arose in the sphere of legislation, commercial and industrial policy and socioeconomic relations"; b) "unification and representation of common interests of industry and trade"; c) "carrying out common actions"[17].

The cited document formulated the organisation's goals in details. The function of representation of interests of the whole industry and trade face to the legislative, Governmental and public institutions was prioritised. Following the established tradition the Convention retained cultural and educational functions as main aspects of its public activities. Nevertheless, one more function appeared: the collection of statistical data as a basis of scientific investigation conducted by the Convention's experts[18].

Thus, the Convention positioned itself as one of the main participants in the provision and elaboration of the legal framework for the industry and trade. It was proclaimed for the first time in the history of the Russian BIAs.

3. Development assistance

The representative function of the entrepreneurial associations was focused exclusively on the creation of favourable conditions for the development of Russian industry and trade. This sort of work was multi-sided and very extensive and characterised the wide spectrum of activities typical for all Russian BIAs. Moreover, many organisations frequently united their efforts in various public actions to achieve results that were more significant.

Formulating its representative function, the Society for Assistance to Russian Industry and Commerce (shortly the Industry and Commerce Society) underlined that the organisation was useful for the "whole Russian commercial and industrial community". Simultaneously, it rendered service to the Government, which required the most authentic

---

16 See *Polnoe sobranie*, *op. cit.*, 3, Vol. XXV, part 1, n. 26310.

17 See *Polozhenie ob obshcheimperskikh S'ezdakh predstavitelei promyschlennosti i torgovli* [*General Rules for Imperial Conventions of Representatives of Industry and Trade*], Sankt-Peterburg, tipografiya V.F. Kirshbaum, 1906, p. 1.

18 See *Ibid.*, p. 3.

data about national well-being. For a long time, the Industry and Commerce Society had been concentrating its own efforts on elaboration of protectionist policy for supporting young Russian industry. It petitioned the Government for tax privileges for the extracting and mining industries. The report stated that the Society's requests had been satisfied, and large-scale iron manufacturing appeared in the Southern region while the Russian coal industry began developing faster. The Government complied with the petition for liquidation of the out-of-date payoff system in the oil extracting industry, and for the entry of private business into that industry. As a result, the influence of this branch was significant. The Ministry of Finance took into consideration the Society's opinion on opening or closing State bank branches in far-distant province. Since the 1870s, the Society had been standing for the elaboration of labour legislation and for limiting the employment of minors in manufacturing. The first law in this series was adopted in 1882. In 1885 the Industry and Commerce Society initiated the creation of one more regional representative association: the Convention of Representative of Iron Factory Owners which promoted the development of metalworking industry. The Industry and Commerce Society leaders were sure that they had made a significant contribution to the solution of almost all important questions facing Russian trade and industry because the majority of petitions were resolved more or less positively[19].

The Convention of Representatives of the Mining Industry of South Russia concentrated mainly on tax policy, which was considered as generally successful. In one case, it was connected with the establishing of preferential tariffs on coal and anthracite transportation by the Russian railways, in another with introduction of progressive income tax in Russia. A number of measures providing a positive institutional environment were of prime importance for the Convention. They related to access railroads, mine industry credit, fire insurance and labour relations. In 1881, it succeeded in setting up the Society of Mutual Credit by Mine Industry Owners of South Russia. On the question of labour, the Convention pursued two interrelated aims: 1) elaboration of measures for attracting and keeping personnel, 2) working out procedures for maintaining relations between industrialists and workforces. In 1884, the Society of Financial Aid to Mine Workers was opened. During the period of its existence, it gave out approximately 470,400 grants as social insurance for the families of workers who lost

---

19 See *Otchet o deyatel'nosti vysochaische utverzhdennogo Obshchestva dlya sodejstviya russkoi promyschlennosti i torgovle s 1867 po 1892 g.*, p. 10. *[Report on Activity of the Society for Assistance to Russian Industry and Commerce from 1867 until 1892]*, Sankt-Peterburg, Tipografiya A.S.Suvorina, 1892, p. 10.

their jobs, became unfit to work or were daisabled by accidents. The problem of health protection was closely connected with the question of the prevention of explosions in mines and collieries. For that purpose, the Convention assigned considerable sums of money to run an experimental station for research into explosive gases[20].

The Society of Factory and Mill Owners of the Moscow Industrial Region paid much attention to the creation of an adequate socio-economic environment in the following aspects: regulation of labour relations, improvement of workers' lives, preventing non-payments, and, finally, the creation of stable turnover in trade and industry. Before the adoption of social insurance laws in 1912, the Society took an active part in the work of the special commission founded by the Ministry of Trade and Industry and in the conferences of Moscow district factory inspectors. On its behalf, the Society of Factory and Mill Owners carried out a series of explanatory public lectures for industrial workers. By the end of 1912, it had organised 26 medical insurance cash departments at Moscow enterprises that served 50,000 workers[21].

As far as credit status was concerned, the Society undertook a number of measures. Firstly, it organised registration of non-payments to stop the bank crediting those enterprises which violated their own obligations. In 1912, it held data on 4,563 defaulters and 5,766 non-payments. After that, the Society, in cooperation with the other associations, organised the archive of the Help Office on Credit Rating. It was a public institute aiming at protection of industrial interests. Within its first year of activity, the Office prepared references on 51,523 firms and physical persons. The report stated that a tight union of numerous commercial and industrial organisations gave to its work a form of mutual credit protection. In the end, the Help Office on Credit Rating brought great advantages to industrialists and merchants[22].

The all-Russian Convention of Representatives of Industry and Trade organised its representative work in several aspects: a) a wide public discussion of acute and urgent questions of economic development to

---

20 See Fomin, P.I., *Kratki ocherk istorii s'ezdov gornopromyschlennikov Yuga Rossii* [*Brief Studies of History of the Conventions of Representatives of Mining Industry of South Russia*], Khar'kov, Tipografiya i litografiya M. Silberberg, 1908.

21 See *Obshchestvo zavodchikov i fabrikantov Moskovskogo promyschlennogo raiona v 1912 g.* [*The Society of Factory and Mill Owners of Moscow Industrial Region in 1912*], Moskva, [npi],1913, pp. 77-83.

22 See *Ibid.*, pp. 84-90; *Spravochnaya kontora o kreditosposobnosti Obshchestva zavodchikov i fabrikantov Moskovskogo promyschlennogo raiona* [*Help Office on Credit Rating by the Society of Factory and Mill Owners of Moscow Industrial Region*], Moskva, Tipografiya P.P. Ryabushinskogo, 1912, pp. 3-5; Central Historical Archive of Moscow (hereafter TsIAM), RG. 1076, inv. 1, f. 15, pp. 4-5.

coordinate entrepreneurs' positions and opinions; b) the preparation by its own initiative or Governmental inquiries of reports, notes and even draft laws on general and concrete questions of economic policy, as well as replies to official drafts; c) the participation in permanent and temporary Governmental commissions and conferences, as well as creating more appropriate conditions for invited entrepreneurs[23].

Prominent business experts, well informed on each disputable matter, asserted trade and industry interests. The Convention eventually created an effective mechanism of influence on the Governmental legislative organs via its members in the State Council and the State Duma.

4. Innovation activities and research programmes

According to the Soviet historian Nikolai Filippov, there were approximately 47 scientific and technical societies in Russia before 1917. His list included associations organised exclusively by prominent Russian scientists and professors from Saint Petersburg, Moscow, Kharkov and Kronstadt. The Russian Technical Society was the first and the most authoritative among them. Filippov did not specify in the list the societies that were founded by entrepreneurs, engineers and technologists working in private enterprises[24]. In this respect, the Society for Supporting Experimental Sciences and their Practical Application deserves recognition. It was aided in 1909 by a merchant from the town of Vologda named Christopher Ledentsov who granted 2 million roubles to the cause in his will[25]. That public organisation provided innovative research, particularly in the field of technical equipment[26].

In parallel with the purely scientific and technical societies, the BIAs successfully operated in the field of applied sciences. The Society for Assistance and Development of the Textile Industry was the largest and the most influential organisation (with the exception of the Saint

---

23 See Shepelev, L.E., *Tsarism i burzhuaziya, op. cit.*, p. 103.

24 See Filippov, N.G., *Nauchno-tehnicheskie obshchestva v Rossii (1866–1917)* [*Scientific and Technical Societies in Russia (1866–1917)*], Moskva, MGIAI, 1976, pp. 206-213.

25 Without taking into account currency exchange rates, in 1914 1 rouble was equalled to 2.16 DM, to 2.67 FF, to 2.54 Kr; and one pound was equalled to 9.46 roubles. See *Rossiya 1913 god. Statistiko-dokumental'ny ocherk* [*Russia in 1913. Statistical and Documentary Reference Book*], Sankt-Peterburg, BLITS, 1995, p. 175.

26 See Morozova, S.G., *Obshchestvo sodeistviya uspekham opytnykh nauk imeni Kh.S.Ledentsova: ego vklad v nauchno-tehnicheskii progress* [*The Society for Assistance to Success of Experimental Sciences Named after Kh.S.Ledentsova: Its Contribution to Scientific and Technological Progress of Russia*], Moskva, Politekhnicheski muzei, 1993.

Petersburg association under the same name). Created by Moscow entrepreneurs and technologists, the Society accomplished representative, scientific and cognitive functions. Scientific activities were prioritised throughout its history.

The laboratory of the Chemical and Dyeing Group was one of the most creative and fruitful structural sections in the Society. Sergei Prokhorov organised that unit in 1891. Moscow University's Professor Oswald K. Miller[27], along with Sergei Nazarov and Vladimir Ogloblin, supervised its work; almost all of the group's members were well-known and authoritative persons in the Russian textile industry as well as in science. In total, the Chemical and Dyeing group carried out 144 sessions (so-called "Discussions") and presented 261 papers. Those papers were devoted to the theoretical problems as well as the vital issues of the bleaching process, cotton-printing and dyeing technology that Russian textile factories faced. At the beginning of the twentieth century, students of the Moscow Technical Institute used to attend the group's sessions, which gathered from 16 to 69 participants. In 1914, its members were preparing to partinipate in the International Congress on applied chemistry but the First World War changed their plans drastically[28]. As far as the laboratory was concerned, it gained authority within business circles very quickly. From 1892, exchange bargains were struck on painted substances owing to the laboratory's certificates. Moreover, due to its activities the Society managed to withdraw several kinds of counterfeit goods from distribution in the Moscow region[29].

There were two more units in the structure of the Society: the Spinning & Weaving Group and the Mechanical & Building Group. Professor of the Saint Petersburg Institute of Transport Engineers Nikolai Belelyubski, a brilliant Russian engineer and bridge builder, assisted the Mechanical and Building unit[30]. Together with the Moscow

---

27 O.K. Miller (1848-1919), was a well-known Russian chemist. He developed the first synthetic sulphurous substantive dye (canarine).

28 See Voznesenski, N.N., *Dvadtsat' pyat' let deyatel'nosti Khimiko-krasil'noi gruppy Obshchestva dlya sodeistviya uluchsheniyu i razvitiyu manufakturnoi promyschlennosti* [*Twenty Five Years of Activity of the Chemical and Dyeing Group by the Society for Assistance and Development of Textile Industry]*, Moskva, Izvestiya OSURMP, 1916, pp. 3, 8, 14, 38, 47.

29 See *Otchet Obshchestva dlya sodejstviya uluchsheniyu i razvitiyu manufakturnoi promyshlennosti za 1892 god* [*Report by the Society for Assistance and Development of Textile Industry for 1892 Year*], Moskva, [npi], 1893, p. 37. *Otcheti Obshchestva dlya sodejstviya uluchsheniyu i razvitiyu manufakturnoi promyshlennosti za 1893 god* [*Report by... 1893 Year*], Moskva, [npi], 1894, p. 35.

30 N.A. Belelyubski (1845-1922) was the first who applied original construction of free cross-section girders in bridge building. In 1900, he was awarded the Grand Prix at the World Exhibition in Paris. See *Otchet Obshchestva dlya sodejstviya uluchsheniyu*

Society of Electrical Engineers, the Group had carried out research dealing with the practical results of usage of diesel engines in the industry. These two organisations prepared a questionnaire that was sent to 2,000 enterprises[31]. Thus, the Society tried to solve one of the most important questions of rapprochement of the production process and science in the name of economic progress and the prosperity of Russian manufacturing.

The second half of the nineteenth century featured improved record keeping and statisitical analysis by Governmental sources, which were stimulated by deep socio-economic modernisation of the country. As a result, high-grade statistical registration allowed the Government to pursue an adequate economic policy and more or less correct administrative decisions. This motivated entrepreneurial associations to start their own statistical surveys and observations.

In 1897, the Convention of Representatives of the Mining Industry of South Russia was one of the first associations to organised its own Statistical Bureau as a structural unit. The Bureau elaborated a detailed programme for monthly statistics on extractions of minerals and the expenditure of enterprises. It made an annual collection of data about technical equipment, numbers of workers, their distribution by professions, and accidents. The Convention's expenditures on statistical research amounted to considerable sums. From 1897-1905, it spent more than 100,000 roubles on these activities[32]. A collection of various data under the title "Russian coal industry" became the most relevant work edited at the beginning of the twentieth century by the Statistical Bureau.

The experts of the Convention of Representatives of Industry and Trade carried out a wide research programme based on data collected by its Statistical Bureau and Permanent Legal Commission, and published the results in the Minutes of Conventions, the Council's reports and in the journal "Industry and Trade". In 1909, the first edition of the valuable and comprehensive statistical directory appeared under the title "The factory enterprises in the Russian Empire". Five years later, it was revised and expanded. A firm and all its industrial enterprises were taken as registration units. In 1912-1914, the Convention's experts generalised the results of the legislation pertinent to industry and trade

i razvitiyu manufakturnoi promyshlennosti za 1892 god [*Report by... for 1892 Year*], Moskva, [npi], 1893, p. 10.

31 See TsIAM. RG. 225, inv. 1, f. 8, back of page 5.

32 See Fomin, P.I., *Kratki ocherk*, *op. cit.*, pp. 21-22.

in extensive analytical reviews[33]. In 1913, the Convention's experts edited two comprehensive volumes presenting statistical data on the national economy for the period 1885-1913: there were sections on population, living standards, industry, agriculture, trade, transport, finance and credit[34].

Various questions about Russian commercial and industrial life were discussed in sessions organised by the Society for Assistance to Russian Industry and Commerce, particularly in relation to railways tariffs, protectionist duties, internal taxes, and oriental trade. The results of these debates were published in the periodical "Commercial collection" and in voluminous annual "Works" in the form of analytical reviews. Scientific articles written by the members of the Society for Assistance and Development of the Textile Industry were usually issued in its own "Proceedings".

5. Cultural and educational activities

The overwhelming majority of entrepreneurial associations included in their charters a paragraph proclaiming a cultural and educational mission. As a rule, it was multilateral and comprised the creation of technical schools and colleges, libraries, museums, exhibitions, the establishment and awarding of prizes and grants, and publishing. These aspects of public activities, especially in the realm of education, were presumably the most pronounced in the old associations because Russian entrepreneurs faced an acute lack of qualified labour during the rapid process of industrialisation. That was why the educational mission took prime importance. There were two ways of solving this urgent matter: by means of private initiative or by means of Governmental efforts. Practical work revealed that education turned out to be a conciliatory platform that united even bitter business competitors. In the end, it united state and society. Large corporations and well-known entrepreneurs usually organised elementary schools attached to their firms while associations concentrated their efforts on institutions of higher learning and secondary technical training schools. They regarded that kind of activity as extremely necessary and important because it created favourable conditions for industrial development.

---

33 See *Promyschlennost' i torgovlya v zakonodatel'nykh uchrezhdeniyakh. 1907-1914* [*Industry and Trade in the Legislative Institutions, 1907-1914*], Sankt-Peterburg, Tipografiya. T-va p.f. "Electrotip. N.Ya. Stoikovoi", 1912-1914, 3 vols.

34 See *Statisticheski ezhegodnik 1912 g. (Soveta s'ezdov predstavitelei promyschlennosti i torgovli)* [*Statistical Yearbook. 1912]*, Sankt-Peterburg, [npi], 1913; *Statisticheski ezhegodnik 1913 g. (Soveta s'ezdov predstavitelei promyschlennosti i torgovli),* [*Statistical Yearbook 1913*], Sankt-Peterburg, [npi], 1914.

In 1868 the Russian Technical Society (RTS) was the first organisation that launched educational activities attracting large firms and entrepreneurs in financing its schools. The RTS was also the most successful in that sphere. At the end of the century, its Permanent Commission on Technical Training had opened 25 elementary and secondary schools of three types: 1) factory schools for children; 2) night classes for adult workers; 3) specialised secondary colleges.

From 1876, the RTS educational institutions received Treasury subsidies because the Russian Government declared them very useful and necessary for the state. For some schools, these assignments constituted approximately 30 per cent of total receipts; the remaining educational expenditures were covered by private donations[35]. It is very important to underline that the RTS also opened 13 local departments in large industrial centres, and each department established schools and night classes. In 1903, the RTS had 63 elementary schools and secondary colleges with about 7,000 pupils in Saint Petersburg alone. At that time, the budget of the Permanent Commission on Technical Training came to 190,000 roubles. The prestige of the RTS schools was such that cities' authorities and local administrations (the zemstvo) set up grants on their behalf[36].

The educational activities of the others were conducted more or less successfully too, though on a small scale in comparison with the RTS. For example, the oldest organisation, the Convention of Representatives of the Mining Industry of South Russia, sponsored institutions of higher learning and secondary training schools. The College of Mines, schools of captains (mine masters) and commercial schools were objects of its primary interest. The Convention spent about 238,000 roubles on these purposes from 1884-1905, and more than 210,000 roubles were transferred to the new College of Mines in Ekaterinoslav, founded in 1899[37].

The Moscow Technical Institute and the Spinning and Weaving College became institutions of high priority for the Society for Assistance and Development of the Textile Industry. From 1896-1899 it

---

35 See Tits, B.N., *Ocherk istorii postoyannoi komissii po tehnicheskomu obrazovaniyu pri Imperatorskom Russkom tehnicheskom obshchestve s ee osnovaniya v 1868 godu do 1 yanvarya 1889 goda [A Brief History of the Permanent Commission on Technical Training Attached to the Imperial Russian Technical Society from the moment of its establishment in 1868 till January 1, 1889]*, Sankt-Peterburg, Tipografiya E.A. Evdokimova, 1889, pp. 200-201, 218.

36 See Filippov, N.G., *op. cit.*, pp. 167-168; Bradley, J., *Voluntary Associations in Tsarist Russia. Science, Patriotism and Civil Society*, Cambridge-London, Harvard University Press, 2009, pp. 177-200.

37 See Fomin, P.I., *Kratki ocherk, op. cit.*, pp. 21-22, 38-42.

spent 231,000 roubles on establishing a specialised secondary training school that was opened in Moscow in November 1901. The College was kept exclusively by the mill owners who voluntarily deducted a fixed sum paid from every working loom at their enterprises. Moreover, the Society's members made donations to a foundation for pupils, and arranged visits to the city museums and to the Moscow Art Theatre[38].

Old Russian entrepreneurial societies succeeded in making numerous temporary and permanent exhibitions of various types. Needless to say, the Russian Technical Society became the recognised leader in this sphere, surpassing the other organisations in the number of its deeds. The Anniversary Exhibition of Electroplating, devoted to the prominent member of the St.Petersburg Academy Boris Jacobi (1889)[39], the All-Russian Exhibition of Printing and Publishing (1895), and the International Aerostation Show (1911) became the most significant events in its history. As regards the others, the situation was as follows: in 1896, the Society for Assistance and Development of the Textile industry organised an experimental station at the All-Russian Exhibition in Nizhniy Novgorod, after which it established a permanent exposition of fabrics at the Polytechnic Museum in Moscow. Two movable teaching show exhibitions for handicraftsmen established by the Society for assistance of Russian Industry and Commerce were recognised as the most important events in Central Russia in the Summers of 1903 and 1905. They gathered 65,500 and 27,500 visitors respectively[40].

---

38 See *Otchet Obshchestva dlya sodejstviya uluchsheniyu i razvitiyu manufakturnoi promyshlennosti za 1899 god [Report by the Society for Assistance and Development of Textile Industry for 1899 Year*], Moskva, [npi], 1900, p. 38. *Otchet o deyatel'nosti Moskovskogo pryadil'no-tkatskogo uchilishcha pri Obshchestve dlya sodejstviya uluchsheniyu i razvitiyu manufakturnoi promyschlennosti, sostojashchego v vedomstve Ministerstva torgovli i promyschlennosti. za 1912/1913 uchebny god [Report on Activity of the Moscow Spinning and Weaving College Attached to the Society for Assistance and Development of Textile Industry for 1912/1913 School Year]*, Moskva, [npi], 1914, p. 64.

39 Moritz Hermann von Jacobi (1801-1874) was born in Potsdam in a Jewish family. In 1835, he was invited to the University of Dorpat (nowadays Tartu) and in 1837 he was sent on business to Saint Petersburg.

40 See Fedorov, S.A., "Otchet o deyatel'nosti stantsii dlya issledovaniya khlopka, pryazhi i tkanei, ustroennoi i organizovannoi po predlozheniyu 'Obschestva dlya sodejstviya uluchsheniyu i razvitiyu manufakturnoi promyshlennosti'" ["Report on Activity of the Station for Research of Cotton, Yarn and Fabrics Organized by the Society for Assistance to Russian Industry and Commerce"], in *Izvestiya Obschestva dlya sodejstviya uluchsheniyu i razvitiyu manufakturnoi promyshlennosti* [*Proceedings of the Society for Assistance to Russian Industry and Commerce*], Moskva, [npi], vol. IV, 1897; *Uchebno-pokazatel'nye vystavki dlja kustarei i remeslennikov 1903 i 1905 gg.* [*Teaching Show Exhibitions for Handicraftsmen in 1903 and 1905*], Sankt-Peterburg, Tipografiya inzh. G.A. Bernsteina, 1907.

Thus, varied cultural and educational activities conducted by numerous entrepreneurial associations helped to solve a number of pressing problems: the propaganda of advanced technologies and experience; the rising of the overall level of industrial development; the proliferation of technical knowledge; the training of workers for large-scale and small-scale industry; the promotion of industrial culture to the handicrafts milieu; the organisation of summer practice for students and schoolchildren in large industrial enterprises.

Conclusion

By the beginning of the twentieth century, there were approximately 150 BIAs. The Russian entrepreneurs created a convenient combination of branch and regional organisations that protected and coordinated the economic interests and efforts of the upper middle and middle classes. The BIAs united businessmen, managers and technicians for solving numerous urgent questions surrounding the rapid economic growth of Russia and the improvement of its socio-cultural context. As Joseph Bradley puts it, "associations and the activities they sponsored were living examples of the economic power, creative spirit, paternalist good works, civic stewardship, and refinement of the middle classes"[41]. In my opinion, this generalisation is wholly apllicable to the Russian situation.

Subject to the forces governing this economic growth, the Russian voluntary BIAs evolved from simple spokespersons of entrepreneurs' interests to active and influential participants in the formulation and development of the principles of domestic economic policy. They contributed to the creation of favourable conditions for national development, tried to protect the interests of the business community and to create a positive social environment. Nevertheless, the Russian entrepreneurs and their BIAs could not completely remove special interest groups from their ranks, even within the framework of a nation-wide organisation.

In the final analysis, the Russian BIAs should be considered as an element of the institutional framework of economic development on the one hand, and, on the other hand, as a sign of the formation of civil society in modernizing Russia.

---

41 See Bradley, J., "Voluntary Associations, Civic Culture, and 'Obshchestvennost' in Moscow", in E.W.Clowes, S.D.Kassow, J.L.West (eds.), *Between Tsar and People. Educated Society and the Quest for Public Identity in Late Imperial Russia.* Princeton, Princeton University Press, 1991, p. 132.

An Overview of the French Business Interest Associations (1880s-1920s)

Pierre VERNUS

Université Lumière Lyon 2

Introduction

The history of Business Interest Associations (hereafter BIAs) in France remained an area of research rather neglected by historians until recently. For instance, a 2007 review of the existing literature on the employers' organisations devoted only 6 out of 128 pages to the history of BIA before the Second World War[1]. While recent research has modified our knowledge on the subject, most of it still deals with national federations or confederations or with organisations located in Paris[2]. Consequently, we still lack a comprehensive understanding of the BIAs in France before 1914. The consequence is that the chronology and the causes of the BIAs' creation, characteristics, structures and functions have been presented in a somewhat skewed and distorted manner, based on several questionable assumptions.

---

1 See Rabier, M., *Revue de littérature: organisations patronales en France et en Europe, Documents d'études*, Paris, Direction de l'animation de la recherche des études et des statistiques, décembre 2007, http://www.travail-solidarite.gouv.fr/IMG/pdf/DE130BIS_organisations_patronales-3.pdf (30 december 2012).

2 For instance see: Fraboulet, D., *Quand les patrons s'organisent. Stratégies et pratiques de l'Union des industries métallurgiques et minières 1901-1950*, Villeneuve-d'Asq, Presses universitaires du Septentrion, 2007; Rust, M.J., *Business and Politics in the Third Republic: the Comité des Forges and the French Steel Industry, 1896-1914*, Ph.D, Princeton University, 1973; Dubos, J., *André Lebon: un homme d'affaires en République (1859-1938). Le patriotisme et l'influence*, collection Carnot, Rennes, PUR, 2001; Lemercier, C., *Un si discret pouvoir. Aux origines de la Chambre de commerce de Paris, 1803-1853*, Paris, La Découverte, 2003; *Id., Un modèle français de jugement des pairs. Les tribunaux de commerce, 1790-1880*, HDR, Université Paris VIII Vincennes-Saint-Denis, 2012, http://tel.archives-ouvertes.fr/docs/00/68/55/44/PDF/Lemercier_manuscrit_inedit.pdf (18 april 2013).

This paper aims to make a contribution towards filling that gap. It deals with voluntary associations that can be divided into two legal categories in France after 1884: the syndicats professionnels (authorised in 1884 by the Waldeck-Rousseau Law) and the associations (Associations Act of 1901). We will focus primarily on the first category because it was the most numerous and because it included the greater part of the local and regional organisations. This chapter relies on data collected in the "Annuaire des syndicats professionnels of 1900", published by the Ministry of Commerce, and on data accumulated in the course of a research project on the syndicats patronaux (employers' unions) in the departments of the Rhone-Alpes region[3].

This paper will initially review the traditional historiography, before introducing new sources and explaining how a new approach of focusing on local level organisations can renew our understanding of the French BIAs. The result will be the presentation of new and challenging findings on the history of the BIAs in France.

1. The French BIAs in the Nineteenth century: traditional assumptions

The long-standing traditional historical view of the BIAs in France, or French organisations patronales, could perhaps be best summarised as follows: French employers have organised themselves late in the day; after resisting free trade, Labour unrest and the growing strength of the Labour movement in the last decades of the nineteenth century were the two major causes that compelled employers to gather together. This interpretation relied heavily on Priouret's and Lefranc's books[4].

As a matter of fact, Priouret, and Lefranc, whose first chapter relied for the most part on Priouret's work, noted the existence of trade associations in the first decades of the nineteenth century and that of chambres syndicales that were set up during the Second Empire. However, they did not attach much importance to these groups because they involved artisans or men of small or medium trade rather than industrialists. They also briefly mentioned some examples of regional or local groups of industrialists such as the Comité des filateurs de Lille (Spinners' Committee of Lille), which was created in 1824, but again paid little attention to them, discarding them as remnants of the

---

[3] See Ministère du Commerce et de l'Industrie, *Annuaire des syndicats professionnels, commerciaux et agricoles*, Paris, Imprimerie nationale, 1900; Vernus, P. (ed.), *Les organisations patronales. Une approche locale (XIXe-XXe siècles)*, Lyon, Institut des sciences de l'homme, 2002.

[4] See Priouret, R., *Origines du patronat français*, Paris, Grasset, 1963; Lefranc, G., *Les organisations patronales en France, du passé au présent*, Payot, Paris, 1976.

nostalgia of the pre-revolutionary corporatist order that were condemned to disappear. Priouret and Lefranc postulated a connection between industrial expansion and concentration on the one hand and the development of the BIAs on the other hand. Moreover, implicitly if not explicitly, they considered that only national organisations were worthy of study because they assimilated national level organisations grouping heavy and/or concentrated industries (the cotton industry, the steel and iron industry, engineering, metalworking, coal mines and so on) to modern forms of organisation. Leading on from this, because they thought that most industrialists – in their view the real patronat – did not support free-trade, they considered protectionist mobilisation as the main cause of the first wave of creation of BIAs bodies. As a result, they emphasised the importance of the protectionist Association pour la défense du travail national (Association for protecting national Labour), founded in 1842 by Auguste Mimerel. Mimerel's action, according to Lefranc, could be explained by the fact that the Nord region progressively assumed the leadership of the movement over the Centre region, Normandie and Paris, whereas the East remained at the head of the cotton industry. Lefranc assumed that Lyon only played a minor role in the attempts to organise business because of the nature of its dominant silk trade and industry, with its foreign-oriented supply and export markets.

For Priouret and Lefranc, the other main chronological landmarks were the creation of the Comité des Forges in 1864, the Union des industries minières et métallurgiques (UIMM) in 1901[5], the Confédération de la production française (CGPF)[6] in 1919 and the Conseil national du patronat français (CNPF) in 1945. Whereas Priouret ended his book at the end of the Second Empire, Lefranc extended his work into the 1970s but applied the same approach by focusing his study on the confederations and the national or Parisian organisations. So by favouring the top associations, their works neglected the bulk of the organisations patronales.

Another idea was that the French BIAs emerged later than employers' organisations in other countries, especially Germany. This theory was developed in the early 1900s by authors connected with the BIAs and who often advocated the reinforcing of employers' organisations so that they could better defend their own interests at a time when the trade unions were becoming more pugnacious and socialists parties were achieving electoral successes. They referred to two major organisational models: firstly, the Confédération générale du

5 About UIMM see the contribution of Danièle Fraboulet in this volume.

6 It was renamed *Confédération générale du patronat français* after 1936.

travail (General Confederation of Labour) formed in 1895, whose cohesiveness was often overestimated by employers; and, secondly, the German employers' associations[7]. So, as Lefranc wrote: "on the social field the patronat fight on two fronts. It resists against the rise of the workers movement, represented by trade unions, and opposes State interference. The activity of their organisations translate and arrange employers' spontaneous reactions"[8]. So, the growth of the Labour movement would have been the second major impulse that urged employers to organise themselves and to create long-lasting organisations at the national level: industry federations and, above all, the UIMM.

More recent research challenged this traditional view and the assumptions on which it relied. It demonstrated that the BIAs were more numerous and more active than had previously been suggested, and that fighting free trade and resisting the growth of the Labour movement and State intervention were not the only incentives for patrons to gather together. They created associations to regulate competition, compile economic information and to settle disputes. By adopting a grassroots and local or regional approach, this paper will contribute to this historiographical renewal.

2. Focusing on local or regional associations

Adopting a local approach can be justified by the fact that the first BIAs grouped people practicing the same activity or range of activities at a local level. Even if there were examples of associations with national aims created as early as the 1840s or even before, long-standing national structures were not developed until after the local system had been refined. This sequence raises fresh questions about why employers organised themselves, about the level and the form of the organising process over time and about the distribution and redistribution of tasks among associations at different levels.

Other reasons can further justify a regional or local approach. Firstly, it facilitates the production of a clearer picture of the diversity of businessmen and associations. Secondly, during most of the nineteenth century the regulation of markets, especially of labour markets, was local or regional and based on local practices and customs. Thirdly, it is not necessarily the case that local associations operated in the same manner as federations or confederations. Fourthly, the local approach promotes not only the consideration of the BIAs from the point of view

7 See Saint-Girons, P., *L'Assurance patronale contre la grève, thèse de doctorat en droit*, Paris, 1908; Blonde G., "La défense patronale en Allemagne", in *Le Musée social. Mémoires et documents*, Paris, Rousseau, 1907, p. 7121.

8 See Lefranc, G., *Les organisations patronales*, *op. cit.*, p. 52.

of industrial relations (as has often been undertaken) but also allows for an examination of the whole range of their functions.

Concerning the chambres syndicales, as already seen, the assumption that patrons organised themselves belatedly was based on a narrow and questionable view of the patronat that implicitly excluded small or medium employers or capitalists. Proceeding from a more extensive definition of patron as an employer that might have been classified as small or as more substantial, especially in industry or trade, more accurately reflects the reality of the commercial and industrial structures of the French economy in the nineteenth century, in which artisans, small and medium enterprises and trades were predominant[9].

The Le Chapelier Law of March 1791 (which banned groups aiming to defend their interests), the law of 10 April 1834, and several articles of the French Code Penal have often been highlighted to explain the late development of intermediary bodies in France, particularly the late organisation of French patrons. Of course, these restrictive laws induced the monitoring of various groups by the French government. Professional associations such as chambres syndicales or clubs were no exception. Workers' trade unions were the main object of this government interference but employers' associations were also affected. In spite of this, a great number of patrons' organisations existed before the Waldeck-Rousseau Law of 1884. During the First Empire, in addition to some activities in the food sector, such as bakers and butchers, the prefect of police in Paris incentivised some trades in the building industry, such as carpenters and masons, to gather together. During the 1860s the Second Empire adopted a more liberal stance and the law of 25 May 1864 legalised the coalitions, the temporary groups formed to co-ordinate strikes, so that trade associations of workers were finally tolerated. This decision applied to employers' associations also, even if they were already accepted in practice by the authorities.

Thus, some chambres syndicales (or syndicats) were created in the first half of the nineteenth century. In Paris they brought together a great number of members, the majority of whom were employers and who progressively became known as patrons after 1870[10]. That the authorities accepted their existence is illustrated by the response of the prefect of the Rhône to a request from the brewers of Lyon to authorise the chambre syndicale they had just created: "I have no objection to allow

---

9 On the history and meaning of the word patron see Daumas, J.C., "Patrons, patronat: les mots et les chiffres", in J.C. Daumas, A. Chatriot, D. Fraboulet, P. Fridenson, H. Joly (eds.), *Dictionnaire historique des patrons français*, Paris, Flammarion, 2010, p. 1237-1244.

10 See Lemercier, C., *Un modèle français*, *op. cit.*, p. 159-177.

the Syndicat des brasseurs (Brewers' Union) operate, like in other brewing centres but I need not to give them an official authorisation. This institution does not need one given its aim. I kept the copy of the association statutes for informational purposes"[11]. The laws restricting the right to form associations were essentially aimed at workers groups that were considered as a potential threat to public order. The authorities were much more tolerant towards employers' groups. This was recognised by the government minister Forcade Laroquette in his report of 30 March 1868 which announced state tolerance for workers' trade unions[12]. He noted that the chambres syndicales of the patrons often had old origins, that their number had increased in recent years and that "applying the same rules to the workers as to the employers administration will not interfere in the setting up of the chambres syndicales". Moreover, administrative authorities or commercial courts frequently consulted the chambres syndicales about technical problems. However, the tolerance of the authorities was precarious, especially when an organisation seemed to be a danger to the regime[13]. Chambers of commerce occasionally resisted the creation of the chambres syndicales for fear of losing their monopoly on representing business interests[14].

Finally, the Waldeck-Rousseau law of 21 March 1884 on the syndicats professionnels repealed the Le Chapelier law and legally recognised these groups. It specified the manner in which they should be formed. The Waldeck-Rousseau law was extended on 12 March 1920 to further clarify the attributes of the syndicats professionnels and the legal status of the unions de syndicats[15].

The bureaucracy and legislation surrounding syndicats professionnels resulted in administrative practices that produced documents useful for historians. During the period of tolerance before 1884 files on trade organisations were compiled. In the 1870s, legislative proposals aiming to legalise professional associations prompted the central administration to calculate the number of these kind of bodies. In October 1876 the Minister of Agriculture and Trade's Bureau of Internal Trade ordered the prefects (the heads of administration in the departments) to compile

---

11 See Archives départementales du Rhône, 10 M.

12 Published in *Le Moniteur*, 31 March 1868.

13 See Agulhon, M., *Le cercle dans la France bourgeoise 1810-1848. Étude d'une mutation de sociabilité*, Paris, Armand Colin, Cahiers des Annales, 1977, p. 28.

14 See Lincoln, A., "Le syndicalisme patronal à Paris de 1815 à 1848: une étape de la formation d'une classe patronale", in *Le Mouvement social*, n° 114, january-march 1981, p. 11-34; Agulhon, M., *Le cercle*, *op. cit.*, p. 28, 32-33, 60-61.

15 See Soubiran-Paillet, F., *L'invention du syndicat (1791-1884). Itinéraire d'une catégorie juridique*, Paris, LGDJ, 1999; Pic, P., *Traité élémentaire de législation industrielle. Les lois ouvrières*, Paris, Rousseau, 1922 (5th edition).

information on the employers' associations and workers' trade unions in their respective regions, listing membership numbers, period of creation and resources. The process was repeated the following year. These early lists were far from perfect, however, and the Bureau complained about omissions. But it consistently requested further lists in the following years. For its part, the Ministry of the Interior, facing as it was the revival of the socialist movement and trade unionism, also requested such lists[16]. Before 1884, then, more or less regular trade association censuses were undertaken.

The law of 21 March 1884 stipulated that syndicats grouping people "practicing the same activity, similar trades or related activities that collaborate to produce some particular products [could] be freely created without the Government's approval". The only condition was that the statutes of the syndicat and the names of the people in charge of its administration had to be registered with the municipality (or in Paris with the prefecture of the Seine departement) where the head office of the syndicat was located.

This legal framework oriented the way patrons organised themselves. For instance, the fact that the members had to practice the same activity or similar trades hampered the formation of inter-branch organisations that were created as associations after the passing of the law of 1 July 1901. Moreover, the syndicats were only able to study and defend industrial, commercial or agricultural interests and could not deal with political issues.

In spite of the liberal provisions and interpretation of the law of 1884, the same administrative practices went on. As early as August 1884 the Bureau of the Ministry of the Interior, responsible for monitoring of the syndicat professionnels, required the prefects to send it a copy of the forms establishing when the syndicats were registered. Furthermore, a special register had to be completed with the date of submission of the statutes, the name of the administrators or directors, and the date of receipt. It seems that the information was not always clearly or fully transmitted and the registers were rudimentary and incomplete. In 1886, the overseeing of the syndicats professionnels came under the responsibility of the Ministry of Commerce: then the Ministry of Commerce and Industry (after 1906, responsibility passed to the Director of Labour in the Ministry of Labour). In 1885 and 1887, the prefects were again required to send a yearly census of the syndicats professionnels that existed in their department. The whole idea was to publish a directory of these associations and this was achieved every

16 For example, the first Bureau of the Direction for General Security sent the prefects such lists in at least 1880, 1881 and 1882.

year from 1889 to 1914. Several categories were distinguished among the syndicats professionnels: the workers' unions (syndicats ouvriers), the employers' unions (syndicats patronaux), the unions grouping workers and employers together (syndicats mixtes) and the agricultural unions (syndicats agricoles). The directories also list the unions de syndicats, that is the organisations grouping several syndicats. These organisations were ordered by department and town. The name, the creation or declaration date, the number of members, the address, the number of women, if any, and the services offered by the syndicat (journal, courses, mutual aid societies and so on) are given.

3. An alternative view of the BIAs

Thus, the monitoring of the syndicats professionnels generated serial documents at the local and national levels. In spite of their limitations, these documents allow a quantitative treatment and the elaboration of an overall picture of the population of these organisations. Such an investigation was undertaken previously for the departements of the Rhone-Alpes région[17] but a systematic exploitation of the informations included in the "Annuaires des syndicats professionnels" will give a global and more pertinent overview of the French BIAs during the last quarter or the last third of the nineteenth century. The first result of a case study of the "Annuaire of 1900" will be considered here.

First of all, counting the syndicat professionnels does not corroborate the idea that employers' organisations (or BIAs) expanded belatedly. In the 1900 directory about 2,100 syndicats patronaux and 50 unions patronales are listed. In the Rhône-Alpes departments, more than 1,800 syndicats patronaux were registered before 1939. These departments accounted for about 10 per cent of this kind of association in France between 1889 and 1930 (the proportion remained stable during this period). The Rhône alone accounted for between one-third and four-tenths of the total, the departments of Loire and Isère for 15 and 19 per cent respectively, and the others departments (Ain, Ardèche, Drôme, Savoie and Haute-Savoie) made up the difference. These proportions roughly reflected the balance of industrial and commercial establishments located in each department.

Concerning the chronology, if we look at the statistics about the syndicats professionnels patronaux collected in the directory of 1900 (the head office of which was in Paris), and for which we know the year of creation (see barplot 1 at the end of the article), we notice that less than 5 per cent were founded in the first half of the century. A surge

[17] That is to say Ain, Ardèche, Drôme, Isère, Loire, Rhône, Savoie and Haute-Savoie. See Vernus, P. (ed.), *Les organisations patronales, op. cit.*

occurred during the Second Empire, so about 28 per cent existed before the law of 1884, another one in the second half of the 1880s and one-third in the second half of the 1890s.

Outside Paris (see barplot 2 at the end of the article), the syndicats patronaux created in the first half of the nineteenth century and still existing in 1900 were less numerous: two were founded before 1848 and 13 per cent before 1884 (mostly between 1870 and 1884). Specific periods of increase can be identified from 1884 for a number of years, at the beginning of the 1890s and again in the last years of that decade.

The directory of 1900 only lists the surviving syndicats or unions at the end of 1899. But the same chronology can be observed for the foundation of syndicats patronaux registered in the Rhone and Isère departements, the number of which increased dramatically during the 1880s and 1890s, then again during the 1900s. The economic depression of the 1880s, the growing volume of social and industrial legislation, and finally the rise of the labour movement at the beginning of the twentieth century could explain the increasing number of new bodies.

Table 1 – Syndicats patronaux in Loire and Rhone

Period of creation	**Loire**		**Rhône**	
	N.	**%**	**N.**	**%**
Before 1884	19	5	52	7
1884-1899	67	19	108	15
1900-1913	88	25	173	25
1914-1918	8	2	20	3
1919-1929	89	25	126	18
1930-1939	88	25	224	32
Total	359	100	703	100

Source: Vernus, P. (ed.), *Les organisations patronales*, *op. cit.*, p. 38.

Of course, as already suggested, not all the syndicats professionnels that were created survived. A lot of them disappeared quickly. But a thorough analysis of the age structure of their populations nuances the idea that these organisations were highly volatile. There is the possibility that registration forms or files might lead to exaggeration or overestimation of the lifetime of the syndicats because it was not compulsory to declare their dissolution. Nevertheless, in 1914 more than a quarter of those syndicats existing in the departments of the Rhone and the Loire had been created at least 20 years earlier. The proportion was around 40 per cent in 1920. Thus, two groups of syndicats are to be distinguished: the first and largest one constituted a more or less ephemeral set but the second one grouped a solid kernel of a minority of long-lasting organisations. This was evident before 1914 and sometimes even before 1884. In the Rhône-Alpes the main economic sectors were already structured by a range of syndicats. For instance, in the building industry 13 syndicats existed before 1884[18]. One of these was the Chambre syndicale des entrepreneurs of Lyon (Chambre syndicale of the building contractors) and it helped to create other syndicats patronaux in the Rhône and the other departements during the following 20 years: in Vienne (1866), Saint-Étienne (1867), Tarare (1870), Valence et Grenoble (1872), Chambéry (1876), Rive-de-Gier (1880), and Bourg-en-Bresse (1882). In the silk industry, one of the major French export sectors, a first organisation, the Réunion des fabricants de soie (Silk Manufacturers' Meeting), was created in 1827 but it was short-lasting. A Society Against Silk Waste Embezzlement was founded in 1845. The Cercle des Teinturiers (Dyers' club) existed in 1855 but it became a syndicat only in the 1890s. The most influential chambres syndicales appeared from the late 1860s onwards with the Association de la fabrique lyonnaise (Silk weaving industry association, Lyon) in 1867, the Union des marchands de soie (Silk merchants' union, Lyon) in 1869, the Union des filateurs et des mouliniers français de la région de Valence (Silk spillers' and throwers' Union of the Valence region) in 1874, and the Union des filateurs et mouliniers de la région d'Aubenas (Silk spillers' and throwers' Union of the Aubenas region) in 1875[19]. Consequently, before the end of the nineteenth century each main activity within the sector had its own syndicat and sometimes several. Because of the concentration of silk industry in the Lyons region, some of these chambres syndicales had a national bearing. In the metalworking industries, the Association métallurgique du Rhône was formed in 1872, followed by the Association métallurgique du département de la Loire ten years after[20].

Concerning the location, from the 1880s onward national sectorial unions of syndicats were created in Paris. If some of them had only Parisian members, others were true nationwide structures. During the same decade local inter-sectorial unions of syndicats were formed in

[18] On the building industry see Robert, F., "La régulation de la concurrence: pratiques syndicales dans les industries du bâtiment du Rhône (1862-1900)", in P. Vernus (ed.), *Les organisations patronales*, *op. cit.*, p. 51-69.

[19] See Vernus, P., "Regulating the activity of a business community: employers' organisations in the Lyon silk industry (1860s-1939)", in *Business and Economic History Online, The Proceedings of the Business History Conference*, 2004, vol. 2 (http://www.thebhc.org/publications/BEHonline/2004/Vernus.pdf).

[20] See Vernus, P., "Pour une histoire du syndicalisme patronal dans la soierie lyonnaise avant 1914: l'Association de la Fabrique lyonnaise", in *Id.* (ed.), *Les organisations patronales*, *op. cit.*, p. 71-103; Fraboulet, D., "L'organisation syndicale de la métallurgie dans le Rhône (1872-1939)", in *Ibid.*, p. 123-144; *Id.*, *Quand les patrons s'organisent*, *op. cit.*, chapter 4.

cities such as Aix-en-Provence, Bordeaux, Limoges, Lyon, Marseille, Nantes, Reims, Rouen, Saint-Étienne, Versailles. Consequently, a trend towards a higher level of organisations could be observed before 1914. Unsurprisingly, most of syndicats patronaux were concentrated in Paris but their influence declined after 1884 (40.2 per cent of the syndicats created before 1884 were located in Paris but only 20.4 per cent thereafter). Further research is needed to determine the logic of location outside the capital city. Except for Lyon, Marseille, Lille-Roubaix-Tourcoing and Bordeaux, the ranking resulting from the number of syndicats created after 1884 did not match that of the population (for example, there is a discrepancy between the two rankings for Rouen). Thus, other variables have to be taken into account and tested, variables such as the status of the city. Was it a prefecture or not? Did it have a chamber of commerce? What was the nature, the diversity and the level of dynamism of its main economic activities? Moreover, the population should be split into sub-categories. Thus, the spatial distribution of the bakers' or butchers' syndicats, respectively around 190 and 100, does not follow the same logic as that of the textile activities.

In the Rhône-Alpes about 80 per cent of the syndicats created before 1884 were concentrated in the Rhone and the Loire departments that were the hub of the majority of regional industrial and commercial activities. As in the rest of the country, the growing number of syndicats in the following years were increasingly geographically dispersed and a lesser percentage of syndicats located in the Rhone department. Lyon, with its high level administrative functions, and its status of large commercial and economic centre with access to national and international markets, was particularly attractive for locating the head office of the syndicats and unions. Some of them were initially established outside Lyon but subsequently moved to the city. The federations of syndicats were more concentrated: two out three were located in the Rhône.

On the other hand, two-thirds of these syndicats represented the interests of commercial activities. The majority represented the selling or trading of foods, catering, drinks and tobacco. The minority belonged to industrial and artisanal activities, and a lesser minority again could be assigned to the services sector. However, the comparison between the sectorial distribution of the BIAs and the weight of the different sectors in a local economy is problematic. Ideally, the list of members should be known and compared with the list of enterprises of the sectors covered by the BIAs. It is not possible to do this work exhaustively because the information is simply not available, but it could be conducted for some major sectors (see Maps 1 and 2 at the end of the article)[21].

The functions fulfiled by the syndicats were numerous and diverse. Protecting the national market against foreign competition, labour unrest or State interventionism in the social and economic fields were far for being the only reasons why patrons gathered together. In fact, free traders organised themselves early, too. In March 1843 the chamber of commerce of Lyon denounced the action of Miremel's Association de défense du travail national and the silk manufacturers initiated a petition against protectionism[22]. Of course, employers also reacted against decisions or events that threatened their positions but it must be highlighted that other incentives were numerous, for instance regulating competition among the actors of a sector or a trade in order to avoid unfair practices and setting up a commercial or industrial police, sometimes by arbitrating or conciliating the disputes between members of the syndicat or the actors of the sector; favouring the diffusion of new technologies; collecting and disseminating commercial information among the members, especially when markets quickly evolved; opposing the setting up of new taxes by municipalities; acting to modifying the legal framework; securing or maintaining the hegemony of a local elite upon the commercial institutions[23]; developing sociability and making cooperation easier; and lastly, for some employers being president of a syndicat, even if small and not representative, was a way to obtain recognition among their peers and/or from public authorities.

A local, regional and a more sophisticated and nuanced quantitative approach allow for a more accurate and informative chronology of the development of the French BIAs. In turn, this facilitates a more complete understanding of their history. If it is right that in Paris the density of the BIAs was higher and that these associations appeared earlier, it is no longer possible to assume that French employers came together belatedly and that free trade, labour unrest and state interventionism were the main causes that compelled them to associate themselves. Despite the progress made here, there is still much scope for research in this area and the promulgation of new ideas and findings.

---

21 Please note that modalities of the membership should be taken into account: usually the members were enterprises rather than individuals.

22 See *L'Echo de la fabrique de 1841*, 28 February and 15 March 1843.

23 For instance, the union of *syndicats*, the *Union des chambres syndicales lyonnaises* was formed in 1885 after the passing of a law extending the electorate for the elections of commercial courts.

Barplot 1. Years of creation, Province

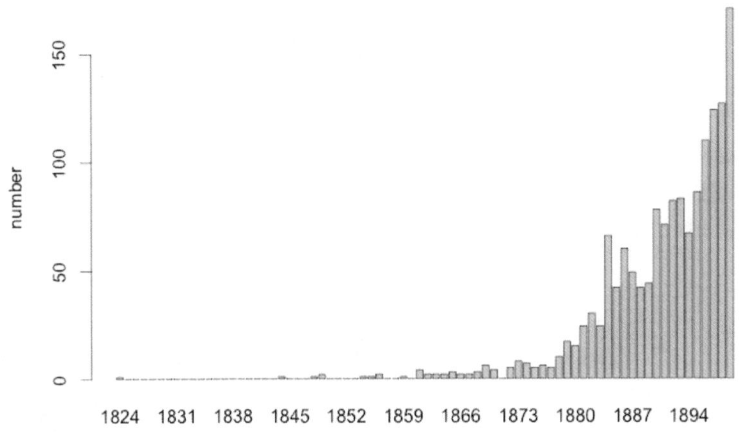

Source: Ministère du Commerce, de l'Industrie, des Postes et des Télégraphes, *Annuaire des syndicats professionnels industriels, commerciaux et agricoles*, Paris, Imprimerie Nationale, 1900.

Barplot 2. Years of creation, Paris

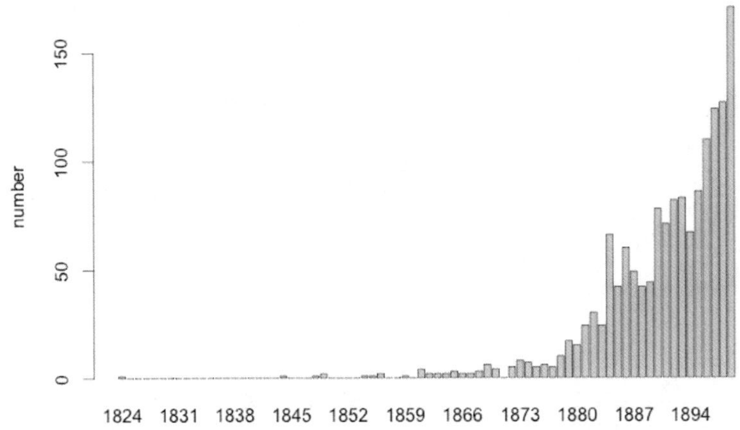

Source: *Ibid.*

Map 1 - Location of syndicats patronaux existing in 1899 and created before 1884 (outside Paris)

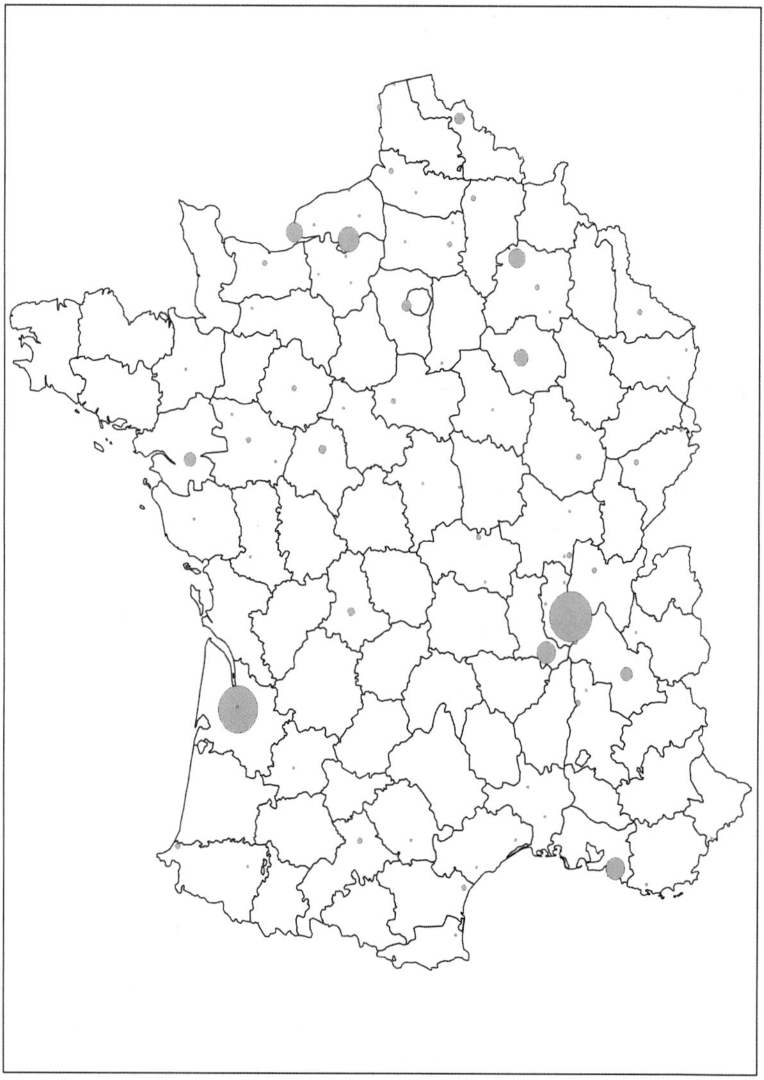

Source: *Ibid.*

Map 2 - Location of the syndicats patronaux existing in 1899 and created in 1884 or after

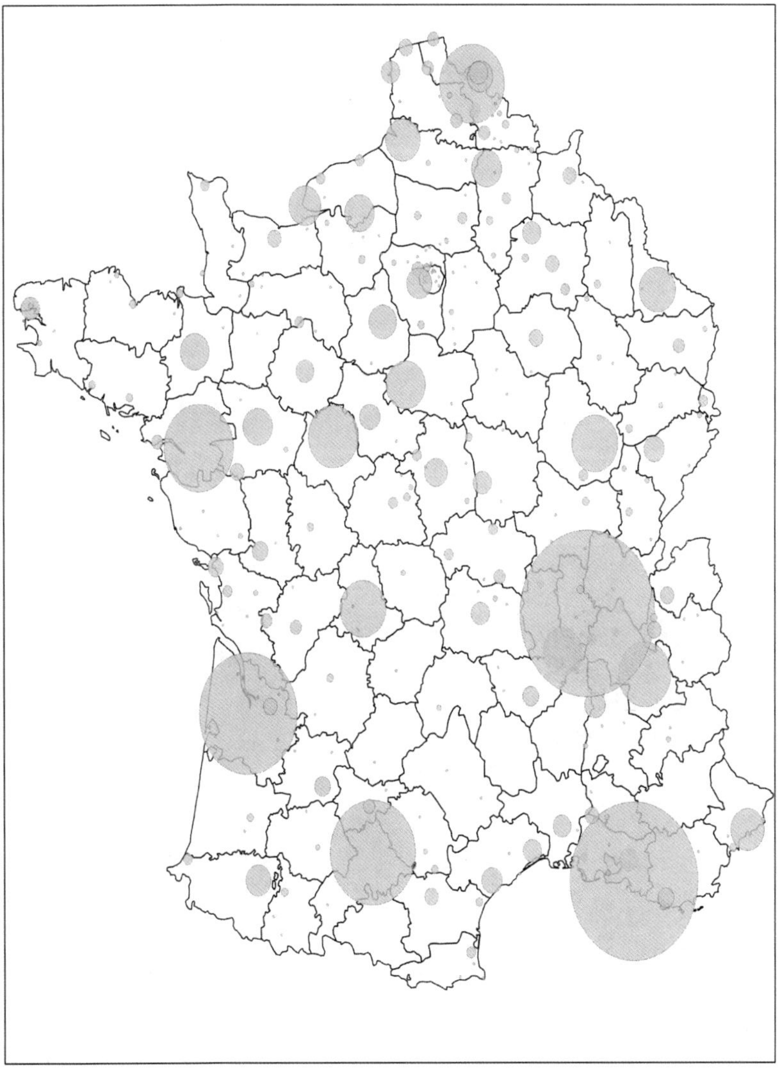

Source: *Ibid.*

Notes on the Genesis and Development of Business Interest Associations in Milan (19th-20th Centuries)

Andrea M. LOCATELLI * & Paolo TEDESCHI **

** Catholic University of Milan*
*** University of Milan-Bicocca Dems*

Introduction

The aim of this article is to consider some aspects of the origin and development of the Business Interest Associations (hereafter BIAs) which had their headquarters in Milan from the 1860s to 1950s[1]. Based on documents held in the archives of the most important BIAs in Lombardy and nationally, as well as in major Italian libraries[2], it demonstrates the unique nature of Milanese BIAs (vertical, horizontal, local, provincial, regional, national), and how they operated[3]: it also illustrates

1 While this article is the result of common research, analysis and reflection by its authors, Andrea M. Locatelli drew up paragraphs 1 and 2 and table 1, while Paolo Tedeschi wrote the remaining text. This article is related to the research project "The Business Associations in Lombardy: Aims, Organisation, Strategies (19th-20th Centuries)" involving researchers from the Catholic University of Milan and the University of Milan-Bicocca DEMS.

2 See the Archives of the Assolombarda (in particular bb. 1652, 1656, 1660, 1663) and of the Confindustria (in particular bb. 1.5/3-1.5/30, 47.1.1-47.1.7 and *Fondo Statuti e Documenti*). See also statutes and documents concerning BIAs at the Biblioteca Braidense (Milan) and at *Sezione Pubblicazioni minori* of the Biblioteca Nazionale (Florence) and the newspaper "L'Industria Lombarda" (published since 1922). Finally, see *Bibliografia dei periodici economici lombardi, 1815-1914*, Milan, Angeli, 2005 (http://pereco.lombardiastorica.it); Ferrari, D. (ed.), *Quasi un secolo fa. Dall'archivio di Assolombarda*, Milan, Assoservizi, 1988; Vidotto, L., *L'organizzazione industriale lombarda nell'ultimo cinquantennio*, Milan, Stucchi, 1959; Savallo, G., *Guida di Milano e provincia 1920-1921*, Milan, Pirola, 1921.

3 The vertical BIAs grouped enterprises belonging to the same productive sector; the horizontal BIAs grouped enterprises having their headquarters in the same area, but belonging to different productive sectors. Vertical and horizontal BIAs were local or provincial or regional or national: this obviously depended on their area of operation (a town, a province, a region or nationwide).

that they were characterised by a high number of members and a great ability to grant services to those members, assisted by an efficient internal mechanism for mediating competing interests. Furthermore, it shows that there were important differences between the factors influencing the evolution of BIAs and their members' attitudes. They depended on the conditions of productive sectors and the quality of firm assets in different sectors and their productivity and ability to increase their earnings. Their leaders used social resources and/or made good use of their rents. The so-called "selective incentives" had a great importance in explaining BIAs' economic and social role: this depended on the benefits linked to the governments' decisions on trade and fiscal policies. Moreover, the active engagement of members in BIAs' activities depended on their position in industrial policy and/or on the development of training programs and technical support services.

The article also analyzes the methods of diffusion and enforcement utilised by Milanese BIAs and the evolution of the activities they undertook in an effort to support manufacturers and improve their market. It highlights the contribution of Milanese BIAs to Lombard (and Italian) economic development and explains how they participated in the definition of new rules favouring industrial development and competition in internal and foreign markets. It concentrates on the experience of Lombardy because this region led national industrial growth and was also a key determinant in the national pattern of industrial associationism (together with Turin). In the early years of the period under review, the social and economic role of entrepreneurs was recognised and appreciated in the local community only: the result was that entrepreneurs defined their relationship with the public within the local dimension exclusively. The situation changed when the BIAs were founded and progressively developed a new industrial context both in Milan and Turin. By the end of the nineteenth century they could affirm the role of industry in the Italian economic system and, considering the competitive nature of enterprises and increasing State interference in the economy, they tried to satisfy the need of entrepreneurs to participate in the solution of social problems concerning the development of the new industrial society (through legislation on accidents in the workplaces, unemployment assistance, general health and social security). The leadership of BIAs knew well that for industrial development to occur there would have to be an agreement with trade unions and public authorities. Leaders of BIAs always attempted to reduce the contractual power of workers but, at the same time, they acknowledged that they had to accept some compromises and find the best way for: a) improving productivity more than wages (they asked for low interest rates on loans for investement and they tried to slow the growth of real wages); b) increasing State protection against foreign products (they called on the government to increase tariffs on imported goods); c) reducing taxation on entrepreneurial activity (they demanded the transfer of some taxes from the earnings of enterpreneurs to those of "rentiers").

1. The origin and development of the first Lombard BIAs and their economic goals

The initial diffusion of BIAs in Lombardy occured between the 1860s and 1870s. Their appearance was linked to the evolution of the economic and social system of the region and its capital. Already in the late 1860s, Lombardy was affected by significant processes of industrialisation with the spread of the factory system within the textile industry. The productive system was multi-dimensional and multi-sectoral and, at the same time, the transformation was polycentric. The entrepreneurial experience was related to the manufacturing tradition: silkworm breeding was common in the hilly areas of Lombardy and meant that there was a labour supply for the emerging firms. The processing of cotton was consolidated by the presence of proto-industry. The location of factories was conditioned to the exploitation of energy resources such as water. The manufacturing business was based on a risk-focused and competitive pattern (the "Manchester model") and used local resources and a local workforce. Entrepreneurs legitimated their presence in Lombard society through social works and civil commitment. A manufacturing system emerged which had different expectations about the management of workforce and trade policies: this pattern affected the prospects for coordination and unity of purpose. Initially, however, labour issues were resolved by means of a direct relationship between the employer and the workers: the textile industry was the main sector and the workforce was predominantly female. So conflicts were rare until the 1890s. Employers encouraged and supported the creation of friendly societies including workers from their factories: they also organised vocational courses and built villages for their workers[4].

During the second half of the nineteenth century, Milan became the main Italian commercial and financial centre. This involved development of manufacturing in many sectors (in particular in textiles, metalworking, manufacturing of rubber and electrical production) and includ-

4 See Zaninelli, S. (ed.), *Storia dell'industria lombarda*, 2 vol., Milan, Il Polifilo, 1988-1991; Romano, R., *La modernizzazione periferica. L'Alto Milanese e la formazione di una società industriale 1750-1914*, Milan, Angeli, 1990; Besana, C., "Da coloni a imprenditori. Attività economiche e dinamiche sociali tra Ottocento e Novecento", in E. Bressan (ed.), *Storia della Brianza*, vol. II, *Economia, religione e società*, Oggiono-Lecco, Cattaneo, 2007, pp. 55-151; Carera, A., "Le radici del 'fare' lombardo e la cultura del lavoro", in A. Colombo (ed.), *Far bene e fare il bene*, Milan, Irer-Guerini, 2010, pp. 115-120.

ed a strong presence of small and medium enterprises (SMEs) as well as widespread homework. The demand of the middle and upper classes allowed the consolidation of activities carried out by craftsmen and workers who maintained a strong artisanal tradition, such as clothing packers and printers. Milan was ruled by a cohesive high society including members of the old aristocracy and major educational and welfare institutions, along with entrepreneurs and big traders. They controlled the city administration and promoted an economic growth based on the development of SMEs and the great factories of the mechanical, chemical, and electrical sectors. However, the project did not foresee the creation of big factories in Milan. The moderate classes came to fear the social consequences of lots of workers in urban areas: so the big factories usually operated in the suburbs of Milan and other Lombard towns[5].

During the 1860s, textile and mechanical entrepreneurs were the protagonists of the economic system in Lombardy and associated with liberal merchants and financiers. In most cases, they aggregated in clubs for the development of commercial and industrial activities. The main aims of the first BIAs were the recognition of the interests of class (e.g. the issue of protectionism) and the affirmation of enterpreuners' identity. Textile employers used all existing institutions, such as chambers of commerce, to defend their interests and to explain their reservations about the launching of early social legislation. They were also present in consultative institutions, such as the Council of Trade, and thus influenced decisions taken by the national government[6].

At the end of the 1860s, local and multi-sectoral BIAs with a national vocation emerged. Integrative associations allowed entrepreneurs to share perspectives on issues that might impact on local economic prospects. Entrepreneurs could not achieve their goals only through intersectoral structures (such as the Chamber of Commerce) and so manufacturers were forced to band together in organisations with their own. This

5 On industrial development in Milan and its suburbs see Dalmasso, E., *Milano capitale economica d'Italia*, Milan, Angeli, 1972, pp. 34-45, 121-125; Fiocca, G. (ed.), *Borghesi ed imprenditori a Milano dall'Unità d'Italia alla prima guerra mondiale*, Rome-Bari, Laterza, 1984; Cova, A., *Da capitale di un regno a capitale di un'economia*, in G. Rumi, A. Buratti, A Cova (eds.), *Milano nell'Unità nazionale (1860-1890)*, Milan, Cariplo, 1991, pp. 311-327; Trezzi, L. (ed.), *Sesto San Giovanni 1880-1921. Economia e società: la trasformazione*, Milan, Skirà, 1997. Porta,. P.L. (ed.), *Milano e la cultura economica nel XX secolo. Gli anni 1890-1920*, Milan, Angeli, 1998.

6 See Moneta, M., "Forme e tendenze dell'associazionismo industriale italiano dalle origini alla costituzione della Confederazione generale dell'industria (1861-1919)", in *Annali di storia dell'impresa*, 1992, n. 8, pp. 261-342; Trezzi, L., "Economia e società. Le esperienze associative", in G. Rumi, A. Buratti, A.Cova (eds.), *Milano nell'unità nazionale, op. cit.*, pp. 415-439.

type of organisation initially solved any conflicts of interest within the association and, then, coordinated members engaged in all economic activities in their dealings with public institutions. Furthermore, BIAs asked for a limited control of public power over agreements among producers on prices (as in the case of the construction of new railway lines) and were insistent on obtaining greater assistance from the public budget for new enterprises combined with a decrease in the burden on high profits. New Lombard BIAs represented and supported the interests of their members in discussion with the economical and political institutions, emphasising taxes and tariffs: they lobbied public authorities and parliamentarians[7]. They also ensured them of more efficient services and productive activity. In particular, BIAs solved tax and bureaucratic issues, provided legal assistance in cases of accidents at the workplace, supplied arbitration or conciliation in disputes among members, and prepared detailed surveys about the conditions and prospects of markets where members operated or could potentially invest.

The BIAs with a solely economic identity (such as those concentrating on labour offices, collective purchasing, or updates on technical or political problems) continued until the First World War, especially in the textile (cotton) and metallurgical sectors. For example, the Associazione Industriale Italiana (founded in 1867) grouped enterprises of different sectors with the goal of promoting and supporting entrepreneurship as a factor in social progress. Their cross-sectoral nature was exemplified by the alliance between bourgeoisie and nobility opened to businesses. Their central committee coordinated the activities of local committees and managed relationships with institutions while creating a network of enterprises to exchange information and increase comparative advantages.

The main BIAs also tried to establish rules of business conduct: so the different statutes included participation in committees for industrial exhibitions and the submission of lists for the chamber of commerce and local governments. Some BIAs operated a common policy replacing state action: the Consorzio tra Industriali Meccanici e Metallurgici di Milano (hereafter Consorzio) grouped mechanical and metallurgical enterprises to answer the law on accidents in the workplace. Initiated in

---

7 On Lombard BIAs' advice on tariffs see Associazione dell'Industria e del Commercio delle Sete in Italia, *Risposte all'interrogatorio industriale per la revisione della tariffa doganale. Categoria della seta: trattura e torcitura, cardatura e filatura dei cascami*, Milan, Bellini, 1886; Circolo Industriale e Commerciale, *Petizione all'onorevole presidenza della Camera dei deputati per l'onorevole commissione parlamemtare incaricata dell'esame della nuova tariffa doganale*, Milan, Reggiani, 1887; *Id.*, *Risposte all'interrogatorio industriale per la revisione della tariffa doganale*: 1886, Milan, Bellini, 1886.

1898, it supplied legal protection for its members, managing a common fund and the insurance for accidents. A new trade union identity was also enshrined in statutes: so some BIAs became representative organisations of their economic sector: for example the Società fra gli Esercenti la Vendita del Vino a Brescia (founded in 1893) and the Consorzio fra gli Esercenti di Gallarate e uniti (1896) began to manage the contract of the duty on alcoholic beverage consumption and so they represented all people selling alcoholic drinks in their dealings with public authorities. Several BIAs started their activity as a friendly society gathering artisans and followed the growth of their members who became big entrepreneurs, such as in the case of blacksmiths and printers. They also promoted cooperatives (especially among SMEs) in order to buy raw materials and/or sell their products and, in this way, to reduce market inefficiencies. BIAs could also resolve contractual difficulties with workers which were related to enterprises by individual contracts: in fact there were no trade unions asking for collective contracts (they only arrived in the late nineteenth century). BIAs also supported courses at business schools and polytechnics as well as vocational trainings courses for officers, employees and workers (giving the priority to people working in member companies). However, this normally happened only for the richest BIAs such as those grouping textile (from 1877 for silk producers and from 1894 for producers of cotton) or mechanical or metallurgical enterprises[8].

Some BIAs tried to protect the interests of industrial enterprises and also those of other "proprietary classes of productive activities": in 1880 the Circolo Industriale e Commerciale di Milano (hereafter Circolo) came into being and grouped owners of factories and shops and merchants and, from 1890, farmers aslo. It absorbed the Associazione Industriale Italiana in 1884 and it enjoyed a prominent position in Milanese high society, representing the most important businessmen in the city[9]. In 1889 the Circolo per gli Interessi Industriali, Commerciali ed Agricoli was also founded. It was an alternative to the previous

---

8 See *Statuto dell'Associazione industriale italiana*, Milan, Società cooperativo-tipografica, 1867; Associazione dell'industria e del commercio delle sete in Italia, *Il convegno serico di Milano*, 1906, Milan, La Stampa Commerciale, 1906.

9 The administration was entrusted to a council of 17 members: it did not explicitly mention the relationship with the trade unions. Members supported the election to local institutions and to the national parliament of candidates who promised to defend the economic interests represented by the Circolo. Among its members were Amman, Bertarelli, Binda, Bocconi, Branca, Crespi, De Angeli, Candiani, Dufour, Frua Gondrand, Hoepli, Joel, Lepetit, Mylius and Ramazzotti. See *Statuto e regolamento del Circolo industriale e commerciale in Milano approvati nella seduta del 13 maggio 1884*, Milan, Maglia, 1884. See also Castagnoli, A., Scarpellini, E., *Storia degli imprenditori italiani*, Turin, Einaudi, 2003.

Circolo and wanted to support the "few big interests of large speculators" and also those "of the majority of the industrialists, traders, merchants and farmers". It did not have a billiard room, but its offices were available on a daily basis as a comfortable place for meeting entrepreneurs and favoured contracts.

Most BIAs were vertical and their members shared the same economic and financial interests. The law did not require a legal identity while the initial joining and annual fees were low and usually related to the size of the firms. Exceptional contributions could be paid by mutual support between members: this allowed the management of BIAs without financial problems. Leaders were elected: each member (corporation, company, individual entrepreneur) only had one vote. The President, the Treasurer and members of the Committee were entrepreneurs (or their executives): they were rarely professionals. At the start, the structures had few staff but numbers increased with the introduction of new functions. They often used external professional advice. This allowed them to provide more services for members and to promote good relations and business between them.

The first experiences of BIAs were influenced by the mutual and cooperative model, which was also spreading among the productive elites. The "collective action" appeared to be aimed at the "common good", rather than simply representing special interests. The goal was economic and cultural, i.e. to promote the spread of cooperation, thrift and education through cooperative banks, cooperative stores, and mutual societies, and by supporting local SMEs. An example of these early BIAs was the Associazione Industriale Italiana and the Associazione della Tessitura Serica Italiana (founded in Como in 1877 and grouping silk industries). The Società fra i Proprietari Tipografi in Milan also aimed "to facilitate the mutual knowledge of partners, promoting the principles of solidarity and mutual assistance among the partners". It also had the goal of enhancing human capital through education, performance awards, and placement, while at the same time seeking to limit competition. The various "colleges" of contractors in the building industry also wanted to increase the professional skills of their members (and of their workers). The Società Orefici, Argentieri ed affini in Milan founded a school of design dedicated to young apprentices interested in working as goldsmiths and silversmiths. Some BIAs promoted and/or supported courses for skilled workers at a vocational school for textile workers or the school of electrical engineering: the school laboratory for the chemical industries was in particular supported by the Unione Saponiere Italiane, founded in 1904 and grouping soap enterprises. This commitment to training continued, even after years of increasing social conflict.

Some BIAs were similar to consortiums: the Associazione Generale dei Fabbricanti di Concimi Chimici (founded in 1900 by producers of chemical fertilisers) provided agreements "to improve the conditions of normal sales" and denounced unfair competition in addition to engaging in promotional activities and providing technical advice. The effort to regulate competition was the basis of other Milanese BIAs, many of which had a national dimension, such as the Consorzio Fabbricanti Candele di Cera (founded in 1891 and grouping producers of candles), the Unione Zuccheri (founded in 1904 and representing producers of sugar) and the Unione Industrie Fiammiferi (founded in 1905 and grouping producers of matches). How to stop the "dangerous and relentless depreciation" of the graphic arts, "to govern the relationship of partners with customers" and "to provide continuous fellowship of members" were goals of the Unione Industriali Arti Grafiche in Milan. Its statute established "mutual respect" obligations among the members and bound them "wherever possible" to stock paper from members instead of outside firms. There was also a register of insolvent customers and even one of lazy workers.

In the early twentieth century, the Associazione tra gli Industriali Cotonieri (hereafter Cotoniera) promoted several agreements among cotton enterprises (Consorzio tessitori in greggio, Consorzio tessitori domestici, Sindacato filatori), but these deals had a limited duration. Moreover, during a period when the cotton sector was depressed, the Cotoniera promoted new trading companies (Società docks cotoni di Genova, Società per la coltivazione del cotone in Eritrea e in Libia) and some consortia in order to balance production and consumption (Consorzio fra filatori di cotone, Unione fra filatori per lo short-time organizzato). The Cotoniera also monitored the fortunes of the sector, collecting statistics from the members and sending them to public administrators. It published its "Bollettino" from 1906 so as to provide new information concerning the cotton sector[10]. Similarly, the Associazione dell'Industria e del Commercio delle Sete in Italia (hereafter Associazione Serica), which grouped silk enterprises, collected statistics and published its "Bollettino" (and also a yearbook) to give members information about the silk sector. The Associazione Serica offered its

[10] The "Bollettino" (this name changed lots of times) published advertisements, legal news, statistics on employment and markets, technical supplements (containing even samples of fabric), and news on business (bankruptcy, constitutions and dissolutions, and corporate meetings). It also provided news about the "Experimental station for the cellulose, paper and vegetable and artificial textile", that is the main research center of the Politecnico di Milano which studied natural and artificial textile fibres with the support of the textile companies and BIAs. See *Bollettino dell'Associazione fra gli industriali cotonieri e Borsa cotoni*, 1906-1910; *Bollettino dell'Associazione cotoniera italiana*, 1910-1913; *Bollettino della Cotoniera*, 1912.

members relevant services (such as placements) and created a number of associate societies (as the Società per la difesa contro i furti di seta ed affini, the Società di mutuo soccorso fra gli addetti all'industria serica, the Società di mutuo soccorso per gli impiegati e i dirigenti). It also sponsored a master for silk managers, and a laboratory for scientific experiments, as well as a cooperative for aging and tasting of silk[11].

Finally, some BIAs encountered problems with public authorities which did not provide an appropriate consideration for SMEs, did not reduce taxes, and did not give fiscal exemptions for raw materials as petrol, gas, electricity etc[12]. There also existed an alternative employers' association to BIAs: the Partito Economico (the economic party), founded in Milan in 1907. Its aim was the support of business interests through the election of employers' representatives to public institutions. However, this party only became a think tank: so BIAs remained the main lobbying instrument to obtain laws favouring enterprises[13].

2. The development of the trade unions and the related changes in the structure of Lombard BIAs

At the end of the nineteenth century the development of BIAs' "trade-union" structures started in a multi-sectoral fashion and had a strong local influence. The formation and extensive growth of trade unions in factories led entrepreneurs to start a path of strengthening and specialisation. Moreover, members explicitly mentioned in statute the organisation of some training courses for workers and the establishment of funds to reward workers' productivity. New BIAs also operated as a place of arbitration for disputes among members: an office was dedicated to this purpose. For instance, the Società fra i Proprietari di Fabbriche di Guanti in Milan (founded in 1893) had to coordinate the interests and needs of 21 glove producers in 1914. This included advising members and mediating between them, and political brokering: one

11 See *Bollettino dell'associazione serica*, 1889. It replaced *La manifattura serica* (published since 1878).

12 See, for example, the Unione esercenti le vetture pubbliche di Milano (founded in 1905 and grouping 458 public drivers), Associazione italiana industriali e negozianti in pelliccerie (founded in 1908 and grouping 165 fur coat industries and shops), the Associazione proprietari sartorie per signora (founded in 1908 and grouping 110 dressmakers); Associazione fabbricanti e installatori gaz, luce elettrica, bronzisti, idraulici (founded in 1899 and grouping 100 installers of gas and electricity, bronzers, plumbers). All data concerning membership numbers refers to 1914.

13 See Besana, C., *Les industriel lombards et les institutions politiques des années 1880 à la première guerre mondiale*, in D. Fraboulet, C. Druelle-Korn, P. Vernus (eds.), *Les organisations patronales et la sphère publique. Europe XIXe et XXe siècles*, Rennes, PUR, 2013, pp. 29-41.

statute provided for the BIA's intervention for the solution of conflict in the workplace.

In the early twentieth century Milanese enterpreneurs did not create a horizontal BIA to discuss new contracts with trade unions. However, in the nearby town of Monza the situation was different: even if Monza only had just over 42,000 inhabitants, there were 14,000 workers employed in factories there. Monza was the core of a district, the Brianza, which boasted about 61,500 manufacturing workers. In Monza, for the first time in Italy, entrepreneurs created a territorial cross-sectoral BIA with "trade-union" goals. In 1902 the Federazione degli Industriali Monzesi (hereafter the Federazione) was created and coordinated four vertical BIAs (hat entrepreneurs, cotton weavers, dyers and managers workshops). It was initially focused "only on disputes between capital and labour", but later it considered "other purposes of general character". Hence, it developed an articulated structure, adopting the organisation model of the trade unions: it was equipped with a presidency and a secretariat and also a stable staff. New BIAs included 44 companies (with 3,600 workers). There were 82 members by 1905 (with about 10,000 workers) and 300 by 1910 (with 15,000 workers). Their influence was gradually extended around all of Brianza: their members employed 25 per cent of manufacturing workers in Brianza. It provided collective services: a commercial office, a laboratory for the testing of yarn, a law office and medical services for the prevention of labour accidents. It made petitions for trade agreements and, from 1910, it published its newspaper, "La Federazione industriale".

The success of this experience depended on multiple factors. The industrial development of Monza was based on simultaneous and integrated growth in sectors linked to traditional Brianza crafts and businesses. Monza hosted many mechanised SMEs which were active in sectors such as the production of felt hats, cotton weaving and dyeing, and the production of machinery and associated parts. From the 1890s reformist socialist and catholic trade unions assumed a leading role: the decline of revolutionary socialism eased relations with BIAs[14]. Hat manufactures were also relevant for the establishment of BIAs with "trade union" aims. Their workforce was mainly male (and strongly

---

14 From 1898, reformist socialist trade unions supported concrete action to improve conditions for workers rather than promoting theoretical change in the wider economic and political system. The leaders of catholic trade unions (created to counter the growth of socialist unions in the textile sector) were the protagonists of bitter clashes with the industrial party over the introduction of the principle of consultation: they looked for a non-confrontational way to solve the conflict between the interests of capital and workers and they wanted to modernise the old paternalistic methods usually used to manage labour relations without protests and strikes.

"unionised"), well paid and had an ancient craft tradition. Enterprises negotiated with the trade unions on preparing a labour contract valid for all firms. Thus, the birth of the Federazione was preceded, at the beginning of 1902, by a new contract for workers and by a new system of regulation of work in all Brianza's factories. Finally, the role of Carlo Ricci (a hat producer who was the President of the Federazione) and Giuseppe Riva (a professor who was the Secretary of the Federation) was also central to these developments[15].

The role of the Federazione was relevant in other contexts too. In 1906 the example of Federazione was partly reflected in the establishment of the Lega degli Industriali of Turin. In the Autumn of 1907, thanks to the direct intervention of the Secretary of the Federazione, a new BIA was established in Bergamo: it was the Federazione delle Industrie Tessili, grouping 19 textile firms (with about 16,500 workers). From 1910, after a rough confrontation with catholic trade unions, the new BIA started a new relationship between employers and workers. The enterpreuners of the district of Bergamo abandoned the direct and unbalanced relationship between enterprises and their workforce: they tried to adequately satisfy their workers' needs through the BIA and new collective contracts[16]. In the area of Gallarate and Busto Arsizio entrepreneurs also tried to replicate the initiative, but they initially failed. At the end of 1913, Giuseppe Riva attended a meeting of entrepreneurs at Gallarate and defined a program for a new BIA. The Federazione Industriali del Gallaratese was then established in January 1914. It included 94 enterprises (with 11,000 workers), which were divided into six sections: weaving, embroidery machine manufacturers, dyers and

---

15 Riva was considered "the soul" of the Federazione. He was a professor of literature in the technical institute of Monza, and the author of essays on the history of Monza and correspondent for the moderate newspapers in Milan. His approach to labour problems was based on the typical pragmatism of the Lombard economic system. He agreed with Ricci that the industrial system was a progressive factor for society. He considered the entrepreneur as an innovator who needed to promote the moral and material life of his employees. Riva identified the social role of the entrepreneur in promoting welfare and philanthropic initiatives. He did not see collective forms of employment as disruptive of social order. Riva considered the workers' trade unions and the BIAs as useful tools for the development of productive activity: so the consultation between employers and workers had to prevent all conflicts and the existence of stable industrial relations was the way for improving "factory life" and allowing enterprises to avoid expensive external arbitration. Riva and Ricci asserted a "job ethics" shared by workers and trade unions.

16 See Besana, C., "L'associazionismo imprenditoriale tra crisi agraria e prima guerra mondiale", in V. Zamagni, S. Zaninelli (eds.), *Storia economica e sociale di Bergamo. Fra Ottocento e Novecento. Tradizione e modernizzazione*, Bergame, Fondazione per la storia economica e sociale, 1996, pp. 258-263.

bleachers, mechanical, master builders, industrial enterprises. It had a president (Alessandro Maino, a cotton entrepreneur) and a secretariat[17].

New BIAs had more fuctions and a strong local identity. They exchanged information about regulations and tariffs, workers laid off and social legislation. All statutes required an entrance fee and the share paid by the members varied according to the number of workers. Sometimes a "fund of resistance" was set up and used in the case of conflict within plants. Several statutes gave to a "governing council" the right to intervene in the case of strike action and, moreover, to establish rules managing competition on labour supply. In 1910, most of the 85 Italian BIAs focused their action on economic goals: support for exploitation of plants, the spread of new technologies and the trade regime. So new BIAs played important roles in addressing market downturns through capacity reduction or rationalisation. They also reduced information costs with collective action and setting standards for buyers. In some cases, quality upgrading was a related function that moved beyond providing members with information for using association incentives to change member behaviour. The achievement of these objectives called for the establishment of second-level structures and for the consolidation of integrative patterns: a renewed commitment influenced the decisions of the political and administrative system. Most BIAs wanted to avoid state intervention on maternity leave, to protect child labour and to revert life insurance proceeds to the public finances in order to establish a pension fund[18].

Lombard (and moreover Milanese) BIAs increased in number and size: they often represented the majority of Italian enterprises and so they used in their name the words "national" or "Italian". The Associazione Nazionale dell'Industria Metallurgica (founded in 1900) grouped metallurgical factories. The Associazione Nazionale degli Industriali Meccanici (founded in 1904) grouped mechanical enterprises although the Consorzio continued to take care of Lombard ones: it had 31 members in 1915 and 40 in 1917 (with 23,800 workers). In 1910 the BIA grouping cotton industries became "Italian" by amending its articles to favour weavers and traders rather than spinners.

---

17 See Sanna, A. (ed.), *Federazione industriali del Gallaratese. L'attività svolta dal 1914 al 1924. Origini e progressi dell'industria e dati statistici. Elenco descrittivo delle ditte fasciste*, Gallarate, Federazione industriali del Gallaratese, 1924.

18 See "Organizzazioni padronali. Italia. Notizie sulle organizzazioni padronali dell'industria e del commercio", in *Bollettino dell'Ufficio del Lavoro* 1909, pp. 1090-1111, "Organizzazioni padronali industriali e commerciali, Statistica delle organizzazioni di lavoratori", in *ibid.*, 1911, pp. 21-34. Some BIAs also suggested to modify the functioning of the Consiglio Superiore del Lavoro (High Council for Labour). See Vecchio, G. (ed.), *Il Consiglio superiore del lavoro (1903-1923)*, Milan, Angeli, 1988.

New BIAs represented the new Italian industrial economy, from traditional sectors (textile, food, mining) to mechanical, chemical and electro-metallurgical ones. The statutes did not mention industrial relations: they only indicated technical-economic objectives. Only BIAs including metallurgic and mechanic entrepreneurs in Milan and Genoa provided for relations with trade unions: they considered all economic and legal issues and also aimed to prevent the causes of conflict. The statutes of new BIAs were copied by the pre-existing BIAs: the structure and the organisation were the same and whatever differences there were depended on the particular skills of members.

In late 1909, a Committee of Milanese entrepreneurs, constituted with a prevailing representation of the Consortium of engineering firms, was involved in the formation of the Confindustria, but the composition of the board of the new national structure clearly indicated the supremacy of Piedmont industry. The aims of the Confindustria were laid down in Article 3 of the Statute. The Confindustria did not affect the autonomy of the individual associations. It was non-political and its aims were: a) to promote the union of BIAs existing in Italy and the establishment of new ones where they did not exist, in order to protect and defend by all appropriate means the collective interests of industry; b) to support the freedom to work; c) to encourage understanding with the workers[19]. Its main goal was the organisation of trade union activity and its structure looked especially to relations with the working class, to contracts, to issues of social legislation and the streamlining of bureaucratic procedures in a liberal fashion. The Confindustria was characterised by the weighty representation of the mechanical sector on its board and its

---

[19] See *Bollettino dell'Ufficio del Lavoro*, 1910, pp. 551-552. The Confindustria was promoted by Louis Bonnefon Craponne and Gino Olivetti who had previously founded the Lega torinese degli industriali (1906) and the Federazione industriale piemontese (1908). They asked for public appreciation of the social and economic role of industry and this implied a new departure in relations with the workforce. The Lombard BIAs which founded the Confindustria in 1910 were the Consorzio and the Federazione. The other founders came from the Liguria (1) and, moreover, from the Piedmont (9). The Confindustria was managed by the General Council (15 members elected by the confederate BIAs) and the Committee (4 members elected by the General Council and the President). About 2,000 companies with 300,000 employees joined it. See Belloni, E., *La Confindustria e lo sviluppo economico italiano. Gino Olivetti tra Giolitti e Mussolini*, Bologne, Il Mulino, 2011; Castronovo, V., *Cento anni di imprese. Storia di Confindustria 1910-2010*, Rome-Bari, Laterza, 2010; Bazzichi, O., *Cent'anni di Confindustria (1910-2010)*, Padua, Libreria universitaria edizioni, 2009; Fiocca, G., *Industriali e Confindustria dalla prima guerra mondiale al fascismo*, Rome, Biblink Editori, 2000.

liberal ideology: its function was to create a more efficient market and one that was primarily entrepreneurial in character[20].

However, the Confindustria did not represent all Italian enterprises. In 1910 some sectorial BIAs, including the metallurgical ones, formed a new national BIA grouping the enterprises whose capital was represented by stocks: it was the Federazione delle società per azioni (hereafter Assonime) which was founded in conjunction with leading companies and chambers of commerce. The Assonime had a "legislative and administrative oversight function": it was a lobby group created by big enterprises for influencing the activity of the Italian parliament and, in particular, obtaining the strengthening of protectionism[21].

The Lombard (and especially Milanese) BIAs' approach also appeared different: the main goal remained the defence of the interests of enterprises in their relations with public authorities. BIAs were conscious that they had to adapt themselves to the new context, but they did not want to change their structures: they wanted to keep the diversity of their experiences and identities. Besides, the Federazione (which became influential across all the central Lombardy) and the Consorzio (which represented the Milanese mechanical and metallurgical enterprises) did not "cover" the interests of all Lombard industrial sectors. Therefore, some Milanese enterprises associated with Assonime, including the cotton factories and the electrical companies (and the most important banks too). They prioritised unitary action on their relation-

---

20 The Confindustria grouped industries from Piedmont including mechanics, textile, graphics, publishing, and a part of the engineering sector. A new generation of entrepreneurs (such as Giovanni Agnelli, Camillo and Gino Olivetti, the Perrone brothers) controlled the Confindustria to protect industrial interests based on the new organisational model of "Taylorism". The most innovative contribution was that of Gino Olivetti (the Secretary of the Confindustria) who promoted the rationalisation of the production system in mechanical engineering. Please note that during the 1970s, the history of the BIAs in Turin was considered as the affirmation of bourgeois ideology in Italy. More recent studies revised this approach and highlighted that the primary objective was negotiation with the trade unions. On the debate concerning BIAs' origins and functions see: Martinelli, A. (ed.), *L'azione collettiva degli imprenditori italiani: le organizzazioni di rappresentanza degli interessi industriali in prospettiva comparata*, Milan, Edizioni di Comunità, 1999; Baglioni, G., *L'ideologia della borghesia industriale nell'Italia liberale*, Turin, Einaudi, 1997; Berta, G., *Il governo degli interessi: industriali, rappresentanza e politica nell'Italia del nord-ovest: 1906-1924*, Venice, Marsilio, 1996.

21 In 1910, 223 companies gave their allegiance to the Assonime. The first president was Carlo Esterle (CEO of Edison, the main Italian electric company). The direct involvement in Assonime of the metallurgical, mechanical and cotton entrepreneurs and leading banks (such as the Banca Commerciale Italiana), implied that the strengthening of protectionism was the main objective. See *Tra imprese e istituzioni: 100 anni di Assonime tra imprese e istituzioni*, Rome-Bari, Laterza, 2010, 6 vol.

ship with workers. They preferred to develop local and sectoral BIAs and represented a real alternative to the Confindustria model.

They also criticised the new social legislation and the Federazione was opposed to participation in consultation structures by the State. They wanted to harmonise state intervention with the needs of Lombard industry and to avoid entrepreneurs having to bear the attendant social costs. They also requested the state to simplify the bureaucratic procedures involved. These issues impacted particularly on the sectors not protected by high tariffs and which struggled against foreign competition. Their argument was that the German model, based as it was on compulsory insurance, provided workers with excessive protection and was too expensive. Finally, the trade unions obliged enterprises to standardise work conditions, in particular costs of output: most members of vertical BIAs also wanted the standardisation of markets and competition rules. This was not appreciated by all the enterprises whose success was due mostly to entrepreneurial skills. In general, employee-worker relationships were a cause of concern for BIAs' members and the war did not change that: someone considered it an opportunity and others a very negative event for domestic consumption and sales in foreign markets.

In Lombardy, the expansion of functions and therefore the size of BIAs was normally related to the development of trade unions with a well-defined cultural and social identity and, moreover, strong relations with friendly societies and cooperatives. From 1891 the Camere del Lavoro (socialist) and, from 1900, the Unioni del Lavoro (catholic) grouped workers of industrial sectors (steel, chemical, textile etc.): they were closely linked to the territory, with responsibility for coordinating action at the departmental level. Their importance progressively increased and obliged Lombard entrepreneurs to create horizontal BIAs operating in parallel with the vertical BIAs[22].

Faced by the major strikes of the early years of the twentieth century, entrepreneurs sought to combine new contract negotiations managed by BIAs with a partially positive response to the request of trade unions

22 On the growth of the dimensions and functions of Lombard BIAs see also Besana, C., Fumi, G., Locatelli, A.M., Tedeschi, P., "Apercus sur les origines des organisations patronales lombardes", in D. Fraboulet, P. Vernus (eds.), *Genese et morphologies originelles des organisations patronales en Europe (XIXe-XXe siècles)*, Rennes, PUR, 2012, pp. 35-52. About the birth and development of trade unions in Milan see Antonioli, M., Torre Santos, J., *Riformisti e rivoluzionari. La Camera del lavoro di Milano dalle origini alla Grande guerra*, Milan, Angeli, 2006; Granata, I., *Crisi della democrazia. La Camera del lavoro di Milano dal biennio rosso al regime fascista*, Milan, Angeli, 2006. About relations between friendly societies, cooperatives and trade unions see Trezzi, L., *Sindacalismo e cooperazione dalla fine dell'Ottocento all'avvento del fascismo*, Milan, Angeli, 1982.

for increases in real wages, reduction of working hours and better conditions inside the factories. BIAs favoured contracts valid for all partners, which were a valuable tool for entrepreneurs not accustomed to regarding trade unions as interlocutors with real bargaining power. The general contracts reduced differences in competitiveness among companies, although these agreements took effect only if adopted by single firms. In a short time the vast majority of firms used models drawn up by BIAs. This trend was linked with the opportunity to maintain social peace in factories (especially large and medium size ones) through the implementation of signed agreements with the trade unions. In addition, the refusal of some entrepreneurs concerning the BIAs' agreement entailed the negation of the organisation's rules by limiting its representativeness and bargaining power. This behaviour was punishable by fines and with the loss of legal assistance.

The first level of Milanese BIAs which negotiated with trade unions were represented by vertical BIAs with a perfect knowledge of the economic and financial conditions of their productive sector: they grouped industrial enterprises only, while other BIAs also grouped the owners of shops and stores and in fact represented most of the members of Milanese BIAs. The new contracts arranged by Milanese BIAs were the reference for most of the companies in Lombardy and in other regions, too. Vertical BIAs with their headquarters in Milan were in particular able to handle new contractual issues with trade unions, although they obviously paid limited attention to the common objectives and strategies of Milanese (and Lombard) industry. The new contracts depended on the relevance of each BIA, that is on the number and dimensions of its members. BIAs representing thousands of enterprises had great contractual power, while BIAs including few entreprises only worked to solve their members' bureaucratic problems. It is evident that BIAs such as the Federazione commerciale italiana (grouping 30,000 retailers in 1914) or the Consorzio (which in the same year grouped 1,800 mechanical and metallurgical enterprises) were more important than other Milanese BIAs and also had a relevant position in the relationship with the other Italian BIAs and in particular with trade unions. So, for instance, leaders of BIAs such as the Associazione industriali metallurgici italiani (founded in 1900 and included 188 metallurgical factories and thousands of workers) were more influential than others Milanese BIAs which represented hundreds of SMEs[23].

---

[23] Milan was the headquarters of the Federazione Lombarda Tabaccai (founded in 1902 and grouping 854 Lombard tobacconists), the Associazione Esercenti in Vino al dettaglio (founded in 1907 and representing 854 wine retailers), the Società Orefici Argentieri ed affini (founded in 1873 and grouping 700 goldsmiths and silversmiths),

Finally the Milanese BIAs' real contractual power also depended on existing links with the Confindustria and, moreover, the other vertical BIAs with structures similar to trade unions. The coordination of their action (that is the creation of a wide network of BIAs holding the same position regarding workers) increased the contractual power of Milanese BIAs, especially if they had few members. As all Milanese BIAs had a great contractual relevance, which they obtained directly (by the number of their members and/or the dimension of their enterprises) or indirectly (by their links to other BIAs), their leaders thought that they did not need a Milanese horizontal BIA for coordinating the activities and interests of Milanese enterprises operating in different sectors.

3. Fascism and the consequent relevant changes of the nature and structure of Milanese BIAs

During the First World War, the functions of BIAs were limited by the creation of the Regional Committees of Industrial Mobilisation (CRMI) which had to plan and organise the industrial production of the "war economy"[24]. Their experience with the CRMI allowed many Lombard (and moreover Milanese) entrepreneurs to face economical and technical problems in different sectors and areas: they in fact had to find and manage compromises, in league with representatives of the government, between enterprises who were often pursuing distinctly opposed interests. This implied that Lombard entrepreneurs had a good training and learnt to manage horizontal BIAs, that is BIAs grouping enterprises having their headquarters in the same area, but, sometimes, very different aims (e.g. the producers of paper, printers and publishers on one hand and the producers of electricity or metallurgical entrepreneurs on the other).

At the end of the First World War, then, facing the growth of the contractual power of trade unions, the entrepreneurs were ready to create new horizontal BIAs. In 1919 they founded a cross-sectoral structure, the Federazione Industriale Lombarda (FIL), grouping 20 vertical BIAs (with more than 200,000 workers). Its offices were in the headquarters of the Consorzio and its main function was to provide guidance to members negotiating with trade unions asking for better

---

and the Società Droghieri di Milano e Lombardia (founded in 1884 and representing 500 Lombard grocers). All data concerning the members refers to 1914.

24 On the CRMI see Segreto, L., "Statalismo e antistatalismo nell'economia bellica. Gli industriali e la Mobilitazione industriale (1915-1918)", in P. Hertner, G. Mori (eds.), *La transizione dall'economia di guerra all'economia di pace in Italia e Germania dopo la prima guerra mondiale*, Bologne, Il Mulino, 1983, pp. 301-334; Tomassini, L. "Mobilitazione industriale e classe operaia", in G. Procacci (ed.), *Stato e classe operaia in Italia durante la prima guerra mondiale*, Milan, Angeli, 1983, pp. 79-102.

working conditions and a new system of employer-employee relations. There was also a special section for SMEs. In the post-War years almost half of the national vertical BIAs had their headquarters in Milan and, with the FIL, they faced a specific challenge from the anarchic and socialist revolutionary organisations occupying factories in September 1920. These events contributed to some Lombard entrepreneurs giving their financial support to the fascist movement. Other members BIAs criticised fascist violences and preferred to support the liberal party. However, the number of entrepreneurs supporting the fascist party progressively increased and, at the end of October 1922 (immedjately after the "Marcia su Roma"), leaders of all BIAs accepted the new Mussolini government. They thought it could reduce the contractual power of trade unions and recreate social peace in factories. They also thought that, after this had been achieved, they could easily eliminate Mussolini: they evidently underestimated him[25].

Mussolini in fact dismantled catholic and socialist trade unions, but he also began to modify the structures and functions of BIAs. In early October 1925, all BIAs with their headquarters in Milan had to give their allegiance to the agreement signed between the Confindustria (whose leader was, since 1923, the Milanese entrepreneur Stefano Benni) and fascist trade unions: they recognised themselves as the sole representatives of employers and workers (so catholic and socialist organisations were excluded). The Act n. 563 of 3 April 1926 further modified industrial relations by creating new fascist BIAs for each productive sector. New BIAs had to be authorised and controlled by the State. The law obliged entrepreneurs and workers to respectively join new fascist BIAs and trade unions: new contracts signed by fascist organisations were valid in all factories. The law also established a new judicial power to solve all disputes concerning the fulfilment of contracts in the workplace: this was in addition to the previous law requiring workers and employers to settle their disputes by arbitration. Strikes and lockouts were prohibited, and later became crimes against the national economy. The local horizontal BIAs had an exclusive competence regarding existing contracts and assisted entreprises in the new "labour courts". All vertical BIAs had to ensure the improvement of the

[25] Is is not possible to list here all the articles of "Corriere della Sera" and "Industria Lombarda" concerning Milanese BIAs' activities and their members' political opinions in the early 1920s. On relations between the fascism and the leadership of BIAs see Melograni, P., *Gli industriali e Mussolini. Rapporti tra Confindustria e fascismo dal 1919 al 1929*, Milan, Longanesi, 1972; Guarneri, F., *Battaglie economiche fra le due guerre* (L. Zani ed.), Bologne, Il Mulino, 1988; Jocteau, G.C., "Gino Olivetti: la Confindustria e il corporativismo. Il ruolo dell'ideologia nel sindacalismo padronale italiano", in *Annali di storia dell'impresa*, 1992, n. 8, pp. 343-378; Fiocca, G., *Industriali e Confindustria, op. cit.*

technical and economical activities of their members, but the Confindustria had the right to modify their decisions. Finally, the new system increased BIAs' financial resources: all enterprises had to pay an annual fee of a day's work for each person employed[26].

The Milanese horizontal BIA became the Federazione Provinciale Fascista di Milano in July 1926 when the new statute was approved and recognised by public authorities. In 1927 its jurisdiction was extended: it included the Brianza (belonging to the department of Milan but previously autonomous and managed by the Federazione degli Industriali Monzesi) and the department of Varese. It became the Unione Industriale Fascista di Milano e della provincia di Varese, grouping 7,798 enterprises (with 306,426 workers). It was divided into sections relating to production (a company operating in different sectors participated in multiple sections) and some representatives of non-Milanese enterprises were present on its Board. It granted new services to its members: it also had a shop reserved for their families.

The Milanese BIAs had a specific relationship with the fascist regime. They were not free and fully depended on the contractual choices of the regime: they could not criticise Mussolini's economic choices such as the excessive revaluation of the national currency. Neither could they use their traditional tactic of lobbying political leaders through newspapers or by financial means: only personal links with Mussolini and fascist leaders were relevant. However, the fascist party was grateful for the financial help received in the early 1920s and it was very attentive to entrepreneurs' interests: so BIAs disposed of a high level of autonomy (if compared to all other associations). This became more evident when vertical BIAs headquartered in Milan, but significant nationally, received the fascist "invitation" to move themselves to Rome, leaving behind in Milan a provincial federation only. Fifteen of them ignored this invitation and retained their main offices in Milan because it was the best location for them logistically and in terms of their financial services.

This partial autonomy was reduced in 1931 because of the arrival of the Great Depression from the USA. All BIAs had to reduce financial resources and to cut almost 30 per cent of services previously granted (inclusing finance provided to Milanese colleges and universities to improve technologies and the quality of future engineers and managers).

---

26 The money was distributed among local BIAs (vertical and horizontal), the national vertical BIAs and the Confindustria. BIAs could refuse the subscription of an entrepreneur or exclude it: this happened if the entrepreneur did not pay regular contributions and/or did not show a "real fascist attitude". The punishment was quite severe: the enterpreneur refused or excluded was reported as a "breach" and his enterprise could not receive public aids.

Instead, they had to give money to public authorities which were involved in the attempt to save the Italian industrial and financial system. The remnants of their independence disappeared in 1934 when a new reform included entrepreneurs and workers in a new unique organisation, the Corporazione, which was not a private association, but a public institution. All organisations grouping employers and workers (as well as artisans and professionals) were collected in 22 Corporazioni "covering" all productive sectors (there were no sections for SMEs). New vertical organisations could conclude contracts concerning their own sector; new horizontal ones became provincial offices coordinating and controlling the local vertical organisations. The new Milanese horizontal organisation (called Unione Provinciale di Milano) coordinated 38 associations representing all productive sectors: it also included the enterprises of transports (private and municipal), the "institutions of public education and training", and the associations of executives. Furthermore, the leaders of new structures were not elected by members, but decided by the fascist regime. The role of Milanese entrepreneurs was partially reduced: even if seven important vertical organisations maintained their headquarters in Milan (in particular those grouping mechanical, metallurgical, textile and chemical producers), the system of Corporazioni definitively attributed more relevance to Rome. Besides, the creation of the IRI, which from 1933 controlled a great share of the Italian factories, increased the role of public enterprises and reduced those of private ones: even if in Milan (and Lombardy) there were few (in number and dimension) public enterprises, at national level the situation was different and this reduced the attention paid to private enterprises' interests. Moreover, private industry was in competition with a player (the State) who could at any time modify the rules[27]. However it was a Milanese entrepreneur, Alberto Pirelli, who substituted Benni as leader of the Corporazione Generale Fascista dell'Industria (the new name imposed on the equivalent of the Confindustria): this

27 The IRI was the public company which, in 1933, absorbed the three Italian great "mixed banks" and a relevant share of Italian industry. The IRI saved the Italian industrial system and transformed Italy into an economy of "State enterpreneurs" (as the most important Italian entrepreneur was the State). It controlled 42 per cent of companies listed in the stock exchange, 90 per cent of boatyards, 40 per cent of iron and steel enterprises, and 30 per cent of electrical ones. See Domenicantonio, F. (ed.), *Intervento pubblico e politica economica fascista*, Milan, Angeli, 2007; Castronovo, V., *Storia dell'IRI*, 1, *Dalle origini al dopoguerra (1933-1948)*, Rome-Bari, Laterza, 2012.

meant that private Milanese enterprises could continue to defend their interests against fascism[28].

With the "new economy of war" from June 1940 all national vertical organisations were obliged to defintively transfer their headquarters to Rome. However, their location changed again after the armistice (8 September 1943) and the consequent birth of the fascist Republic of Salo. All national organisations grouping employers had to go to Milan where they were coordinated by the new Confindustria Alta Italia. The corporative system was abolished and, in February 1945 the Confederazione generale del lavoro, delle arti e della tecnologia was created: its goals were the safeguarding of productive interests and the removal of the antagonism between employers and workers. New rules about the "socialisation of business" were planned, but in April 1945 the fall of the fascist regime closed the project. However, even if from the Autumn 1943 to Spring 1945 the new organisations grouping entrepreneurs and workers did not conclude relevant contracts, this period was very important for the Italian BIAs' future because a lot of entrepreneurs supported the anti-fascist movement (giving money to members of the resistance and even using false documents attesting to the indispensability of some workers in order to avoid their deportation to Germany or their conscription to the fascist army). This was illegal and the entrepreneurs risked German reprisals, with some actually being imprisoned. This strong break with fascism meant that many enterprises received the raw materials and electricity supplies from the occupying US forces necessary to continue production during the first post-war months. Young anti-fascist entrepreneurs were also well positioned to assume relevant functions in post-war reconstruction: the financial support given by their fathers to fascism could be overloked or forgotten so that it was possible to rebuild the Milanese BIAs which had existed in the early 1920s and to give a new economic and social role to entrepreneurs[29].

28 The Milanese horizontal BIA had to stop the publication of "L'industria lombarda" which was fused at the end 1934 with "L'Organizzazione industriale" and edited by the Corporazione Generale Fascista dell'Industria.

29 On the Milanese entrepreneurs' economic thought during the post-war reconstruction period see: Bolchini, P., "Banche, mercato finanziario e industria nella Ricostruzione", in *Milano fra guerra e dopoguerra*, Bari, De Donato, 1979, pp. 35-76; Longoni, G.M., "'Modello americano' e 'Buon senso antico'. La formazione di una nuova cultura dell'impresa a Milano negli anni Cinquanta", in *Nuova rivista storica*, 1994, pp. 327-368; De Luca, G. (ed.), *Pensare l'Italia nuova: la cultura economica milanese tra corporativismo e ricostruzione*, Milan Angeli, 1997.

4. Post-war reconstruction and the new functions of Milanese BIAs

The activity of renewed horizontal BIA in Milan started immediately after the fall of fascism. The provisional government formed by the anti-fascist parties named Giovanni Falck as extraordinary commissioner of the Unione Milanese. The new leadership was not elected and only included people who did not previously have a responsibility in fascist organisations: all new leaders belonged to the "interim board" and were linked to the "movement of national liberation". A new statute was drafted on 25 June 1945 and the Associazione Industriale Lombarda (hereafter Assolombarda) was created: a board of directors was elected during the first assembly as well as a treasurer and a director of a "research department". Membership was voluntary, registration fees and contributions were related to the number of employees (managers, employees and workers had the same relevance for this purpose). According to this rule, electrical and chemical members provided more funds. The Assolombarda quickly expanded: in March 1946 it had 5,394 members (with more than 331,700 workers). There were not great differences from the fascist period: the membership was almost the same because the "purges" of fascists only involved a dozen entrepreneurs who were replaced by some commissioners elected by the company executives. Entrepreneurs closely related to the fascist regime normally left the direction of enterprises to heirs (or to faithful managers) at the end of the war: this eliminated all political obstacles to the allegiance of new BIAs and allowed them to group the majority of existing enterprises.

In the Assolombarda there were 31 local BIAs which were sectorial and only grouped Milanese entrepreneurs working in various sectors. Each BIA could be divided into sections depending on any sector subdivisions. There was also a BIA grouping all entrepreneurs from small sectors with few adherents and related to industrial districts on the periphery of the Milan department (that is Monza, Legnano, Lodi). There were also some differences from the fascist period: the non-industrial organisations including managers and institutions of education and training had disappeared. Most Milanese BIAs extended their jurisdiction to neighboring provinces and, in some cases, throughout the Lombardy. The BIA including mechanical and metallurgical enterprises was the most important, with 1859 members and 160,000 workers[30].

[30] In 1948 members of the *Assolombarda* were divided into 31 local vertical BIAs which were called *Sindacati* (as in the trade unions) and grouped the Milanese producers of goods and services. They were: Abbigliamento [clothes], Albergatori [hoteliers], Alimentari [food], Alimentazione Dolciaria [pastry makers], Ausiliari del

The Assolombarda also assumed the leadership of all new Lombard horizontal BIAs which were mostly founded in the two mounths following the end of the war. Only in Brianza was the arrival of the new BIA delayed until 1946: its members previously belonged to the Assolombarda and now they could receive services without going to Milan (as had been the case prior to fascist rule)[31]. The leaders of the Assolombarda also organised the reconstruction of local and national vertical BIAs whose structures had been destroyed by the war. The Assolombarda created a close relationship with all national vertical BIAs headquartered in Milan: there were 39 in December 1945 and 51 in September 1947 (see table 2). As the Confindustria included 92 vertical BIAs, the national relevance of the Milanese BIAs is clearly evident. They included all strategic industrial sectors (mechanical, chemical, electrical) and traditional ones (textile and food), as well as innovative sectors like the electrotechnical industry. To cater for exceptional cases, the Associazione Nazionale Esercenti Industrie Varie included all entrepreneurs who did not belong to a productive sector with enough members to justify the foundation of a sectorial BIA[32]. It was also the case that other national BIAs which had their headquarters in Rome or in Piedmont (such as those entrepreneurs producing glass, cars, wool, etc.) had a second office in Milan. Finally, there were also three BIAs

---

Traffico [traffic wardens], Calzature [shoes], Cemento, Calce e Gesso [cement, lime, gypsum], Ceramica, Abrasivi [ceramics, abrasives], Chimici [chemicals], Concia [tanning], Confezioni in Serie [clothing], Edili [building], Elettrici [electricity], Fabbricanti Carta e Cartoni [paper, cardboard], Gomma, Conduttori [cables], Grafici e Cartotecnici [graphics, paper], Installatori [installers, technicians], Laterizi [bricks], Legno [wood], Marmo, Pietre [marble, stones], Metalmeccanici [metallurgical, mechanical], Mugnai, Pastai, Risieri [flour, pasta, rice], Orafi [goldsmith], Pellettieri [leather industry], Sabbia ed affini [sand and similar], Tessili [textiles], Tessili Artificiali [artificial textiles], Tessili Vari [various textiles], Trasporti [transport], Varie [miscellaneous], Vetro [glass]. For information concerning the activities of the Assolombarda during post-war reconstruction see "L'Industria Lombarda" (the publication of which restarted in 1946) and also the list of archives in note 2.

31 These were, in 1948, 13 Lombard horizontal BIAs linked to the Assolombarda (date of foundation): Unione degli Industriali della provincia di Bergamo (28-5-45); Associazione Industriale Bresciana (9-6-45); Unione Industriali di Como (1-6-45); Associazione Industriali della provincia di Cremona (5-5-45); Unione Industriali Lecchesi (7-5-45); Associazione Legnanese dell'Industria (12-6-45); Associazione Industriali della provincia di Mantova (1-6-45); Associazione degli Industriali di Monza e della Brianza (15-2-46); Associazione degli Industriali di Pavia (4-8-45); Unione Industriali Valtellinesi (14-5-45); Associazione degli Industriali della provincia di Varese (1-5-45); Associazione Vigevanese Industriali (1-5-45); Associazione Industriali Oltrepò Lombardo (26-6-45). See Confindustria, *Annuario 1948*, Rome, Failli, 1948, pp. 1040-1053.

32 The Associazione Nazionale Esercenti Industrie Varie included enterprises producing brushes, lamps, pens, pencils, buttons, combs, toys, doormats, etc. See Confindustria, *Annuario 1948*, *op. cit.*, pp. 1022-1023.

with their headquarters in Lombardy, but not in Milan: they were strictly linked to the main industrial sector of their department, specifically the production of bricks (in Bergamo) and of silk (in Como)[33].

The services provided by the new horizontal Milanese BIA were more expansive than had been the case in the early 1920s and it had to enlarge its offices. In the months immediately following the war, when transport and tele-communications were exceptionally difficult, they also hosted the agency of national entrepreneurs association (the Delegazione Alta Italia di Confindustria) which managed relations between Rome and the enterprises of northern Italy. In addition, from 1945 to 1947 most of the new BIAs in the Assolombarda signed contracts recognised for all companies in northern Italy. The Assolombarda also advised public authorities and provided them with technical support supporting their efforts to identify overstaffed workforces and to calculate the real wages that enterprises would have to pay to neutralise inflation. Finally, it continued to finance the Milanese universities (to guarantee to its members high quality engeneers and managers for the future) as well as some new vocational training courses reserved for its members' managers, employees and workers (to improve their professional skills and increase the competitveness of member enterprises).

The special relationship that it enjoyed with other Lombard BIAs allowed leaders of the Assolombarda to take a prominent role in the industrial reconstruction of Lombardy, and because this region was crucial for the Italian economy, they assumed national importance. In the second half of the 1940s they were involved in all debates and negotiations concerning new laws and future policies for the internal market (in particular tariffs on foreign goods), finance (in particular the real cost of industrial credit and support for investments in technological innovation), and labour (in particular increases in real wages and the reduction of social wage costs). Leaders of the Assolombarda were called on by members of the "assemblea costituente" (the first Italian free parliament after the downfall of fascism) to advise on strategies to follow during the post-war period and on which productive sectors and infrastructure to prioritise. Of particular significance was their involvement in all decisions concerning the use of ERP funding. The Italian government could not develop an effective plan of reconstruction for Lombardy nor a system of loans and grants without consulting the

---

33 These were the Lombard vertical and national BIAs with their headquarters outside of Milan [sector] (date of foundation): Associazione Nazionale degli Industriali Laterizi [bricks] (Bergamo, 7-11-45); Associazione Nazionale tra gli Industriali Tintori, Stampatori, Apparecchiatori e Coesionatori di Seta e Rayon [dyers, printers, dressers and cohesioners of silk and rayon] (Como, 1-8-45); Associazione Italiana Fabbricanti Seterie [silk producers] (Como, 7-9-45). See *Ibid.*, pp. 981, 1015-1016.

Assolombarda. The Assolombarda used its offices to manage applications for ERP assistance from Lombard enterprises. The leadership of the Assolombarda tried to use the ERP to renew plants rather than to repair and improve roads, railways, power lines, and telephone lines. While the Assolombarda declared that public enterprises should receive more than private enterprises, the reality was that the greatest companies (Milanese ones included) received most of the ERP aid. There was some dissension between Assolombarda leaders and public authorities about the distribution of ERP aid and the use of the "counterpart fund" created by the sales of "grants" received by the Marshall Plan: the board of the Assolombarda criticised the Italian government for favouring public enterprises[34].

The leaders of the Assolombarda represented a significant proportion of the leadership of the Confindustria: they controlled the direction of the board along with the entrepreneurs of Piedmont (whose leaders were FIAT's managers) and the representatives of public industry (the growth of which continued during the post-war period). They occasionally adopted conflicting positions: Milanese and Lombard BIAs pressed the Confindustria to increase the power of vertical BIAs compared to horizontal BIAs. Only in 1955, when Alighiero De Micheli, the president of the Assolombarda, became the leader of the Confindustria, did the two BIAs reach a harmonious note[35].

However, Milanese BIAs were also sometimes divided amongst themselves. A major problem related to the lack of attention given by the leadership of the Assolombarda to SMEs during post-war reconstruction and the distribution of ERP aid. The special session for SMEs was reformed in 1946, but this did not halt the creation of a new BIA,

---

[34] Some leaders of the Assolombarda were members of the committee which had to manage the "grants" and "loans" linked to the Marshall Plan: the offices of the Assolombarda drew up the lists of goods requested by Lombard enterprises and also helped them to obtain financing linked to the counterpart fund. On these activities and the discussions between leaders of the Assolombarda and public enterprises on the system of distribution of ERP aid see Tedeschi, P., "Notes on the Marshall Plan in Lombardy: Technological Innovation and Vocational Training", in F. Fauri, P. Tedeschi (eds.), *Novel Outlooks on the Marshall Plan. American Aid and European Re-Industrialization*, Bruxelles, PIE Peter Lang, 2011, pp. 59-90; *Id.*, "Gli industriali lombardi e il piano Marshall: verso un 'nuovo sistema d'impresa'", in A. Cova (ed.), *Il dilemma dell'integrazione. L'inserimento dell'economia italiana nel sistema occidentale (1945-1957)*, Milan, Angeli, 2008, pp. 403-449.

[35] On the strategies of the Confindustria during post-war reconstruction and the 1950s see Abrate, M., "La politica economica e sindacale della Confindustria (1943-1955)", in S. Zaninelli (ed.), *Il sindacato nuovo. Politica e organizzazione del movimento operaio in Italia negli anni 1943-55*, Milan, Angeli, 1981, pp. 445-547; Mattina, L., *Gli industriali e la democrazia. La Confindustria nella formazione dell'Italia repubblicana*, Bologne, Il Mulino, 1991.

the Associazione Piccole Imprese (API), which dealt exclusively with solving the difficulties of SMEs and represented their interests vis-a-vis public authorities. SMEs had different expectations than the great companies. For example, they wanted to low-interest loans from banks even when they did not have appropriate securities and they also had different relations with their workforce (SMEs were directly familiar their workers' skills and the entrepreneur negotiated job conditions directly with the worker). The birth of the API and, moreover, the discussions about the distribution of financing linked to the "counterpart fund" changed the structure of the Assolombarda because most of the Milanese SMEs passed to the API, which had its own budget. Accordingly, while the average dimension of members of the Assolombarda obviously increased, its financial resources were reduced. This did not happen to the Milanese vertical BIAs as they had the same objectives for great companies and SMEs. The result was that the latter remained linked to vertical BIAs (which received from the API a proportion of its members' fees)[36].

Further divisions were linked to problems in labour relations and to the creation of new European institutions. Some members of the board of the Assolombarda were in fact the promoters of the Lombard Group of the UCID (the Union of the Christian Entrepreneurs and Managers) and of the Italian section of the European League for Economic Cooperation (ELEC). The UCID wanted to realise a new relationship between entrepreuners and workers with the goal of improving both productivity and real wages. The ELEC, for its part, wanted to promote the early stages of the process of European economic integration, that is the creation of the ECSC (and later the EEC). The European integration was considered to represent a great opportunity for the development of the enterprises because it would allow them to sell their product in a wider market. However, many Milanese entrepreneurs did not want to increase real wages, thereby reducing their profits, and were afraid that the prospective new European market, without tariffs limiting foreign competition, would further threaten them[37].

---

36 On the Milanese SMEs which became members of the API and on the activity of this latter group during the post-war reconstruction period see the "Notiziario dell'API".

37 The main goal of the Italian section of the ELEC was the development of cultural and economic cooperation among European countries. The UCID wanted to better organise the productive factors, thus creating better conditions for workers. On their activities during the period of post-war reconstruction see "Operare" (the newspaper of the UCID); Tedeschi, P., "Une nouvelle Europe à construire: la section italienne de la LECE du 1948 à la création du Marché Commun", in *Journal of European Integration History*, 2006, n. 1, pp. 87-104; *Id.*, "Nuove imprese e nuovi imprenditori per essere competitivi nella 'nuova Europa': il gruppo lombardo UCID e

Some leaders of the Assolombarda assumed important functions in the creation of European institutions and divisions were gradually overcome. During the negotiations on the ECSC, Assolombarda engineers were attached to the Italian delegation in Paris for verifying all technical clauses of the agreement impacting on the new community for coal, iron and steel. The Assolombarda asked for and obtained the graduality of the process of elimination of tariffs. This allowed the strongest Lombard enterprises to renew their plants and to compete with the foreign enterprises which always had the advantage of proximity to mines producing raw material. They also informed members about new rules and about the main features of the foreign markets: they organised new foreign language courses for their members' managers, employed and workers[38].

On the issue of employers' relations with workers and their trade unions, the Assolombarda helped all Milanese BIAs to renew most of the existing contractual clauses concerning dismissals, wage equalisation between different areas, the restoration of internal committees including workers, and the establishment of the automatic mechanism of adjustment of wages to match inflation. During the 1950s, the main mission was the defense and promotion of the role of private enterprises over those of public bodies and the restoration of the mechanisms of the free market as key factors in the growth of businesses, specifically a reduction of the contractual power of trade unions. Leaders of the Assolombarda tried to profit from the divisions existing among the Italian trade unions (the communist and socialist CGIL on one side, and, on the other side, the catholic CISL and the republican and social-democrat UIL). Leaders of the Assolombarda argued that real wages could only increase if there was increased productivity and that they should be compensated if forced to supply the former in the absence of the the latter. As possible alternative they demanded the reduction of taxes on the profits of industrial enterprises along with their social costs. This

l'integrazione europea negli anni '50", in *Bollettino dell'Archivio per la storia del movimento sociale cattolico in Italia*, 2007, n. 2, pp. 227-250.

38 On Italian BIAs' attitudes to the integration of European markets see: Petrini, F., "Les milieux industriels italiens et la création du marché commun", in *Journal of European Integration History*, 2003, n. 1, pp. 9-35; *Id.*, *Il liberismo a una dimensione. La Confindustria e l'integrazione europea 1947-1957*, Milan, Angeli, 2005; Tedeschi, P., "Aux origines de l'intégration européenne: les AFL Falck, les industriels italiens de l'acier et la création de la CECA", in M. Dumoulin (ed.), *Economics Networks and European Integration*, Bruxelles, PIE Peter Lang, 2004, p. 189-214; *Id.*, "Les industriels lombards et les nouvelles règles du Marché Commun dans les années '50: risques et opportunités", in E. Bussière, M. Dumoulin, S. Schirmann (eds.), *Europe organisée, Europe du libre-échange? Fin XIXe siècle – années 1960*, Bruxelles, PIE Peter Lang, 2006, pp. 107-147.

obviously implied higher taxes for banks and "rentiers" and their idea was that it would benefit workers' standard of living.

However, the Assolombarda had to face the increasing influence of the CISL on governments supported by the Democrazia Cristiana (DC). The left wing of the DC promoted social reforms and the enlargement of corporate social responsibility, and highlighted the role of private enterprises in Italian social and economic development. As all BIAs maintained low real wages, in 1958 the government created the Intersind to group public enterprises. It dealt exclusively in negotiations with trade unions while the provision of all other services remained in the hands of existing BIAs: its aim, evidently, was to reduce the contractual power of BIAs and to support trade unions like CISL and UIL which were closely related to the government (and opposed the growth of the CGIL)[39].

Conclusion

In the period analyzed by this article the history of Milanese BIAs is divided into four different phases. The first was in the second half of nineteenth century and it is characterised by the foundation of the first BIAs incorporating the main enterprises of the first wave of Italian industrialisation. The second phase, in the opening decades of the twentieth century, involved major advances in the number of members, dimension of offices and types of services provided. A particular feature of this stage was the development of new structures to combat the growth of trade unions. The third phase was "the fascist phase": Mussolini's government progressively reduced the freedom of BIAs and it definitively eliminated them in 1934 when it created the Corporazioni which grouped entrepreneurs and workers in what were essentially

39 In 1960 the Intersind arranged its first separate contract with trade unions and allowed higher wages to workers in the mechanical or metallurgical public industry. In this way it obliged private enterprises to negotiate similar conditions to avoid workers' protests and strikes. On the Intersind's aims and strategies see Sapellli, G. (ed.), *Impresa e sindacato. Storia dell'Intersind*, Bologne, Il Mulino, 1996. About relations between the Assolombarda, the Intersind, and the DC see Martinelli, A., "Organised Business and Italian Politics: Confindustria and the Christian Democrats in the Postwar Period", in P. Lange, S. Tarrow (eds.), *Italy in Transition: Conflict and Consensus*, London, Frank Cass, 1980, pp. 67-87; Tedeschi, P., "Quelques considérations sur les relations entre les organisations patronales et les institutions politiques en Italie: le cas d'Assolombarda du second après-guerre au début des années 1960", in D. Fraboulet, C. Druelle-Korn, P. Vernus (dir.), *Les organisations patronales*, *op. cit.*, pp. 269-279. *Id.*, "Industriali lombardi, imprese pubbliche e Stato dalla Ricostruzione alla nascita dell'Intersind", in A. Cova, G. Fumi (eds.), *Intervento pubblico, dirigismo e programmazione economica in Italia: continuità e cambiamenti (1922-1956)*, Milan, Angeli, 2011, pp. 547-590.

public institutions. The final phase was represented by the "BIAs' new genesis" at the end of the Second World War. BIAs based in Milan, and the Assolombarda in particular, increased in scale and offered new services during the period of post-reconstruction and into the 1950s.

During the early stage of Italian industrialisation, Lombard entrepreneurs created BIAs for the "defence of business interests against public authorities" (regarding taxes and tariffs in particular) and to support the free market to facilitate economic growth. The provision of efficient services would encourage productive activity in plants, allow for the funding of vocational schools and promote the formation of cooperatives. BIAs helped the development of SMEs and large companies and promoted innovation. In Milan finance capital was closely linked to rental profits and the creation of BIAs was taking place within an economic and social system which did not appreciate the industrial entrepreneurs' attitudes. Milanese BIAs also provided services to manage workforces because trade unions did not exist (and could not enforce collective contracts).

Structural changes accompanied changes of emphasis in the new century and were linked to the development of trade unions: Milanese BIAs had to adapt their structure to the new labour market so as to create a new model for industrial relations. BIAs organised their offices to help members in stipulating new contracts with trade unions: BIAs allowed their members to have a greater negotiating power than would have been the case for individual enterprises formulating contracts. Furthermore, BIAs reduced bureaucratic costs and, by pressurising public authorities, obtained a small reduction of taxes and an increase in investment in infrastructure.

However, the fascist regime strongly modified relations between BIAS, public authorities and trade unions. While business interests were supported by Mussolini, all BIAs lost their autonomy with the introduction of full state control over their structures and goal. The creation of the Corporazioni transformed BIAs into public institutions. The fascist model of Italy as "State entrepreneur" meant that public companies represented the main part of the national productive system, so that private industry competition in the internal market was modified.

At the end of Second World War a new horizontal BIA was born in Milan. The Assolombarda had a great influence on reconstruction and later on the strategic decisions of other BIAs, both in Lombardy and at a national level. The services provided for members were much more extensive than previously and involved a new relationship with the public authorities. The Assolombarda helped them to manage ERP loans and grants (and the linked counterpart fund). Moreover, its managers and engineers participated in the negotiations concerning the creation of the ECSC. The membership of the Assolombarda increased even if there were some problems with the SMEs which developed an autonomous BIA (the API) and even if the relationship with public authorities progressively deteriorated because of their doubts about the real social and economic relevance of private enterprises in Italy.

The final goal of the BIAs remained constant during the period under review: to provide services for member companies and to increase their efficiency and competitveness. So, from the 1860s to the First World War, Lombard BIAs (and Milanese ones in particular) helped the development of enterprises by increasing their contractual power in relation to the public authorities and trade unions. BIAs helped Milan and Lombardy to become the most important areas in Italian Industrial. Thus, BIAs representing the Milanese enterprises assumed great importance and this was confirmed during the fascism era when BIAs were transformed under the Corporazioni. Finally, during the period of post-war recostruction and in the 1950s, Milanese BIAs increased their economic and social standing even if they did not obtain the high level of consensus they desired. They helped their members to increase profits and to improve the skills of their workforces. Finally, even if they did not follow all the UCID's suggestions about better industrial relations, they had to improve the quality of life of workers by providing higher wages after the formation of Intersind in the early 1960s.

Table 1 – BIAs with their headquarter in Milan in 1914:
[E = Economic goals; M = Mixed goals including industrial relations;
N = National; R = Regional]

Name, (year of foundation), [sector]	
Società Mutua Cooperativa fra i Proprietari di Forni di Milano e provincia (1863) [friendly society of bakeries]	M R
Associazione Industriale Italiana (1867) [general industry]	E N
Associazione Tipografico-Libraria Italiana (1869) [printers, publishers]	E N
Società fra Proprietari Fabbri Ferrai (1872) [blacksmith]	E R
Società Orefici, Argentieri ed affini (1873) [goldsmith, silversmith and alike]	E R
Mutua Associazione Italiana fra i Fabbricanti e Negozianti di Cappelli (1875) [hat manufactures and shops]	E N
Associazione fra Industriali Cotonieri e Borsa Cotoni (1877), then Associazione Cotoniera [cotton industry and trade]	E R
Associazione dell'Industria e del Commercio delle Dete in Italia (1877), then Associazione Serica Italiana (1914) [silk industry and trade]	E N
Associazione Nazionale Conciatori e Rifinitori Italiani (1880) (first two years in Turin) [tannery]	E N
Associazione dei Fabbricatori di Carta ed Arti affini nel Regno d'Italia (1880) [paper industry and alike]	E N
Associazione degli Industriali delle Arti Tessili (1880) [textile industry]	E R
Circolo Industriale e Commerciale (1880), then, Circolo Industriale, Agricolo e Commerciale (1890) [general industry, agriculture, trade]	E R

Collegio dei Capomastri ed Imprenditori (1887) [building]	E R
Associazione Tramviaria Italiana (1889?) [tramways]	E N
Circolo per gli Interessi Industriali, Commerciali e Agricoli (1889) [general industry, trade, agriculture]	E R
Associazione fra gli Utenti di Caldaie a Vapore (1890) [steam boilers]	E N
Unione delle Ferrovie Italiane d'Interesse Locale (e di tramvie) (1892) [railways, tramways]	E N
Società fra i Proprietari Tipografi di Milano (1893) [printers]	M R
Società fra i Proprietari di Fabbriche di Guanti e Affini (1893) [gloves industry and alike]	M R
Associazione degli Industriali d'Italia per Prevenire gli Infortuni del Lavoro (1894) [workplace injuries prevention]	E N
Consorzio fra Industriali Meccanici e Metallurgici di Milano (1898) [mechanical, metallurgical industry]	M R
Associazione Fabbricanti e Installatori Gaz, Luce Elettrica, Bronzisti, Idraulici (1899) [installers gaz and electricity, bronzers, plumbers]	M R
Associazione fra Commercianti, Esercenti ed Industriali di Milano (1899) [dealers, merchants, entrepreneurs]	M R
Associazione fra Esercenti Imprese Elettriche in Italia (1899) [electricity]	E N
Associazione fra gli Industriali Metallurgici Italiani (1900) [metallurgical industry]	E N
Associazione Generale dei Fabbricanti Italiani di Concimi Chimici (1900) [chemical fertilisers producers]	E N
Federazione dei Trasporti (1900) [transport]	E N
Unione Saponerie Italiane (1902) [soap industry]	E N
Unione fra Industriali Costruttori in Ferro e Fabbri Ferrai (1903) [ironsmith]	M R
Unione Industriali Arti Grafiche ed affini di Milano (1903) [graphic arts and alike]	E R
Associazione Liniera Italiana per l'Incremento dell'Industria del Lino, della Canapa, della Juta ed affini (1906) [linen, hemp, iuta industries and alike]	E N
Federazione Nazionale dei Costruttori Edilizi e degli Imprenditori di Opere Pubbliche e Private (1906) [building]	E N
Federazione fra Fabbricanti di Nastri in Milano (1906) [ribbons industry]	E R
Unione Industriali Articoli in Pelle (1907) [leather industry]	E R
Unione Italiana Fabbricanti Birra (1907) [beer]	E N
Associazione Lombarda fra Industriali dei Trasporti (1907) [transport]	M R
Lega fra Industriali in Laterizi di Milano (1908) [bricks]	M R
Associazione Proprietari Sartorie per Signora (1908) [dressmaker]	M R
Associazione Italiana Industriali e Negozianti in Pelliccerie (1908) [fur coats industry and shops]	E N
Associazione Trasporti Automeccanici (1909) [transport]	E N
Associazione fra gli Esercenti l'Industria dei Pavimenti in Legno (1909) [wooden floor industry]	M R
Associazione fra Industriali e Commercianti di Latticini (1910) [dairy industry]	E R
Unione Industriali Cotonieri (1911) [cotton industry]	E N
Associazione Nazionale fra gli Industriali Meccanici e affini (1914) [mechanical industry and alike]	E N

Source: please refer to footnote 2, at the beginning of this chapter.

Table 2 - National BIAs with their headquarters in Milan in 1948

Name [Sector] (Date of foundation)
Associazione Canapieri [hemp industry] (25-7-45)
Associazione Costruttori Italiani di Macchinario per l'Industria Tessile [textile machines producers] (12-10-45)
Associazione Costruttori Macchine da Cucire [sewing machines producers] (19-2-46)
Associazione Cotoniera Italiana [cotton industry] (6-7-45)
Associazione degli Industriali delle Conserve Animali [cold cuts industry] (14-7-45)
Associazione degli Industriali Filatori di Cascami di Seta [spinning silk waste industry] (8-9-47)
Associazione del Legno e del Sughero dell'Alta Italia [wood and cork] (26-7-45)
Associazione Fabbricanti Italiani di Utensileria Meccanica [producers of mechanic tools] (21-3-46)
Associazione Industria Marmifera Italiana e delle Industrie Affini [marble industry and alike] (11-6-45)
Associazione Industrie Siderurgiche Italiane [steel industry] (1-7-46)
Associazione Italiana degli Industriali dell'Abbigliamento [clothes industry] (8-5-45)
Associazione Italiana dei Filandieri [spinning silk industry] (26-10-45)
Associazione Italiana dei Torcitori della Seta e Affini [twisting silk industry and alike] (21-9-45)
Associazione Italiana della Pellicceria [producers of leather clothes] (30-5-45)
Associazione Italiana Editori [publishers] (29-3-46)
Associazione Italiana fra gli Industriali Molitori [flour industry] (1-7-45)
Associazione Italiana fra gli Industriali Pastificatori [pasta industry] (1-7-45)
Associazione Italiana fra gli Industriali Risieri [rice industry] (15-6-45)
Associazione Italiana Industriali Jutieri [iuta industry] (14-6-45)
Associazione Italiana Industriali Prodotti Alimentari [food industry](14-5-45)
Associazione Italiana Lattiero-Casearia [dairy industry] (19-11-45)
Associazione Italiana Produttori Maglierie e Calzetterie [knitwear, hosieries] (6-6-45)
Associazione Italiana Produttori Seme Bachi [silkworm seeds producers] (14-12-46)
Associazione Italiana tra gli Industriali delle Acque e Bevande Gassate [water and sparkling beverages] (31-8-45)
Associazione Italiana tra i Fabbricanti di Carta e Cartoni [paper, cardboard industry], (11-7-45)
Associazione Miniere e Cave [mines and quarries] (22-6-45)
Associazione Nazionale Calzaturifici Italiani [shoes industry] (24-5-45)
Associazione Nazionale degli Industriali della Ceramica e degli Abrasivi [ceramic and abrasives industry] (21-12-46)
Associazione Nazionale degli Industriali Tintori, Stampatori e Finitori [dyers and printers, staining and imprinting and finishing industry] (19-6-45)
Associazione Nazionale dell'Industria Chimica [chemical industry] (31-7-45)
Associazione Nazionale Esercenti Industrie Varie [miscellaneous] (10-5-45)
Associazione Nazionale fra Commercianti ed Industriali di Ricuperi Tessili [textile waste industry and trade] (6-8-45)

Associazione Nazionale fra i Produttori di Cellofan [cellophane industry] (31-7-45)
Associazione Nazionale fra le Industrie della Gomma Conduttori ed Affini [producers of caoutchouc, cables and alike] (20-12-45)
Associazione Nazionale Imprese Distributrici Energia Elettrica [elecricity] (24-7-45)
Associazione Nazionale Industria Meccanica Varia ed Affine [various mecanic industry and alike] (25-5-45)
Associazione Nazionale Industriali dell'Ottica, Meccanica Fine e di Precisione [optical industry, precision mechanic industry] (22-2-46)
Associazione Nazionale Industriali Manufatturieri delle Pelli e del Cuoio [leather industry] (23-5-45)
Associazione Nazionale Industrie Elettrotecniche [electrotechnic industry] (20-8-45)
Associazione Nazionale Installatori di Impianti Termici e di Ventilazione, Idrici, Sanitari, Elettrici, Telefonici ed Affini [installers of heating and ventilazion systems, water and sanitary ones, electrical and telephonic ones and alike] (21-9-46)
Associazione Nazionale Produttori Tessili Vari [various textile producers] (3-11-45)
Associazione Nazionale tra i Produttori di Alimenti Zootecnici [animal feed producers] (12-12-45)
Associazione Nazionale tra i Produttori di Fibre Tessili Artificiali ed Affini [artificial fibre textiles industry and alike] (6-7-45)
Associazione Produttori Cemento e Fibrocemento [cement industry] (28-5-45)
Federazione Italiana degli Industriali del Cappello [hats industry] (21-5-45)
Industrie Siderurgiche Associate [steel industry] (24-7-46)
Unione Costruttori e Riparatori Materiale Mobile Ferrotramviario [railways and tram-ways, builders and repairers] (3-10-45)
Unione Costruttori Italiani Macchine Utensili [machine tools producers] (21-12-45)
Unione Industriale Fabbricanti Birra [beer producers] (19-12-46)
Unione Nazionale Fonderie non Ferrosi [foundries for nonferrous metals] (28-5-46)
Unione Nazionale fra i Costruttori di Macchine Agricole e loro parti [producers of agrarian machines and their components] (9-8-45)

Source: Confindustria, *Annuario*, *op. cit.*, pp. 935-1040.

Origins and Shifting Functions of Business Interest Associations

The Dutch Case in the Twentieth Century

Bram BOUWENS & Joost DANKERS

Utrecht University

Introduction

The BIA is here defined as an organisation of employers or companies working for the common interest of its members[1]. They typically perform activities to advance or defend interests of business collectively. These activities would be unduly costly or time consuming for an individual company to carry out by itself. The Dutch BIAs played a key role in the organisation of social relations, the famous "poldermodel", which is seen as a decisive factor in Dutch economic success. Often these organisations started at the end of the nineteenth century as rather small, local societies of entrepreneurs. They soon aggregated into regional and national organisations that became powerful actors in the Dutch society and a typical feature of the Dutch business system.

The BIAs unite different functions. These functions and their relative importance can change over time under political or economic pressure. In 2003 VNO-NCW, the largest Dutch federation of employers, together with the management consultant Berenschot presented a model that distinguished five different functions of the BIA. In this article we will use this model to analyse the changing functions of BIAs over time. Many BIAs started as a "society", promoting common values, offering a

1 See van Waarden, F., "Regulering en belangenorganisaties van ondernemers", in F.L. Holthoon (ed.), *De Nederlandse samenleving sinds 1815; wording en samenhang*, Assen/Maastricht, Van Gorcum, 1985, pp. 227-233; Lypczynski, J. and Wilson, J., *Industrial Organization; an Analysis of Competitive Markets*, Harlow, Pearson Education, 2001, pp. 59-61; Schmiter, P.C., Streeck, W., *The Organization of Business Interests; studying the Associative Action of Business in Advanced Industrial Societies*, Köln, Max-Planck-Institut, 1999, p. 9.

network and platform for discussion. Entrepreneurs in the same industry discuss common problems and issues. The BIA organises conferences, lectures and other societal activities that bring together these members and give them a common identity. A second function evolves from this: lobbying in the interest of the membership. The BIA acts as a "diplomat", working on behalf of its members and trying to influence political decisions. The function of the BIA as a "guild" also develops logically from the societal function. The BIA can force its members to accept internally binding agreements on for example quality of goods and services, professionalism and codes of conduct. Mutual agreements in the interests of all members, certification, screening and codification contribute to the creation of a closed professional group. Membership of the BIA in this case is seen as a hallmark for quality. But these agreements can also go somewhat further and cover for example prices or production to suppress competition. In that case the BIA becomes a cartel organisation. Parallel to this function in making internal agreements between members is the "negotiating function" of the BIA. A major task of the BIA is making deals and agreements with other parties, especially trade unions and governments, but also organisations of consumers. As we shall see these external binding agreements are sometimes even considered to be the origin of the BIA. The fifth and last function is that of "service provider". The BIA can have an important role in providing information and services for their members, for example in case of social and fiscal regulations[2].

During the twentieth century the Dutch BIAs adopted different functions according to the changing social, political and economic conditions. In this article we will explore and analyse the way the BIAs performed and modified their functions during the twentieth century. What activities did the BIAs undertake to create added value for their members and how were the changes in their function influenced by the political and economic environment?

1. From society to guild: the roots of BIAs

Since the end of the nineteenth century the Netherlands counted hundreds of organisations working in the interest of an industry or a professional group. Associations of businessmen already existed before the 1880s. Very often these were regular societies, organising businessmen from different industries in a rather informal way. In most cases these associations were regionally organised and they promoted shared interests on for example infrastructure, taxes, trade-policy or education

2 See Schmidt, D., van den Toren, J.P., de Wal, M., *Ondernemende organisaties; balanceren tussen belangen*, Assen, Van Gorcum, 2003, pp. 29-31, 56-66.

of employees. From the 1880s onwards the number of BIAs boomed and a horizontal concentration of organisation of business took place. Also the nature of joint actions changed. Businessmen from same crafts or industries tried to incorporate their individual perspectives into organisations of a more economic homogeneity. Their organisations developed into more formal organisations with offices and employees. Many of these early BIAs became important institutions that played a central role in their branch on a regional or national level.

The Dutch sociologist Van Waarden explained the increase of BIAs at the end of the nineteenth century as a direct consequence of the agrarian crises of these years. The fierce competition within many trades and industries stirred the foundation of these organisations. The members of the different associations tried to abash low quality products and falsifications and raise the standards of the specific craft. This would allow price subsistence and discourage newcomers to enter the market[3]. The BIA in this period clearly functioned as a guild, protecting the interests of a specific industry. To what extent they indeed managed to gain an influential position was depending on different factors like the unanimity between members concerning their collective goals, the composition of the membership, especially the ratio of smaller and larger companies[4].

Traditionally, the emergence of BIAs has been explained as an action of businessmen to countervail the success of trade unions. Especially within the theory on corporatism this is seen as one of the most important incentives for the emergence of BIAs. Structure and performance of BIAs are in this vision induced and determined by other organisations, like the state or trade unions[5]. During the 1910s trade unions increased exceedingly in the Netherlands and the number of employees that joint these unions tripled to 683,000. In 1920, about 40 per cent of the employees belonged to one of the trade unions[6]. At the same time the number of BIAs increased rapidly during the first decades of the twentieth century. Between 1907 and 1920 the Ministry

3 See van Waarden, F., "Regulering en belangenorganisatie van ondernemers", *op. cit.*, pp. 232-233.

4 See Lypczynski, J., Wilson, J., *Industrial Organisation, op. cit.*, pp. 59-61; Scherer, F.M., Ross, D., *Industrial Market Structure and Economic Performance*, Boston, 1990, pp. 97-102. See also: Levenstein, M.C., Suslow, V.Y., "What determines Cartel Success?", in *Journal of Economic Literature*, 2006, n. 1, pp. 43-95.

5 See for example van Waarden, F., *Organisatiemacht van belangenverenigingen; de ondernemersorganisaties in de bouwnijverheid als voorbeeld*, Leiden, Rijksuniversitat, 1989. p. 35.

6 See Windmuller, J.P., de Galan, C., van Zweeden, A.F., *Arbeidsverhoudingen in Nederland*, Utrecht/Antwerpen, Het Spectrum, 1990 (7th edition), pp. 58-59.

of Economic Affairs counted an increase from 342 to 1666. It is clear that in this situation the external binding function of the BIA became paramount. Representation of employers and presenting a strong partner in negotiating with the unions was an important function of the BIA in this period.

2. BIAs in the interwar period

A major problem in analyzing BIAs is the instability of these corporations. Associations fell apart and disappeared, dissenting groups split off and formed new alliances, other associations were created and existing forms of co-operation were centralised or decentralised. The administrators of the Ministry of Economic Affairs that tried to collect information must have been as puzzled as much historians are nowadays. The administrative problems were solved after 1920, when the government only collected the data of the most important and stable associations. As a result in 1936 the Ministry of Economic Affairs presented 748 associations of shopkeepers, craftsmen, manufacturers and traders. Most of these associations were founded during the First World War and during the crisis of the 1930s[7].

The concentration and stabilisation of the BIAs during these years was a reflection of the centralisation process that strengthened the position of the trade unions[8]. As a result of the strengthened position of the unions the number of collective bargains grew in the 1920s and 1930s. The growing influence of the government on the social-economic affairs during the First World War and especially during the 1930s also stimulated this process[9]. It should however be noted that most agreements between employees and employers still had a strong local or regional nature. The extent or magnitude of the bargains increased during the interwar years, which can also be seen as a driving force behind the organisation of employers and the growing number of BIAs. For many firms membership of an association became more attractive, especially after 1937, when the government introduced the Act on Collective Wage Agreements. This law made these collective bargains compulsory for all employees in the industry concerned. The wage agreements got a more public character and became binding also

7 See *Verslagen en mededelingen van de Afdeling Handel van het Departement van Landbouw, Nijverheid en Handel; Overzicht van de in Nederland bestaande patroonsverenigingen*, Den Haag, 1936: National Archives The Hague, inv. 2.06.001, number 3986.

8 See van Zanden, J.L., Griffiths, R.T., *Economische geschiedenis van Nederland in de 20e eeuw*, Utrecht, Het Spectrum 1989, pp. 88-89.

9 See van Zanden, J.L., *Een klein land in de twintigste eeuw; economische geschiedenis van Nederland 1914-1995*, Utrecht, Het Spectrum, 1997, pp. 82-86.

for those employers and employees not represented by negotiating partners. If a firm wanted to have influence on the wages that they were going to pay, the only way was to become a member of the BIA and voice its opinion[10].

Graph 1: Dutch BIAs of shopkeepers, craftsmen, manufacturers and merchants in 1936, year of foundation, 1890-1936

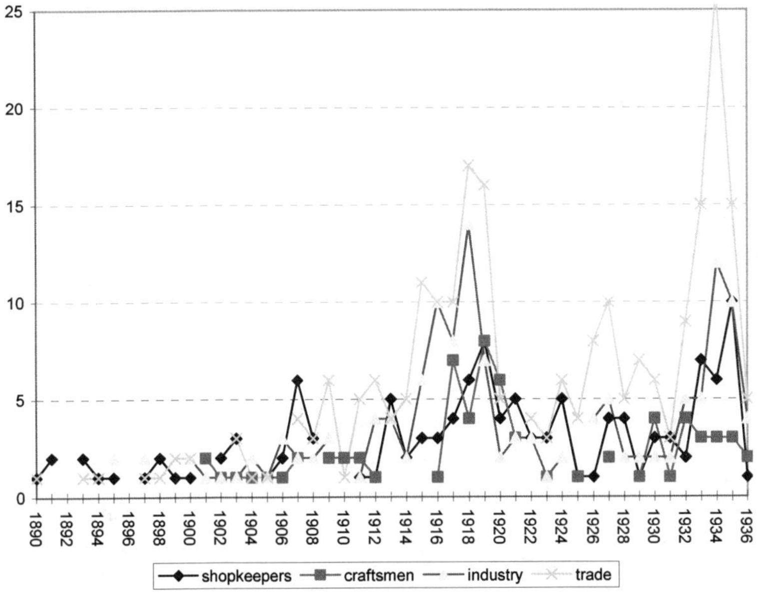

Source: van Waarden, F., "Regulering en belangenorganisaties", *op. cit.*., p. 235.

At the same time, the emergence of BIAs reflects the economic development of the first decades of the twentieth century. Most associations were founded during the First World War and its direct aftermath and during the economic crisis of the 1930s. One could argue that the BIAs like cartels were particularly *Kinder der Not*, founded to eliminate risks, to protect the existing business interests and to control increasing competition. Especially firms that relied on trade were attentive to these developments of the business cycle and were the first to unite. Shopkeepers, craftsmen, wholesalers, international merchants, service providers and manufacturers organised themselves during these periods (see graph 1). The organisation of BIAs was obviously a general

10 Windmuller, J.P., de Galan, C., van Zweeden, A.F., *Arbeidsverhoudingen in Nederland*, *op. cit.*, pp. 72-73.

strategy of all categories of entrepreneurs during this period of economic decline.

One of the functions that seem to be of all times is lobbying. During the interwar years businessmen tried to influence the policy of the government, whether local, regional or national through their associations. The BIAs were also self-regulative organisations in the way that they formulated the institutional context of the industry. The association was an instrument and an alternative to the regulating process of the government. Through self-regulation the industry tried to prevent state-intervention. In fact the government stimulated the formation of BIAs and during the crisis of the 1930s it relied heavily on them for the implementation of laws and regulations. Finally – and last but not least – many associations gathered information on prices, sales, production and other facts that could be of importance for its members. BIAs were an ideal scaffold to make arrangements on prices, production and sales. One could argue that the continuing price decline of these years was an important incentive for businessmen to form associations. Many associations tried to maintain prices by curtailing production. During the 1930s the Dutch government promoted, like many other governments, these internal binding agreements[11].

Graphs 2 and 3 illustrate the shift in functions between 1900 and 1930 and the increasing importance of the guild function and to a lesser degree the function of negotiator. The five functions of BIAs (society, diplomat, guild, negotiator and service provider) are for each period rated from 1 to 5. These numbers reflect the importance of the various functions. The higher the number in the web, the more significant the function is in the overall distribution of functions in the selected period.

The functions of the BIA during these years clearly reflect the changing socio-economic and political circumstances. In the first three decades the societal and diplomatic functions of the BIA clearly became less pronounced. At the same time its function as a negotiator gained importance, due to growing organisation of labour, but also as a result of changes in the law and regulations. However the rise of BIAs in the Dutch case should not be seen as a countervailing force to the rising organisations of the working people exclusively. The BIAs that were founded in this period were primarily organisations that could prevent the industry from fierce competition. Internal binding agreements became more important during the crisis, thus stressing the function as a guild. Before the Second World War most associations indeed focused on these guild activities. The composition of these functions was severely shaken by the changes during the Second World War.

11 See Bouwens, B., Dankers, J., *Tussen concurrentie*, *op. cit.*, pp. 96-100.

Graphs 2 and 3: Selected functions Dutch BIAs (1900 and 1930)

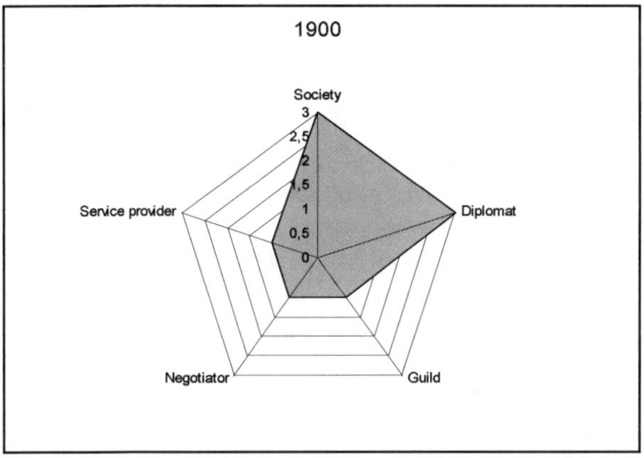

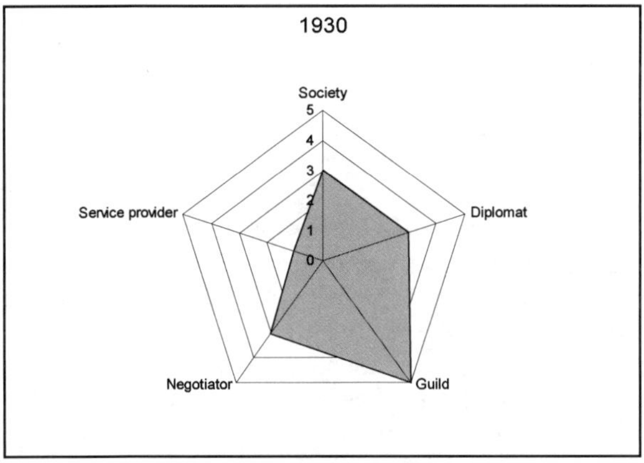

Source: Bouwens, B., Dankers, J., *Tussen concurrentie en concentratie; belangenorganisaties, kartels en fusies en overnames*, Amsterdam, Boom, 2012, pp. 54-59.

3. War and recovery: BIAs in the interlude

The Netherlands were occupied by German national-socialistic troops from May 1940 till May 1945. The occupants intended to copy their own corporatist and authoritarian system to the Dutch business system. They dissolved the existing organisations of employers and employees and disowned their properties. All trade unions were brought together in a single organisation that was a duplicate of the national-socialistic labour-union in Germany. Employers were also pressed to organise themselves in an authoritarian-corporatist way and to become a member of a so-called Vakgroep [Professional Group] or Hoofdgroep [Main group] that organised all companies in their industry. Voluntary

BIAs were replaced by compulsory organisations. This enforced organisation in fact functioned as an instrument for the occupier to get a firm grip on Dutch business.

After the war this compulsory organisation with its division of Dutch business into six main groups with numerous professional groups, was temporarily maintained. Many groups and sub-groups continued their activities under a slightly different name and often survived well into the 1950s. Apparently the collaboration that had been forced upon the employers during the war had not been an entirely negative experience[12]. In the after war period cooperation characterised Dutch economy. The recovery of heavy war damages required teamwork of employers, employees and government. Improving productivity and stimulating industrialisation were seen as a condition for economic recovery. Employers and employees had to work together closely to reach common economic goals and spread prosperity. The leftist government after the war wanted to propel collaboration into all aspects of Dutch business. A law on the organisation of Dutch economy was proposed and initiated in 1950. In this public-private organisation, the so-called Publiekrechtelijke Bedrijfsorganisatie (PBO), employers and employees in a certain industry collectively decided on wages, prices, distribution and other conditions. In this way representatives of capital and labour would collaborate to create the most optimal conditions for production and distribution. This collective effort was first and foremost directed at the common interest and prosperity of the Dutch population[13]. The Social Economic Council was the top of this organisation. It was an institution with an equal representation of employers and employees besides the delegates of the government. The Council gave – and still gives – advice to the government on all essential social and economic questions[14].

The attempt to organise Dutch business according to the socialist design of a planned economy and the catholic ideal of cooperation between employers and employees, however failed. Because the interests of employers and employees on many subjects proved to be opposite,

---

12 See van Waarden, F., "Regulering en belangenorganisaties", *op. cit.*, pp. 236-238.

13 See van Zanden, J.L., *Een klein land in de 20e eeuw; economische geschiedenis van Nederland 1914-1995*, *op. cit.*, pp. 170-182; Sluyterman, K.E., *Dutch Enterprise in the Twentieth Century. Business Strategy in a Small Open Economy*, London/New York, 2005, pp. 133-144.

14 See Geertsema, W.J., *Wet op de Publiekrechtelijke Bedrijfsorganisatie*, Amsterdam, C. van Santen, 1950, Introduction; Maas, P.F. (ed.) *Parlementaire geschiedenis van Nederland na 1945, deel 3; het kabinet-Drees-Van Schaik, 1948-1951; liberalisatie en sociale ordening*, Nijmegen, Gerard Noodt Instituut,1991, pp. 437-438; SER, *Met raad en daad; visies op de toekomst van de overlegeconomie op nationaal en sectoraal niveau*, Den Haag, SER 2000, pp. 27-29.

the public-private organisation was actually a rather marginal success. Only in sectors like trade, food and agriculture this type of organisation became successful. This was because these branches were strongly affected by European regulation and thus dependent on cooperation with the government. In most industries businessmen rejected the idea of a private-public organisation. The liberal sentiments in Dutch economy were apparently too strong to accept a fully coordinated economy. In most industries loyalty of employers as well as employees proved to be first with their fellows, and second with the company in which they worked. Thus the work councils in which employees inside the company were represented proved to be more successful. As a consequence the BIAs, as well as the trade unions that had been flourishing in the 1930s, were revived[15].

4. Repositioning the BIAs

During the first half of the 1950s most BIAs were re-established and took up their activities of the decades before the war. The exact numbers of organisations is rather unclear. The Social Economic Council counted 894 alliances of employers in 1980, but van Waarden and de Vroom reviewed these figures and made an estimation of 1660 BIAs[16]. Compared to the pre-war records these figures indicate a significant increase[17]. A process of both differentiation and concentration took place at the same time and caused the increase of the total number of organisations. The differentiation was mainly due to the introduction of new commodities and services that were unknown or not so widespread in the decades before the war. Producers of for example cosmetics, packaging materials, liquid gas or even theatre productions organised themselves. These associations were relatively small and unknown to the consumers of their products. Several industries and services that lacked a BIA before the war now founded an association. Examples of these are the assurance companies, the producers of rubber and plastics and the chimneysweepers. Specialisation, differentiation, but also internal conflicts and new regulation caused the growth of the

15 See van Zanden, J.L., *Een klein land in de 20^{e} eeuw*, *op. cit.*, pp. 170-182; Sluyterman, K.E., *Dutch Enterprise in the Twentieth Century. Business Strategy in a Small Open Economy*, *op. cit.*, pp. 133-144.

16 See de Vroom, B., van Waarden, F., "Ondernemersorganisaties als machtsmiddel (I)", in *ESB*, 1 August 1984, p. 667.

17 See *Verslagen en mededelingen van de Afdeling Handel van het Departement van Landbouw, Nijverheid en Handel; Overzicht van de in Nederland bestaande patroonsverenigingen*, The Hague, 1936, National Archives, inv. 2.06.001, number 3986.

number of BIAs[18]. As a response many federations combining the interests of larger numbers of BIAs came to the fore. In the corporatist climate of these years these federations put a heavy weight in representing the collective interests of Dutch industry to the government and labour unions. They were invited by the government to discuss the future of the Dutch economy and represent the interests of the industry at large. These federations were important in the tripartite negotiations with employees and government in the Social Economic Council. For the individual members of the BIAs the federations were less visible. In their perception the real work was done by their own specific organisations[19].

Research in the 1980s made clear that almost every firm with 30 employees or more was a member of a BIA. Moreover, many firms combined memberships of different associations at the same time and joined local, regional and national organisations. The level of organisation was much higher than before the war, and also compared with the trade unions the level of organisation of employers surpassed that of employees[20]. At the end of the 1970s the printing industry and the paper and board industry were for example completely organised. Also the diary industry, the chemical industries and the metal industries were highly organised and reached percentages of respectively 99, 95 and 85 per cent[21].

This process of differentiation and concentration in the population of BIAs urged the individual BIA to rethink its position. Graph 4 illustrates the major functions of the BIA in 1950. It makes clear that the developments that started in the 1930s continued after the Second World War. The negotiating and guild functions of the BIA were strengthened further, while its functions as a society and diplomat decreased. During the 1950s the BIA started to develop its function as a service provider.

---

18 See van Waarden, F., "Regulering en belangenorganisatie", *op. cit.*., pp. 238, 259-260.

19 See Bos, W., *Werkgeversorganisatie; ondernemingsorganisatie; plaats en funktie van de werkgeversorganisatie/ ondernemingsorganisatie in het Nederlandse sociaal-ekonomisch bestel*, Rotterdam, Universitaire Pers, 1971, pp. 18-23.

20 See Nobelen, P.W., *Ondernemers georganiseerd; een studie over het Verbond van Ondernemingen in de periode 1973-1984*, Den Haag/Moordrecht, 1987, pp. 80-81.

21 See de Vroom, B., van Waarden, F. "Ondernemersorganisaties", *op. cit.*., pp. 664-670.

Graph 4: Selected functions of Dutch BIAs (1950)

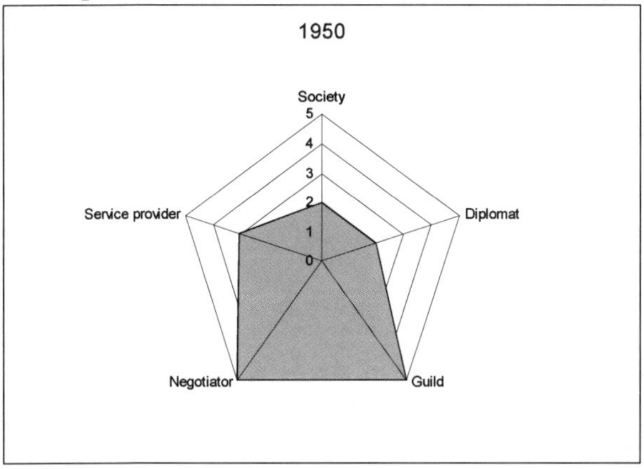

Source: See Bouwens, B., Dankers, J., *Tussen concurrentie*, *op. cit.*, pp. 152-160.

The federations took over the most important negotiating functions of the BIA and negotiated with the unions. On the other hand, for the individual BIA lobbying in the interest of its members and applying pressure on political decision making continued to be imperative. The BIA kept its diplomatic function as an intermediary between government and industry. Social security legislation, tax-regimes, international affairs, company laws and environmental issues were discussed and negotiated between government and BIA as representative of its industry. The tradition of self-regulation persisted as an alternative for strict legislation. During the late 1960s and early 1970s, when the economy made a downward spiral the BIA became an even more crucial partner for the government. Lobbying, collecting data and negotiating with, government, but also consumer organisations and NGO's was just one side of the medal. Especially in structurally weak sectors such as textile, clothing, strawboard and footwear the BIA co-operated with the government to restructure the industry, while at the same time protecting the interests of its members.

The BIA also gained a crucial role in distributing and clarifying the complex legal and fiscal information. Thus the function of the BIA as service desk in this period came more to the fore. Several new issues came about and turned out to be subjects that were ideal to handle within the BIA. The social security legislation, changes in pension funds, the use of representative advisory boards in firms, new tax legislation and environmental issues, were a only a few of the new subjects the industry had to cope with and in which the BIA could play an important role. For the associations it was also essential to convince their members their activities were important. Communication as an instrument to promote the societal function of the BIA and the common identity of an industry became one of the main activities of many organisations. The number of associations that published a magazine increased enormously after the mid 1950s. Every self-esteeming BIA had its own periodical and organised a trade fair[22]. These activities could easily be widened to consumers and serve multiple objectives. Collective advertisements were very popular these days. Between 1946 and 1955 over forty collective campaigns were introduced to convince the consumer to smoke cigars, drink beer or buy toothpaste at the drugstore and not at the supermarket[23].

Finally the guild function of the BIA was continued in this period and to a certain extent even strengthened. Due to intensified communication and collective advertisement membership of the BIA more and more became to be seen as a sign of professionalism and quality. Numerous organisations had their own symbols and indicators to mark members as qualified. At the same time many BIAs continued the coordination of internal binding agreements on prices and production. These collusive practices were again stimulated by governmental policy. Controlling wages and prices was fundamental to the recovery of the export position of Dutch business. The government convinced trade unions to restrict wages and to compensate for this, prices were also kept low. As long as prices were kept under a general maximum all kinds of agreements were acceptable to the government. This made agreements on production or for example the division of markets, attractive for Dutch business. Apart from contributing to more efficient production, this clearly also was advantageous to most companies. The BIA played an important role as a platform for these agreements. These agreements were more secretive because cartels became more suspicious and competition policy became part of the political agenda. After the 1970s the number of cartel agreements decreased[24].

---

22 See for example: Algemeene Vereniging voor de Centrale Verwarmingsindustrie, *Verwarming en Ventilatie* (from 1949 onwards); Vereniging van het Slagersbedrijf, *De Slagerij* (1952); Vereniging De Nederlandse Bloemisterij, *Vakblad voor de bloemisterij* (1952).

23 See Jacobs, M.G., Maas, W.H., *Heineken 1949-1988*, Amsterdam, Heineken, 1991, pp. 22-31; Schreurs, W., *Collectieve reclame in Nederland*, Leiden/Antwerpen, Stenfert Kroese, 1991, pp. 41-51.

24 See Bouwens, B., Dankers, J., "The Invisible Handshake; Cartellization in the Netherlands, 1930-2000", in *Business History Review*, 2010, n. 84, pp. 751-771.

5. BIAs in a period of liberalisation and globalisation

During the last decades of the twentieth century Dutch BIAs still had a crucial role in the organisation of society and business. Corporate concentration was high. Most businessmen joint one or more associations. The exact number of BIAs is still difficult to determine and figures differentiate. The most moderate estimations mention however 1,100 BIAs at the beginning of the new millennium[25]. In this period the federations merged in even bigger organisations. VNO-NCW, the largest federation, counted 150 BIAs and combined the interests of 115,000 employers. Compared to foreign developments, Dutch entrepreneurs belonged – together with their colleagues in Germany, Austria, Belgium and Sweden – to the most coordinated and cooperating businessmen in Europe[26].

These federations played a key role in resolving the economic crisis of the 1970s and early 1980s. One of the highlights was the "Akkoord of Wassenaar" in 1982. Associations of employees, employers and the government recognised that cooperation was essential to recover economic growth. The pact they concluded encouraged wage moderation in exchange for a reduction in working hours to fight unemployment and increase profitability of industry. This resulted in renewed economic growth and the success of the Dutch 'polder model' attracted much international attention[27].

For many industries business perspectives changed radically in these years. Globalisation, the growing impact of European policy and the global development towards a more liberal market economy created new possibilities and threats for businessmen and their associations. Developments more directly related to the industry also had their impact on the tasks and functioning of BIAs. Concentration, specialisation and internationalisation restructured many industries and often put stress on the position of the BIA. A striking example is the experience of the Dutch paper and board industry. All producers of paper and board were member of a BIA that was founded in 1904. This association turned out to be very useful for its members, combining the functions as mentioned

---

25 See Tros, F.H., Alberda, W., Dercksen, W.J., *Arbeidsverhoudingen in Nederland*, Alphen aan de Rijn, Kluwer, 2006[7], pp. 164-195; Schmidt, D., van den Toren, J.P., de Wal, M., *Ondernemende organisaties*, *op. cit.*, p. 35.

26 See van Waarden, F., "The Societal and Historical Embeddedness of Dutch Corporatism", in *Id.*, Lehmbruch, G., *Renegotiating the Welfare State; Flexible Adjustment through Corporatist Concertation*, London, Routledge, 2003, pp. 78-79.

27 See Visser, J., Hemelrijck, A., *A Dutch Miracle: Job Growth, Welfare Reform and Corporatism in the Netherlands*, Amsterdam, Amsterdan University Press, 1997, Introduction; Camijn, A., Bruggeman, J., *Ondernemers verbonden; 100 jaar centrale ondernemingsorganisaties in Nederland*, Wormer, Inmerc, 1999, pp. 265-267.

above. But since the 1980s many foreign competitors acquired the Dutch owned firms and transferred decision making to other parts of the world. Some of these multinationals were not convinced of the advantages of their membership. They resigned and by this indirectly undermined the position of this wellknown BIA[28].

The transformation into a global economy and the policy of deregulation, privatisation and competition forced Dutch BIAs to re-position. Graphs 5 and 6 show this process of shifting functions. Most strikingly the guild function almost completely disappeared. This was mainly due to changing legislation which made cartel agreements illegal. The negotiating function, which was weakened during the 1960s and 1970s when the trade unions and organisations of employers found it difficult to reach agreements, was strengthened again. At the same time the graph shows the growing importance of the position of the BIA as a service provider during the 1980s and 1990s.

The traditional functions of the BIA did not only alter, they became also more complex. With the internationalisation of many industries their common identity and interest were not always obvious. Most BIAs and their members considered lobbying as the core business of the association. But European integration made lobbying also more international and promoted cross border cooperation of the national associations. BIAs felt the need to be present in Brussels, where 80 per cent of the rules related to business were made[29]. Moreover, lobbying was no longer a matter of trying to influence politicians, but increasingly also policymakers of NGO's, other BIAs and different stakeholders of the industry. Cooperation with other associations to reach a common goal and cooperation with partners that operated in the same value chain frequently occurred[30]. As diplomat and service provider most BIAs still generated added value for their members. The internationalisation of the industry and the economic crisis that made contributions of firms to BIAs expensive, made the future of many associations uncertain and forced them to reorganise themselves.

---

28 See *Annual reports VNP* [Dutch Paper and Board Association], 2003-2010

29 See van Schendelen, M.P.C.M., *Machiavelli in Brussels; the Art of lobbying the EU*, Amsterdam, Amsterdam University Press, 2003; Kok, F., Kramer, P., van der Maas, T. (eds.), *Het Brussels labyrint; hoe Nederlanders lobbyen in Europa*, Amsterdam, Prometheus, 2004, 7-12.

30 See Dahl, R.A., *Polyarchy; Participation and Opposition*, New Haven, Yale University Press, 197, pp. 33-37; Schmidt, D., van den Toren, J.P., de Wal, M., *Ondernemende organisaties*, *op. cit.*, pp. 19-20.

Graphs 5 and 6: Selected functions of Dutch BIAs (1980 and 2000)

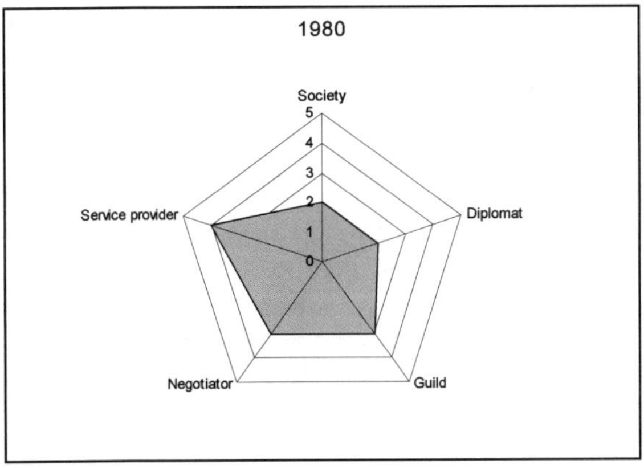

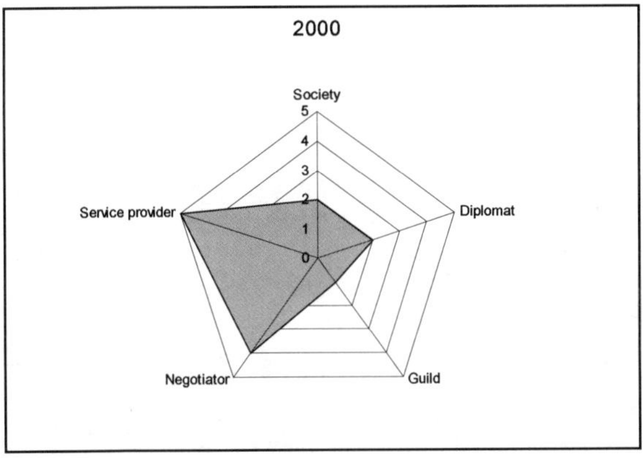

Source: See Bouwens, B., Dankers, J., *Tussen concurrentie, op. cit.*, pp. 152-160, 207-215, 261-264,

Especially the use of external and internal binding agreements changed fundamentally after the 1980s. The collective organisation of labour relations was among the most important motives for businessmen to join a BIA. After 1993 the Dutch social partners agreed to negotiate labour issues on a lower level of industries. The result was that many rather specialised BIAs became more important in dealing with labour relations[31]. New instruments were developed to make use of the wish of the industries to regulate the business themselves. Deregulation was the order of the day. As a result BIAs also became involved in reaching

[31] See Bruggeman, J., van der Houwen, P., *Voorbij Wassenaar; de Stichting van de Arbeid, 1982-2005*, Den Haag, Stichting van de Arbeid, 2005, pp. 97-99.

societal goals. BIAs entered new fields of interest dealing with issues on energy, recycling and sustainability. By touching these activities BIAs often prevented governmental interference and strict legislation[32]. In this respect organisation beyond the border of the BIA and cooperation with other interest groups was essential.

Whereas external binding agreements now belonged to the core activities of BIAs, the nature of internal binding agreements changed fundamentally. During the last decades of the twentieth century deregulation and a more open competition were seen as the driving forces behind economic growth. The EU stimulated competition and started a fierce prosecution of all sorts of cartel-like agreements. Dutch government also formulated a law to retaliate this kind of collusion. Cartel agreements on prices, production and markets became a taboo. As a result the interference of BIAs with internal binding agreements that long time belonged to their main activities ceased to exist[33].

Conclusion

BIAs in the Netherlands have a long tradition and they are a typical element of the Dutch business system. During the twentieth century the position of the BIA changed frequently and their functions evolved accordingly. They were founded in different socio-economic situations, but the intensified cooperation of businessmen was often related to periods of economic or political crisis. As a result BIAs were, as we showed in this article, founded in waves.

BIAs combined different functions. The combination of these functions could change over time in relation to the political and economic context. At the end of the nineteenth century BIAs came into being as informal societies that were often locally oriented. They were social networks bringing together members of the same trade and promoting their common interests in a very general way. This societal function became less important as the BIA gradually developed into more formal institutions with a regional and often national scope. This development was stimulated by the rise of trade unions and BIAs can thus partly be seen as a countervailing action of employers. The BIA had an important function as a negotiator which function in the Dutch model was preserved during most of the twentieth century. At the end of the century this function proved indeed again instrumental for economic recovery and the success of the Dutch "poldermodel".

---

32 See Bouwens, B., *Op papier gesteld; de geschiedenis van de Nederlandse papier- en kartonindustrie in de twintigste eeuw*, Amsterdam, Boom, 2004, pp. 321-322.

33 See Schmidt, D., van den Toren, J. P., de Wal, M., *Ondernemende organisaties*, *op. cit.*, pp. 132-133.

Apart from this the BIA soon developed a diplomatic function, promoting specific interests of its industry. This function was encouraged by the growing governmental interference during the First World War and its aftermath. During the crisis of the 1930s BIAs became an important representative of the industry and also a partner in formulating and enforcing regulation. Self-regulation through the BIA was seen as an alternative to governmental regulation. This was a broadly shared opinion which contributed to the revival of the BIA after the Second World War. Self-regulation throughout the century was a feature of Dutch economy and the BIA was essential to this.

Part of this self-regulation also was the making of internally binding agreements. To prevent governmental regulation members of the BIA made agreements on qualities and conditions of their products and services. This guild function could however easily shift into more cartel like agreements on prices and production. As we saw binding internal agreements belonged to the most important functions of the BIA. Before the Second World War these internal agreements were even stimulated by the government. After the 1960s cartels became more suspicious and gradually their use was restricted. Due to European policy these agreements were completely banned at the end of the century and the BIA at least publicly, lost its function in this respect.

Lastly the service function of the BIA clearly gained weight during the last decades of the twentieth century. The growing complexity of social and fiscal regulation gave the BIA a crucial task in the information and support of its members. At the same time the existence of the BIA was threatened. This created a paradoxical situation. On the one hand companies and especially small and medium sized enterprises came to be more dependent on their association for services and support in a complex world. Internationalisation and globalisation on the other hand, made the position of national BIAs more difficult. Thus the functions of Dutch BIAs shifted throughout the twentieth century. The BIA proved to be a flexible instrument that adapted itself to changing political and economic conditions, but constantly working in the interest of its members.

The Employers' Organisations in the French Metalworking Industry and their Strategies (1901-1940)

Danièle FRABOULET

Université de Paris 13 – Sorbonne Paris Cité

Introduction

The UIMM, the Union des Industries Métallurgiques et Minières (Union of Metalworking and Mining Industries), renamed the Union des Industries et Métiers de la Métallurgie (Union of Metalworking Trades and Industries) in 2001, came into being with the twentieth century. It soon became one of the most powerful employers' confederations in France, maintaining its influence throughout the twentieth century and into the twenty-first[1].

Employers in the metalworking industry founded different types of management organisations over the course of the nineteenth century, both regionally and nationally. The most significant of these, the Comité des Forges de France (CFF, founded in 1864), represented ironmasters' interests in government. However, a rift eventually developed as the interests of producers and transformers of raw materials or semi-finished goods diverged on the issue of customs; the situation was exacerbated by individual rivalries and the inertia of Robert de Wendel, CFF president from 1898 to 1903[2]. Other factors were the Waldeck-Rousseau government's accession to power in 1899 with the Socialist Alexandre Millerand as Minister for Trade and Industry, the rise of the trade union movement among workers, and increasing numbers of

---

1 See Fraboulet D., *Quand les patrons s'organisent. Stratégies et pratiques de l'Union des industries métallurgiques et minières 1901-1950*. Villeneuve-d'Ascq: Septentrion, 2007; *Id.*, "L'UIMM: organisation, stratégies et pratiques du patronat métallurgique (1901-1940)", in *Vingtième siècle*, 2012, n. 114, April-June, pp. 117-135.

2 See Rust, M.J., *Business and Politics in the Third Republic: the Comité des forges and the French Steel Industry, 1896-1914*, Ph.D dissertation, Princeton University, 1973.

strikes. Though a number of national professional trade unions had already been constituted or were in the course of being so, there was seen to be a need for widespread reaction to the threat posed by a decree of 17 September 1900 establishing labour councils. These councils brought together union and management representatives to give their opinions on working conditions and arbitrate disputes when negotiations broke down.

The Chambre syndicale des constructeurs de matériel de chemin de fer et tramways (the Trade Association for Manufacturers in the Rail and Tram Industries), founded by Edmond Duval in May 1899, headed up the opposition movement in the metalworking industry. With the support of his dynamic general secretary Robert Pinot, Duval invited the leaders of ten or so employers' organisations from the major metalworking and mining industries to join him in forming a more pugnacious group. The UIMM, which came into legal being on 5 March 1901[3], brought together professional trade associations representing the metalworking sector, reflecting the wide range of its activities, along with regional organisations representing all or some local trade associations. The UIMM's links with the CFF were strengthened when Robert de Wendel died in 1903 and Baron de Nervo succeeded while remaining vice-president of UIMM.

The aim of this paper is to explore the strategies used by the UIMM to make its voice heard:

a) Strategies aimed at the state. The aim from the outset was to set up a group to influence government policy and therefore form a lobby whose power depended in part on its internal coherence. The paper will analyse the UIMM's role in major social policy debates.

b) Strategies in dealing with the labour movement. What means of action, negotiation, and repression did the UIMM call on, given their highly detailed knowledge of workers' movements in its sector?

The paper explores these questions up to the late 1930s, as the arrival of the Vichy government marked the start of a period, which saw the UIMM ally itself closely to the new government's drive for social and economic renewal, while displaying considerable overall hostility to the establishment of any "integral" corporatism that would force organisations like the UIMM from the political, social, and economic scene.

---

[3] In accordance with article 5 of the act passed on 21 March 1884.

1. The prerequisite: a powerful organisation

In order to make its voice heard, the UIMM had to unite the interests of the main employers' organisations in a sector that was at the heart of industrial changes in nineteenth- and early-twentieth-century Europe. To begin with, the UIMM arranged for the leading trade associations (the CFF and the trade associations for shipbuilders and manufacturers of rail and military equipment) to appoint the same secretary general, Robert Pinot, in 1904, while moving them into its own headquarters. The UIMM, the railway material manufacturers' trade association, and (from 1907) the CFF also shared the same president, Florent Guillain, who took over from Edmond Duval.

In the early years, the leaders strove to strengthen the young federation by recruiting new members, which implied acknowledging that the sector was diversifying and the number of trade bodies increasing. Since economic issues stoked tensions already heightened by the First World War, the UIMM decided in 1919 to focus all its efforts on social and fiscal issues. Membership rose at an uneven rate across the period under study, with numbers rising faster at times of war and labour disputes and falling during the crisis of the 1930s: there were 55 members in 1919, 323 in 1931, and 297 in 1936[4]. The upswing of economic activity shortly before the Second World War did not lead to a rise in membership. However, it is difficult to talk in terms of a fall, given the effects of concentration associated with the crisis. In the years from 1922 to 1927, regional groups (often newly formed) became more numerous than professional trade bodies. That tendency was then reversed until 1938.

Membership rose as the UIMM consolidated its internal organisation. The services gradually became more comprehensive and came to be run by permanent members of staff[5], most of them highly qualified legal experts. By 1919 the UIMM had three departments in addition to the secretariat, dealing with workers' social issues, fiscal issues and litigation, and general information. Three new services were opened in the 1920s and dealt with international issues, liaising with provincial members, and organising according to scientific principles; these were joined by two more in the mid-1930s, with responsibility for applying

4 Membership numbers per trade association are unknown, making it impossible to tell how many companies were members of the UIMM.

5 Not counting the chief executive officer, permanent staff member numbers were as follows: 7 in 1920, 18 in 1929, 20 in 1936, 29 in 1939. See the staff directories in the UIMM archives. See also Dard, O., Richard, G. (eds.), *Les Permanents Patronaux: éléments pour l'histoire de l'organisation du patronat en France dans la première moitié du XXe siècle*, Metz, Centre de Recherche Histoire et Civilisation de l'Université de Metz, 2005.

legislation for workers, apprenticeships, technical education, and health in the workplace. Other bodies linked to the UIMM were set up in parallel to help members with various issues: there were insurance funds against forced unemployment, strikes, and workplace accidents; a retirement fund; the Metalworkers' and Miners' Anti-Tuberculosis Association; Caisse Foncière de Crédit (a land fund providing loans); a central committee for family allowances; a committee for training unemployed youths, and so on. These were run as mutual insurance companies, non-profit organisations (under the terms of the 1901 Act), or limited companies. Almost all of them had their headquarters at the UIMM premises when they were founded, and in most cases for many years afterwards. The range of services on offer was intended to attract new members and help promote and protect a sense of fellowship among employers in the sector.

Developing such a range of activities implied an increase in resources. However, the lack of archival material makes analysing the organisation's finances difficult. Funding initially came solely from membership subscriptions but later from other sources, part of which remain shrouded in mystery.

The success of this policy was down to the organisation's leaders, particularly the general secretary, a title that changed to chief executive officer (délégué général) in 1918. Only two people held this post between 1901 and 1939 – Robert Pinot, long the UIMM's lynchpin, and Alfred Lambert-Ribot. Both were legal experts who had studied law and political science, and both began their careers as high-ranking civil servants, at the Caisse des dépôts and Musée social in Pinot's case and the Conseil d'Etat for Lambert-Ribot. They also held posts that brought them into contact with the world of politics: Pinot was secretary to two monarchist members of parliament representing the Orne département, while Lambert-Ribot was deputy chief of cabinet to the Minister for Labour Albert Métin in 1913 and the Minister for Public Works Albert-André Claveille in 1917. Most of the heads of department held law doctorates.

The same period saw six presidents at the head of the organisation: their role was less significant, though by no means negligible. Following the death of the founding president Edmond Duval, Robert Pinot and the governing board chose men whose high-ranking duties outside the industry would lend the young UIMM the gravitas it needed to be an effective lobbying body. All these men were highly qualified (four had graduated from the Ecole Polytechnique, one from the Ecole Centrale, and one was a legal specialist)[6], reflecting both the importance of the companies they headed up and the high level of technical knowledge required by the various sectors of the industry. Like all Union board members, they all sat on the boards of several professional or inter-professional industry bodies, such as the Confédération générale de la production française (CGPF). They also sat on the boards of various other organisations and institutions such as the Banque de France, chambers of commerce and commercial courts, the Conseil National Economique, and so on. Being on the board of such a range of organisations indicated that the men enjoyed considerable respect in the world of business, while extending their networks in the broad sense, explaining why they were increasingly co-opted onto further bodies. In other words, the choice was made from those with abundant capital – social or otherwise.

It was not always easy building such cohesion: the Union's development was marked by tensions and crises between federations and between industrialists depending on the size of the company and the various industry sectors. The organisation's internal structure was adapted to help overcome such problems.

The UIMM could not hope to influence public decision-making in favour of employers by simply calling on the traditional networks of family, contacts, and understandings. It had to become a fully-fledged lobbying organisation.

2. An influential pressure group

Close links between the political and economic elite are nothing new, but such links did change and develop in the late nineteenth and early twentieth centuries[7]. They became institutionalised from the First World War on, due to increasing state interventionism and the rise of employers' organisations. The UIMM was in fact founded to defend the metalworking industry against the Waldeck-Rousseau government.

The increasing quantity of parliamentary work and the need to keep track of government decisions meant that the secretariat had to maintain constant vigilance. It was important to be familiar with all the proposed bills on social and fiscal issues: detailed studies were made of them, together with surveys of members and international comparisons. The

6 On the organisation's presidents and vice-presidents, see Fraboulet, D., *Quand les patrons s'organisent*, *op. cit.*, p. 65-80.

7 See Fraboulet D., *Quand les patrons s'organisent*, *op. cit.*, pp. 121-156; *Id.*, D., Richard, G., "Au Parlement: représentation et lobbying", in J.C. Daumas, A. Chatriot, D. Fraboulet, P. Fridenson, H. Joly (eds.), *Dictionnaire historique des patrons français*, Paris, Flammarion, 2010, p. 1186-1191.

UIMM claimed expert status both internally, through publications such as manuals on social legislation and social and fiscal information (among other topics), and externally, advising other stakeholders on social and economic issues. It also had to decide which problems were priorities for the organisation – not an easy task given the differing concerns of members, the political mood of the day, and potential rivalry between various institutions – while maintaining the cohesion of the group as a whole.

It was vital to be well-informed so as to make sure that information reached both the various organisations and wider public opinion. As a result, considerable attention was devoted to media representing employers' interests and the agenda-setting quality press. Funding was provided for journals such as "L'Usine" and "La Journée industrielle". Local, regional, national, and industry sector bulletins published the results of membership surveys on the issues of the day while giving advice. Alongside these bulletins were information sheets on specific points, for instance implementing decrees on salaries, and the UIMM membership directory. It is hard to evaluate the financial investment made in the quality press, as such spending often came from specific companies paying for advertising, for example. However, this does not exclude the possibility of direct intervention in the form of press releases, articles, interviews, press campaigns, and so on. Employers did what they could to manage press relations, but often found it difficult to rectify an unflattering public image.

More direct intervention in the political field took on a variety of forms. Since the UIMM had been set up to try to influence government policy, its leaders naturally spent significant energy securing effective access to decision-makers. Few industrialists held national political mandates[8], mainly because such duties were so time-consuming. The need for political ears at all levels thus meant using the networks of members and permanent members of staff in the form of personal contacts, repeated individual or collective approaches to ministers, members of parliament, legislative commissions, and locally elected officials, and involvement in political and economic institutions. Another method was making grants to individuals and employers' organisations such as the Comité républicain du commerce et de l'industrie, founded by Senator Mascuraud, which acted as a mediator between employers and the Radical Party until at least 1911, and Ernest Billiet's Union des Intérêts Économiques. This support played a not insignificant role in shaping the later stances of the members of

8 François de Wendel is the best-known of the few who did.

parliament in question[9]. That said, the relationship between the political and business world was highly complex, and the members of parliament that the UIMM helped elect did not always keep their promises. The need to be represented in institutions, whether on a temporary or permanent basis, seems less a matter of wanting to wield undue influence than of wanting to listen to, inform, and build contacts with men from different spheres of activity.

Another strategic practice was to play institutions against each other: the Senate (where the metalworking industry enjoyed more support) against the Chamber of Deputies, for instance. Examples of issues at play here include the debate on workers' pensions in 1909 and cutting the working day to eight hours. Once a law had been passed, the next step was to apply pressure high up in the civil service to influence how it was implemented administratively. This was easier, as leading employers and high-ranking civil servants often shared the same backgrounds and had studied at the same places. Administrative appeals, for example applying to the Conseil d'Etat for a decree to be cancelled, were the last resort.

Rebuilding France after the destruction of the First World War meant major interests were at stake. As a result, UIMM leaders became particularly involved in two international organisations at this point – the International Labour Organisation and the International Labour Office. Pinot and Lambert-Ribot were regular CGPF delegates at International Labour Conference deliberations from 1919 on and represented French employers at the International Labour Office. They played an important role in the Bureau de documentation et de coordination des délégations patronales (an information centre that also co-ordinated employers' delegations), set up in Brussels in 1920.

As the most organised branch of industry, the metalworking sector's influence spread far beyond the profession, becoming the government's key interlocutor in all negotiations on social issues. Though the employers' position varied little from a paternalist understanding of professional relationships[10], the UIMM did strive for pragmatism in its dealings with public institutions. They bowed to the necessity of agreeing to new legislation when circumstances did not favour them, but carried on trying to influence how it was applied. One such instance

9 Studying political party financing is particularly tricky given the lack of source material and the fact that negotiations were conducted in secrecy.

10 They were powerfully shaped early in the century by Frédéric Le Play's doctrine, which strove to reconcile the need for social reform and the need to preserve the company director's authority and independence. See Le Play, F., *Vues générales sur la statistique, suivies d'un aperçu de statistique générale de la France*, Paris, Martinet, 1840.

was the struggle against shortening working hours[11]: the UIMM tried to delay the eight-hour working day (voted into law on 23 April 1919) for as long as it could, then wielded its influence to shape the regulatory decrees while putting in requests for exemptions. It made occasional efforts to join extant employers' organisations in managing new bodies such as retirement and insurance funds, while at times state intervention was held to be of use, for financing professional training or for maintaining law and order in the fight against labour disputes, for example. Over the first decades of the twentieth century, the UIMM was almost always on the defensive in the face of increasing legislation and trade unionism. The defence of employers' interests can be summed up in a few key points: defending business against outside interference (whether from the state or from employees), maintaining employer control, and limiting employer contributions as much as possible.

Employers realised that the Union was an indispensable tool in setting up an effective, permanent pressure group, counterbalancing the role of trade unions and state interference in the sphere of social reform.

3. A permanent struggle against the workers' movement

One of the reasons why the UIMM was founded was the struggle against trade unions. The same techniques were used as for the state: the UIMM had to be thoroughly familiar with its adversaries, show its strength, foment discord between the leaders and the ordinary members, underline their contradictions and past mistakes, and highlight the good work of programmes implemented by employers. The strategies used ranged from intimidation to support for those unions deemed to be co-operative or even useful in putting down revolutionary elements.

Employers paid considerable attention to the development and organisation of the workers' movement: a number of studies were devoted to the issue, not just by the UIMM but also by regional groups[12]. Dossiers were compiled, principally on the CGTU, the CGT, and the Communist Party, the three groups held to pose the greatest threat, with the intention of judging their progress and influence over employees. Information was drawn mainly from the national, regional, local, and foreign media: cuttings were compiled on a systematic basis and regular surveys conducted, particularly on the state of Communist propaganda in the provinces. This long-term policy of gathering information gave industrial employers regular, detailed information on potential threats, such as the 1924 creation of factory cells, described as "veritable secret

11 See Fraboulet, D., *Quand les patrons s'organisent*, *op. cit.*, p. 205-218; Fridenson, P., Reynaud, B. (eds.), *La France et le temps de travail*, Paris, Odile Jacob, 2004.

12 The UIMM in fact drew on this for inspiration.

societies", and the move towards uniting the SFIC and SFIO in the early 1930s, together with union reunification as the new CGT was infiltrated by cadres trained by the CGTU and the Communist Party.

This knowledge of the workers' movement allowed employers to counter demonstrations and disputes by various means[13], ranging from protection against forced unemployment to confrontations, via calls to non-unionised workers to return to work, ordinary conciliation procedures, press campaigns designed to shape public opinion, and developing social programmes in competition with those set up by workers' organisations. Another aspect of the UIMM policy when faced with the massive strikes of 1936 was to fund the Comité de prévoyance et d'action sociales (CPAS), whose aim was to bring together individual members in the fight against Communism.

Financial protection was under consideration from the beginning of the twentieth century: mutual insurance was thought to be the best way to hold out against workers downing tools. In 1907-08, the UIMM set up six, then eight, specialist funds, unconnected to trade associations but linked to each other through a centralised fund run by the metalworking industry. The "fairness of the cause" was assessed before employers might be granted recourse to a lock-out or be reimbursed for general costs.

Another form of protection was to use force with the help of the state in guaranteeing freedom of labour and property. However, once the Front Populaire came to power, it was no longer possible to use state-sanctioned force to remove workers from the factories they were occupying.

Carrying out checks during hiring, sidelining trade unionists and strikers when re-hiring, and recourse to the courts were all means of minimising the risk of recurrence. Industry employers used them during the strikes of 1938, considering the strikes to be driven by political rather than professional reasons. Striking was considered a wrongful breach of contract and strikers were thus dismissed.

Trying to undermine the united front of adversaries while supporting non-Communist workers' organisations and members of the reunified CGT was another tactic used by employers, who for a while saw Christian trade unions (particularly the CFTC from November 1919 on) as the solution to combating their revolutionary counterparts. However, they were to be disappointed by the CFTC's "extremist" positions. Another strategy was to draw support from middle-ranking management and from technicians. Not only were their aspirations and needs distinct

13 There were 438,466 strikers in 1906, 1,300,000 in 1919, and 2,400,000 in 1936.

from those of the workers, but the fact that they were divided into different categories – engineers, technicians, employees – also gave some scope for manoeuvre. The development of these unions, bound up with the rationalisation of working practices, was also closely studied by the UIMM. However, the leaders did not see them as representing an effective counter-measure to the threat posed by other unions.

The UIMM constantly reminded its members that preventing and managing disputes required employers to be exemplary in following the rules, and punishments were considered for those who failed to be so. Disputes had to be referred immediately to the regional employers' organisation, professional chambers, and (in serious cases) the UIMM itself[14]. The UIMM occasionally patted itself on the back for the way its members followed the rules, helping foil strikes in the Paris region in 1919, for example[15]. More commonly, it criticised employers for lacking in solidarity, as in 1936. Many employers then indicated their dissatisfaction with their organisations by challenging the Accord Matignon, which required a reorganisation of employers' confederations.

Attempts at conciliation were made in parallel with these various strategies. Consultation with social partners was sometimes entered into voluntarily, but more often reluctantly. Such consultations became more commonplace from the First World War on, due to the rise in trade union membership and state intervention. Numerous collective labour agreements were signed in 1919, but numbers immediately began falling the following year, as employers' organisations took advantage of the failure of strikes in 1920 and political and union rifts that weakened the workers' movement. The advent of the Front Populaire and the disputes of 1936 forced employers to consider a different approach to their relationship with employees. The UIMM then engaged in negotiations not only profession-wide, but on a national scale. Its leaders argued for a new policy educating employees about the economic and financial needs of companies and working with employees to set up social programmes. The development of such programmes was part of the paternalist tradition that was now carried out collectively. It attracted new members, particularly small and medium-sized companies, as it enabled them to draw on shared services and therefore lower their own costs; it also meant they were more effective in speaking on behalf of company directors and counteracting trade unions who were

14 See UIMM archives. Waline archive (27 11 11), "Structure patronale", May 12, 1939, p. 14.

15 See UIMM archives (39 21 01). Note dated 3 July 1919 to be sent to regional chambers.

increasingly matching employers' organisations in terms of social provision.

Professional relationships remained difficult despite conciliation procedures from 1938 to the outbreak of war, with a cycle of disputes, repression targeting Communists and trade unionists, negotiations, and arbitration. The outbreak of war in September 1939 did not lead to the advent of universal harmony: employers considered that a new type of working relationship was necessary and inevitable. The national Revolution provided the opportunity a few months later.

In the early decades of the twentieth century, employers' organisations in the metalworking industry came to be a key interlocutor for government and other employers' organisations; they were also the principal partner for trade unions representing employees. Their unity was based on building an organisation that, though structured, remained flexible, and on the selection of a high-calibre management team. Becoming indispensable to members meant increasing the range of services on offer while dividing duties between the regional and national employers' organisations it represented and between various other bodies. Members needed to believe that faith in their leaders and following the rules they laid down were the price to pay to achieve meaningful collective action. This meant using techniques and tactics to try and influence public policy in an ever-expanding arena, to work towards acceptance for the employers' viewpoint over that of other economic stakeholders. Being active on a number of fronts implied creating a significant arena for debating and developing new strategies. In contrast with the inflexibility of its discourse (being master in one's own home and limiting employers' contributions), the UIMM adapted its practices and strategies in accordance with changes in economic circumstance and shifts in the attitude of its social and political partners. Its was a pragmatic position, then, leading it to tone down its traditional paternalism and to delay the implementation of workplace legislation for as long as it could. It was a key partner in the nation's defence, and its voice was heard more clearly in ministries as international tensions rose: there were increasing numbers of exemptions to the forty-hour working week, and the industry applauded new government decrees such as those of November 1938. Following the defeat of 1940, the majority of metalworking industry organisations (with the exception of the CFF and the Comité des Houillères) escaped the Vichy government's decision to dissolve employers' organisations. It seems they were vital to the Vichy government's plans for social and economic reorganisation. While the national Revolution handed them an approach to professional relationships in line with their own ideals, banning strikes, corporatism and the risks of statism led them to delay the implementation of institutions that they mistrusted. They came out of the war in a stronger position, as industrialists had grown used to bowing to the directives issued by trade union organisations, in need as they were of their support in those difficult times. Following a short period in the background, the metalworking industries being at the heart of efforts to rebuild and modernise France, the UIMM adapted to the new context of state intervention and a planned economy with the support of national and regional unions, becoming the key instrument for French employers across the board to engage in social programmes. It once again took on a dominant role both as regards the government and in reconstituting the employers' movement.

The Growth and Role of Employers' Associations in the UK (1916-1945)

Comparisons and Contrasts

Philip OLLERENSHAW

University of the West of England, Bristol

1. The emergence of peak employers' organisations in UK

"Against the iron pressure of economics and modern conditions, the unit is feeble and ineffectual; the group, the society, and the collective effort are authoritative. British manufacturers must be organised, therefore, if they are to hold their own in the world's markets of today"[1].

This rationale for collective action was published by the Federation of British Industries (FBI) in 1922, six years after its formation in 1916. The First World War was profound enough in its effects to alter the relationship between capital and labour and between both of these and the state. In UK, increasing state control of the economy, growing trade union density, size and militancy, and great uncertainty about Britain's place in the post-war world, presented employers with unprecedented challenges. The scale and nature of the conflict would mean correspondingly severe post-war readjustment. During the First World War, and also during the Second one, British employers' organisations were at least as concerned with post-war reconstruction as they were with the wars themselves. This paper focuses on the growth and role of two peak employers' organisations, the FBI and the National Confederation of Employers' Organisations (NCEO) established in 1919, from their inception through to the end of the Second World War. It also considers aspects of the relationship between these organisations

1 See *The Federation of British Industries: What it is and What it Does*, London, FBI, 1922, p. 3.

and other employer associations, how far their membership and activities overlapped and how they attempted to influence parliament[2].

In terms of the historiography, one of the most influential contributions in this area has been that of Keith Middlemas. Middlemas argued that a "new form of harmony" in the British political system "was established with great difficulty" in the period 1916-26 and lasted until the 1960s. The Middlemas thesis of corporate bias in British politics can be briefly summarised as suggesting that that the FBI and NCEO, together with the Trade Union Congress (TUC), entered into a "continuous contract" with government which largely bypassed established political parties for the purposes of economic management and kept both fascism and communism relatively insignificant. The evidence for this is ambiguous and has been forcibly challenged for the interwar period[3]. Even so, Middlemas's focus on the "political importance of non-party, non-parliamentary activity" is certainly welcome[4].

With regard to lobbying parliament, a significant precursor of the FBI and NCEO organisation was the Manchester-based Employers' Parliamentary Association (EPA), established in December 1911 to counter what its leader, Sir Charles Macara, called the government's "German scheme of National Health Insurance" introduced earlier in the same year[5]. The EPA claimed that the National Insurance Act had generated "general dissatisfaction" because of the burden it placed upon industrial employers. Although the first task of the EPA was to lobby for the postponement or significant modification of national insurance, its remit extended to include pressing for "the recognition of the right of great bodies of employers to be consulted before important industrial legislation is undertaken"[6]. The EPA was strongest in northern England and the Midlands and included representatives from many industries such as textiles, hosiery, clothing, engineering, quarrying and building.

2 For a general survey of the period 1916-1945 see Blank, S., *Government and Industry in Britain: The Federation of British Industries in Politics, 1945-65*, London, Saxon House, 1973, chapter 2.

3 See Middlemas, K., *Politics in Industrial Society: the British Experience Since 1911*, London, Andre Deutsch, 1979, especially chapter 13. For some contrary evidence see Turner, J., "The Politics of Business", in *Id.* (ed.), *Businessmen and Politics: Studies of Business Activity in British Politics, 1900-1945*, London, Heinemann, 1984; Dintenfass, M., "The Politics of Producers' Co-operation: the FBI-TUC-NCEO Talks, 1919-1933", in *Ibid.*

4 See Turner, J., "The Politics of Business", *op. cit.*., p. 2.

5 See Davenport Hines, R., *Dudley Docker: the Life and Times of a Trade Warrior*, Cambridge, CUP, 1984, p. 106.

6 See Macara, C., *Social and Industrial Reform*, Manchester, Sherratt and Hughes, 1920 (8th edition), p. 378.

During its relatively short life of five years (it was merged into the FBI in 1916), the EPA established six branches and had affiliation with a number of trade associations. It argued the case for manufacturers in parliament and rejected compulsory arbitration in industrial disputes, preferring the use of the National Council established in 1911 to bring representatives of capital and labour together.

Amongst its most far-reaching proposals involved support for a British Trade Bank. Such a bank had been advocated by the Faringdon Committee in 1916. Historically "conservative banking methods" had served Britain well but it seemed clear that there was a need for supplementary financial methods to assist British trade and industry. The EPA suggested that in the post-war world Britain could learn much from German banks with their willingness to provide accurate information on foreign markets, provision of long credits and "exercise [of] a benevolent supervisory function" over a customer's trade. "The bed-rock fact remains that long credit transactions are only possible with accurate local knowledge of trade in foreign countries. If increased trade with Russia, Italy, South America, and other countries is desired, long credits are necessary. Under the present system they are impossible. The proposed British Trade Bank, if quickly established, will supply the need"[7].

Macara himself disagreed with the FBI and resigned during the merger, but his resignation did point to an important fault line which would become visible on many occasions in the history of employers' organisations in early twentieth century Britain: those businessmen who favoured tariff protection and the sizeable if diminishing free-trading lobby represented most obviously by Lancashire's cotton interests (of which Macara was a representative)[8]. The EPA was also notable for its concentration on state social welfare, which would also become an abiding interest for the FBI and the NCEO, related directly as it was to taxation and the "burden" that industry had to bear. Also noted is how employers' organisations were viewed by some of their labour and socialist critics. The growth in support for the Labour Party, which adopted a nominally socialist constitution in 1918, also helped some employers in the FBI to establish the British Commonwealth Union (BCU) which formed a Parliamentary Industrial Group to press for rapid erosion of state controls after the war as well as safeguarding of British manufacturing and strict controls on trade union action. Support for the BCU grew because some FBI members felt that established channels of communication with sympathetic (mainly Conservative) MPs were too

---

7 See *Ibid.*, p. 396.

8 See *Ibid.*, pp. 379-434.

limited[9]. With the FBI and the NCEO a further important consideration is the balance of their efforts between the domestic, British, front and the international/imperial arenas. The period 1916-1919 not only provided the incentives for peak employers' organisations in Britain, it also set the tone for many policies which would endure throughout the period to 1945.

The FBI emerged against a background of well-established, industry-based employers' organisations, many of which were formed to co-ordinate relations with employees. It was a meeting of one of these, the British Electrical and Allied Manufacturers' Associations (BEAMA), that proved to be the springboard for the formation of the FBI and for a key figure, Dudley Docker, to publicise the cause of businessmen in government, to put the case for a Ministry of Commerce, and for some British emulation of European corporatism[10]. The FBI was an organisation of British manufacturers, though exceptions would sometimes be made to this general rule, (in the case of shipowners, for example) and there would also be early discussions about precisely what constituted a "British company". Thus, for example, in September of 1916 both the Westinghouse Brake Company Ltd and British Thomson Houston Ltd were uncertain if they were eligible for membership "owing to the proportion of their Capital held by persons other than British subjects"[11]. The growth of the FBI membership is indicated in Table 1, while some evidence of the industrial profile of its members is provided in Table 2.

Table 1 - Membership of the Federation of British Industries (1916-1932)

Date	Firms	Associations	Controlled Establishments	Total
1916	50	3	-	53
1917	494	73	-	567
1918	793	152	15	960
1919	946	174	15	1,135
1920	1,222	166	13	1,401
1921	1,567	168	-	1,735
1922	1,729	166	-	1,895
1932	2,442	151	-	2,593

Sources: *The Federation of British Industries*, *op. cit.*, p. 9; *The Times*, 1 November 1932.

9 See Modern Records Centre, University of Warwick, (hereafter MRC) MSS 200/F/1/1/6, Minutes of the Executive Council of the FBI, 12 February 1919.

10 See Davenport Hines, R., *Dudley Docker*, *op. cit.*, pp. 105-106.

11 See MRC MSS 200/F/1/1/5, Minutes of the Executive Council of the FBI, 12 September 1916.

Table 2 - Membership of the Federation of British Industries (1922)

Group	Associations	Firms and individuals	Total
Mining, quarrying and allied trades	4	63	67
Mechanical engineering	15	411	426
Shipbuilding, marine engineering, constructive steel works and allied trades	6	126	132
Electrical engineering	4	110	114
Iron, steel and allied trades	47	461	508
Textiles	38	272	310
Glass and clay products	6	31	37
Printing, printing ink manufacturers, type founders, process workers and allied trades	2	39	41
Chemical fertilisers and explosives	7	120	127
Foodstuffs and tobacco	8	71	79
Agriculture	-	8	8
Building trades	4	37	41
Rubber, asbestos, leather and allied trades	11	128	139
Public utility	7	48	53
Miscellaneous	3	113	116
Non-ferrous metals	11	86	97
Oils and fats	3	38	41
Papermaking, manufacturers of stationery, envelopes etc	1	52	53
Banking and insurance	-	27	27
Woodworking	1	47	48
Cutlery, jewellery, electro-plate and allied trades	3	39	42
Brewing, distilling and allied trades	3	84	87
Fisheries	1	-	1

Source: *The Federation of British Industries*, *op. cit.*, p. 11.

The second half of the First World War saw the British economy come under ever more wide-ranging government control but at the same time saw increasing levels of unofficial and official strike action by trade unions, together with the rapid development of the shop stewards' movement[12]. The number of working days lost doubled between 1916 and 1917, but the 1919 figure, 35 million, was six times higher than that for 1917 and two years later the figure had risen to almost 86 million. The uneven incidence of strike activity was a powerful influence on the

12 See Hinton, J., *The First Shop Stewards' Movement*, London, George Allen & Unwin, 1973.

hardline attitudes of some employer organisations, most especially those in metals, engineering and shipbuilding, which had experienced the most working days lost of any sector in 1917, 1919 and 1921[13]. 1920 also saw the formation of the Communist Party of Great Britain. This was conducive to a strident "right to manage" stance by the particularly hardline and very influential Engineering Employers' Federation (EEF) led by its uncompromising President, Allan Smith, a Scottish trained lawyer and Conservative MP for Croydon South 1919-1923.

2. The division of labour between the FBI and NCEO

Any organisation such as the FBI had to make an early decision on its labour policy and in particular how it might avoid conflict with already established industry-specific employers' organisations. In October 1916, at one of its earliest Executive Council meetings, it was unanimously accepted that "it was most necessary to avoid all conflict with the existing associations" and that the FBI should take every opportunity to reassure officials of other employer organisations that the FBI was "in no way inimical to them or their interests"[14]. Although it set up a Labour Sub-Committee soon after it was established, the FBI in 1917 agreed that "In regard to Labour matters the Federation of British Industries will not concern itself or interfere with any questions affecting working conditions or rates of pay except at the request of the Employers' Associations or Federations established to deal with such questions". This immediately set limits to its interventions. However, wage increases and the rising tide of labour unrest, combined to force further organisations by employers and to a basic distinction between "commercial" and "labour" areas of responsibility. Such a distinction was inherently problematic from both a conceptual and operational point of view and it would sometimes cause difficulties for the FBI and for its individual members in later years.

By the spring of 1918 the FBI and the EEF had resolved to define the term "labour questions" and, amongst other decisions, resolved that all industries "should be fully organised for Commercial and Labour questions respectively", that the co-ordination of employers' organisations for labour questions should be encouraged and led by the FBI and the EEF. There would, moreover, be liaison between the FBI and the new co-ordinating body for labour questions "to ensure joint action on

13 See Mitchell, B.R., Deane, P., *Abstract of British Historical Statistics*, Cambridge, CUP, 1962, pp. 71-72.

14 See MRC MSS 200/F/1/1/5, Minutes of the Executive Council of the FBI, 17 October 1916.

matters affecting Labour jointly with other considerations"[15]. The new body for employers' organisations to consider labour questions was the NCEO which became the British Employers' Confederation (BEC) in 1939[16].

The NCEO's constitution of 1919 set out its initial objectives which gave it broad scope for action:

"1) To secure the fullest co-operation of all Employers' Organisations in dealing with questions arising out of the relations between employers and their workpeople;

2) For this purpose (a) to act jointly by federation or otherwise, and to co-operate with any Association or Federation in furtherance of the objects of the Confederation; (b) to watch over all legislative measures which may affect, or tend to affect, the interests of employers; and (c) to do all other such other things as are in the opinion of the Confederation, incidental or conducive to the above object"[17].

If immediate and pressing labour problems were important in leading to the formation of the NCEO there was a further factor which helps to explain its precise timing. This was the initiative by Lloyd George, the British Prime Minister, to set up a National Industrial Conference in February 1919[18]. This included 600 trade unionists and 300 employers, along with Government ministers and civil servants to try to forge a consensus on industrial and labour policy at a time when radicalism was in the ascendant. In the end the National Industrial Conference, which finally collapsed in 1921 did so because of clear differences between employers and unions, as well as the government's unwillingness to take a positive lead[19].

There was, moreover, a suspicion that the government used the NIC as a way to buy time until post-war industrial militancy had peaked. However, at the outset employers had no wish to be outmanoeuvred by organised labour and it is clear that the need to organise rapidly in time for the National Industrial Conference was a powerful influence on the

---

15 See MRC MSS 200/F/1/1/6, Chairman's Report of the Organisation and Management Committee to the Executive Council, 8 May 1918.

16 See MRC MSS 200/B/3/2/CI, J.M. Bryce to "Certain Employers' Organisations", 6 March, 8 April 1919.

17 See Ibid., The Constitution of the National Confederation of Employers" Organisations, 13 June 1919.

18 See MRC MSS 200/B/3/C/C299, R. Nugent to Secretaries and Representatives of all Associations, 27 March 1919.

19 See Lowe, R., "The failure of industrial consensus in Britain: the National Industrial Council, 1919-1921", in *Historical Journal*, 1978, n. 28, pp. 649-675.

emergence of the NCEO[20]. The collapse of the NIC was a missed opportunity, but it may be that consensus in such a fraught period as that of 1919-1921 was impossible to achieve. As Rodney Lowe has written, however, there were important long term consequences for the demise of the NIC since "the search for an authoritative industrial forum, such as a permanent national industrial council might have provided, was not concluded until 1962 with the creation of the National Economic Development Council"[21].

Early in its existence the NCEO had to respond to the formation of the International Labour Organisation (ILO), under the auspices of the League of Nations in 1919, and the need to participate in its affairs. At that point the NCEO claimed that, as far as labour questions were concerned, the British government viewed it as "the industrial organisation most representative of employers", and continued to do so thereafter. Membership of the NCEO was limited to the central employers" organisations in each industry which had responsibility "for relations between employers and employed". For voting purposes, the number of votes depended on the size of the association. Thus, while all associations up to 50,000 members had one vote, each additional 50,000 members brought an extra vote. The first membership list indicates that 39 employers' organisations with a total membership of 3.65 million had joined the Confederation. By far the largest members were those in the traditional industries. In rank order the top five were the Engineering and National Employers' Federation (c. 800,000), the National Federation of Building Trades Employers (400,000), the Federation of Master Cotton Spinners Associations (225,000), the National Federation of Iron and Steel Manufacturers (196,000) and the Cotton Spinners and Manufacturers' Association (180,000). There were also very small associations affiliated to the NCEO, the three smallest were the British Hemp Rope Manufacturers' Association (7,000), the British Sugar Refiners' Association (5,769) and the British Paper Stock Merchants' Association (4,248)[22]. In the period 1931-1932, some 45 employers' organisations in different industries subscribed to the NCEO, which by then claimed represented 7 million employees, or 60 per cent of the total industrial population of Britain[23].

---

20 See MRC MSS 200/B/4/3/2, *The National Confederation of Employers' Organisations: A Short Description of its Work*, London, Waterlow and Son, 1931, p. 3.

21 See Lowe, R., "The Failure of Industrial Consensus", *op. cit.*., p. 653.

22 See MRC MSS 200/B/3/2/CI, The National Confederation of Employers' Organisations, Constitution and Membership, 13 June 1919.

23 See *The National Confederation of Employers' Organisations: A Short Description of its Work*, *op. cit.*., p. 3.

Organisationally, the NCEO had a President and Vice-President and the two key committees were the Executive Council, comprising members from industries grouped together to ensure broad representation, and a General Purposes Committee meeting monthly, or more often if necessary, which dealt with "any issue requiring immediate attention". In addition, other committees were formed to deal with particular questions or areas of work. Within a few years ten such standing committees were in existence to reflect the evolution in the NCEO's business. The committee structure of the NCEO in 1932 is shown in Table 3.

Table 3 – NCEO Committee Structure in 1931

Council

↓

General Purposes Committee

↓

Standing Committees:

↓

Factories - Trade Boards – Hours - Industrial Organisation Unemployment - Parliamentary - Education - International - Membership Health Pensions and Workmen's Compensation

Source: *The National Confederation of Employers' Organisations: A Short Description of its Work*, London, Waterlow and Son, 1931.

As a further indication of its activity, in 1931-1932, the NCEO had provided twelve delegations to the Prime Minister, or other ministers and government departments. Moreover, the continued existence of the ILO ensured that the NCEO's activities always had an international dimension. In its first ten or twelve years, a representative selection of questions addressed by the NCEO would include: hours of work, factory law, the school leaving age and juvenile employment, the Coal Mines National Industrial Board, the provision of works canteens, workers' compensation; trade disputes and trade union legislation; the cost of living index and ILO work[24].

The division of responsibility between the FBI and NCEO did not mean that there was no contact between the two. In 1919 a liaison committee was established to discuss matters of common interest and where both "commercial" and "labour" questions were involved. The existence of this committee, which also decided that certain representatives of the FBI and NCEO should become members of each other's councils, certainly blurred the distinction between the publicly

24 See *Ibid.*

declared separation in areas of responsibility. Three questions referred to the Joint Committee early in 1920 were transport workers' wages, unemployment insurance and the enquiry into Workmen's compensation. The Joint Committee did not, however, fulfil expectations and had become dormant by October 1920. Nevertheless, regular contact was maintained between the two, in both meetings and regular correspondence, and it seems unwise to accept at face value a watertight separation of "commercial" from "labour" questions[25]. Individual members sometimes raised objections to the FBI's unwillingness to intervene in labour matters. For example, in the year before the General Strike steelmakers Stewarts and Lloyds complained to the FBI about unofficial strikes and the political levy from trade unions to the Labour Party[26]. Moreover, some employers found the FBI stance on labour questions distinctly unhelpful. One of these was leading British textile industrialist Samuel Courtauld, who in 1942 declared that even "the Federation of British Industries, which is the principal employers' organisation dealing with the Government, is a very lop-sided affair, because it is debarred from interesting itself practically in all questions of wages (which are left in the hands of the British Employers' Confederation), and consequently all its dealings and discussions with or about Labour tend to be purely academic"[27].

He went on to suggest that if the FBI was to be the main body representing employers, and he was personally in favour of there being only one such body, "steps should be taken to abolish this anomaly" so as to make the FBI all-embracing[28].

3. Employers' organisations and talks with trade unions

During and after the 1926 General Strike frequent discussion between the FBI and NCEO took place, but both welcomed The Trade Disputes and Trade Unions Act passed in 1927 which placed very considerable restrictions on trade union action. In an effort to provide a new framework for industrial relations after the General Strike, the Mond-Turner talks from 1927 necessarily included individuals who were also members of peak employer organisations as well as the TUC.

---

25 For an example of such a distinction see Holland, R.F., "The Federation of British Industries and the International Economy, 1929-39", in *Economic History Review*, 1981, n. 34, p. 287.

26 See MRC MSS 200/F/1/1/10, Minutes of a Meeting of the FBI Executive Committee, 9 December 1925.

27 See Courtauld, S., "An Industrialist's Reflections on the Future Relations of Government and Industry", in *The Economic Journal*, 1942, n. 52, p. 6.

28 See *Ibid.*

The talks, named after Sir Alfred Mond of ICI and Ben Turner of the TUC illustrated the range of opinion within the FBI and NCEO particularly with regard to the questions discussed which included rationalisation of industry, compulsory conciliation in industrial disputes, security of employment, the disclosure of commercial information to trade unions as well as worker representation in management. Mond selected his employers carefully and most came from very large firms and some were notably progressive in their views on industrial relations[29]. Fourteen had been active in the FBI but significantly only three in the NCEO. The latter felt itself aggrieved at being marginalised and some its key members remained resolutely opposed to joint discussions and certainly to major concessions on industrial relations.

There were few representatives from small firms in competitive industries or from those who dealt first hand with trade unions. Moreover, although the NCEO dealt with labour questions and the FBI publicly did not, there were many meetings between the two during the course of the Mond-Turner talks. The overlap in membership also became obvious on occasions like this. Thus, for example, in engineering, the British Engineering Association which was a member of the FBI focussed on "trade and economics" while the Engineering and National Employers Federation, a member of the NCEO, dealt "exclusively with labour questions". The overlap in membership, however, was in the order of 90 per cent, but even so it was quite possible that the two associations would return different opinions on the Mond-Turner talks[30]. The Interim Report of the Mond-Turner talks has been described as "a remarkable statement of progressive employer thought" and recommended trade union recognition, condemned victimisation of trade union members, supported the idea of a tripartite National Industrial Council, encouraged the rationalisation of industry and criticised the 1925 return to the gold standard at pre-war parity. Reception to the Interim Report highlighted the full range of views within the NCEO, from acceptance, through to qualified approval and finally to rejection – that latter being most obvious amongst the Engineering Employers Federation and Shipping Federation[31]. Within

---

29 For an examination of talks and their outcomes see McDonald, G.W., Gospel, H., "The Mond-Turner Talks, 1927-33", in *Historical Journal*, 1973, n. 14, pp. 807-829; Gospel, H., "Employers' Labour Policy: a Study of the Mond-Turner Talks", in *Business History*, 1979, n. 21, pp. 180-197.

30 See MRC MSS 200/F/1/1/16, Minutes of the Special Committee Appointed by the Grand Council of the Federation of British Industries to consider the recommendation of the Mond-Turner Conference for a National Industrial Council, 31 July 1928.

31 See Gospel, H., "Employers' Labour Policy", *op. cit.*., pp. 185, 192.

the FBI and NCEO, the division of opinion defied clear categorisation such as "expanding/contracting, sheltered/unsheltered, capital/labour intensive". Although the Mond-Turner talks are widely regarded as failing to produce any significant results there were further discussions between the FBI, TUC and NCEO after 1928 but each group guarded its independence and the talks did not lead to any reform of industrial relations. [32] Michael Dintenfass has returned a negative verdict on the various sets of discussions between 1927 and 1933 and has used them to challenge the Middlemas thesis of corporate bias[33].

Research into employers' organisations in Britain between 1916 and 1945 shows that there were strong personal connections between the key office holders of all the main employers' organisations and that it therefore makes little sense to analyse any one of them in isolation. Amongst the other organisations established during or just after the First World War might be noted the National Association of Controlled Firms, with some 3,000 members; the National Alliance of Employers and Employed (financially supported by the FBI) founded in 1916; and the relatively long-lived Economic League. The latter was a broadly-based pro-capitalist, anti-socialist organisation which provided a large-scale blacklisting service to employers in order to minimise employment of socialists and communists. Like the NCEO the Economic League (originally known as National Propaganda) was set up in highly tense year of 1919, at the suggestion of Sir Reginald Hall, then a Conservative MP for Liverpool West Derby. Allan Smith of the EEF was present its first meeting (as were Cuthbert Laws of director of the Shipping Federation and Evan Williams, chairman of the Mining Association) and during the interwar period there were close links between the Economic League and the NCEO, as well as with the FBI. Like the FBI the Economic League had a regional organisation and its most active support came from engineering employers in the north-west of England. Organised into a Central Council and fourteen regions in 1925 the former had a number of past-presidents and vice-presidents of the FBI and one past president of the Association of British Chambers of Commerce[34]. During the General Strike the Economic League worked with the FBI to supply the government with information about coal stocks, the availability of transport and the provision of strike-

---

32 See *Ibid.*, pp. 188, 193.

33 See Dintenfass, M., "The Politics of Producers' Co-operation", *op. cit.*., pp. 90-92.

34 See the excellent study by McIvor, A., "'A Crusade for Capitalism': the Economic League, 1919-39", in *Journal of Contemporary History*, 1988, n. 23, pp. 631-655.

breakers[35]. The shadowy nature of the Economic League reminds us of the limitations of available archival evidence with which to assess the links between employers' organisations and how decisions were reached. During the Second World War, for example, much was discussed over private lunches and dinners, sometimes under the leadership of a leading industrialist such as Sir Charles Craven, a key figure in Vickers, the principal British armaments manufacturer. At one such dinner in October 1941 it was clear that the BEC and the Economic League were secretly discussing how best to respond to the ILO Conference in Geneva due to take place in November.

The BEC, like many other employers' organisations, had become seriously alarmed about rising public expectations about social security embodied in the 1941 Atlantic Charter and elsewhere. As Sir John Forbes Watson of the BEC put it to Clive Cookson of the Economic League: "I hold the view that whatever may be the principles at stake after the war, it is on the labour question of wages, working conditions, social services and standard of living that they will find their outward manifestations and that it is there that the issue will have to be joined"[36].

Labour and socialist critics of the FBI often pointed to the difference between its public statements and its actions. In the 1920s perhaps the most direct critique of the FBI, its connections with other organisations and its role in parliament, from the left was made by the London-based Labour Research Department. In two pamphlets of 1923, entitled "Labour and Capital in Parliament" and "The Federation of British Industries" respectively the Labour Research Department provided a forensic examination of the FBI, its alleged influence in the policy-making process and aspects of its anti-labour politics[37]. Both pamphlets drew heavily on the FBI's own publications, especially its Bulletin, to add weight to its case, and "Labour and Capital in Parliament" was to some extent based on the "Directory of Directors". According to this research, the 1918 General Election returned 70 directors of firms affiliated to the FBI as Members of Parliament. These MPs worked to influence parliament and, in the short term, especially its postwar reconstruction policy. Amongst the aims of the FBI in this area were the

35 See *Ibid.*, p. 644. For some evidence of the role of employers' organisations in the General Strike see McDonald, G.W., "The role of British industry in 1926", in M. Morris (ed.), *The General Strike*, London, Penguin Books, 1976, pp. 289-317.

36 See MRC MSS/200/B/3/2/C940/1, Sir John Forbes Watson to Clive Cookson, 16 October 1941.

37 See Labour Research Department, *Labour and Capital in Parliament*, (Studies in Labour and Capital, n. 3), London, Labour Publishing Co., 1923; *The Federation of British Industries* (Studies in Labour and Capital, n. 5), London, Labour Publishing Co., 1923.

reduction of the "crushing burden" of taxation on industry; the reduction of Excess Profits Duty; the continuation of restrictions on imports; the abolition of Government controls on industry and trade; and state aid to sound British firms[38]. So influential was the FBI alleged to have been that, according to "Labour and Capital in Parliament", it established "a direct control of the machinery of government between 1919 and 1922". The result was that while the FBI prevented any move towards nationalisation of industry, it was also able to maintain prices and increase unemployment through restrictions on overseas trade, to redistribute the burden of taxation from employers to workers and to reduce public expenditure and divide organised labour through its sponsorship of alliances between employers and workers[39]. The last point was a reference to the FBI's involvement in the National Alliance of Employers and Employed, established in the autumn of 1916 with a view to promoting more harmonious relations not merely for the rest of the war but into the postwar reconstruction period too. Many trade union leaders remained circumspect or hostile to the idea[40]. The FBI certainly supported the National Alliance financially, for example voting a £500 subscription in March of 1917[41].

The Labour Research Department's critique of the FBI received quite wide press notice, not least in the Labour-supporting *Daily Herald*, in a article entitled "Behind the Mask of the FBI"[42].

4. The FBI in its wider context

The remit of the FBI was: "The safeguarding, encouragement, development and protection of the interests of British manufacturers and Producers, both at Home and Abroad. To centralise and facilitate the interchange of views between Manufacturers and Government Departments, Public Bodies, Institutions and Associations, in all matters affecting Industry directly and indirectly. To protect Industry as a whole from Legislation which may affect it adversely and promote improvements in administration. To provide a central medium of information, advice and assistance available for the use of its Members"[43]

The first three of these points implied a clear acceptance of the need to lobby parliament and government in particular. The significance of

38 See *Labour and Capital, op. cit.*, p. 14.

39 See *Ibid.*, p. 17.

40 See Clegg, H.A., *A History of British Trade Unions Since 1889*, Vol. 2, *1911-33*, Oxford, OUP, 1985, pp. 231, 252.

41 See MRC MSS 200/F/1/1/5, Minutes of the FBI Executive Council, 16 March 1917.

42 See *Daily Herald*, 26 September 1923, 2, 6, 10 October 1923, 18 January 1923.

43 See *The Federation of British Industries, op. cit.*, p. 2.

export-dominated staple industries in the FBI, and associated concerns about post war prospects, meant that amongst early priorities were improvements to the British consular service as well as developing its own system of commissioners to promote British business abroad[44]. The FBI rationale for overseas organisation was it was "a service run by manufacturers for manufacturers" which was "far more prompt, detailed and efficient than can be rendered by any Government commercial organisation which is compelled to serve many competing interests and is hampered by the necessity of avoiding any action which may cause local embarrassment"[45]. As the FBI admitted, the ideal would be to have commissioners in every market, advised by experts and where necessary also supported by sub-commissioners. Such a structure would require a presence in more than a hundred countries and an estimated cost of £1 million, a sum which was clearly impossibly high for the FBI. Instead, it decided to divide the world into 21 areas which would serve as initial locations for commissioners and once these had been established, to move on to "the systematic breaking-up of the areas into more convenient spheres of activity". In selecting the 21 areas, a number of factors including the size of the market, the "degree of development" of the population, the state of political relations, the extent of foreign competition and the balance of trade between Britain and the area in question. After due consideration, commissioners for the Near East (based in Athens); Spain, Portugal and North Africa (Madrid); the east coast of South America (Rio de Janiero); the East Indies (Singapore); southern Africa (Pietermaritzburg) and the west coast of South America (Valparaiso) were selected to be the first centres for FBI commissioners. Other temporary arrangements were made with Denmark, The Netherlands and Switzerland until resident commissioners could be appointed. Another aspect of the FBI's global conception of its role in furthering British manufactures and trade was to welcome overseas buyers to the Federation's London headquarters where they could be put into contact with the most appropriate manufacturers.

Commissioners were expensive and so too was the fourth area of activity, the provision of information to member firms. These were areas where it was almost impossible to predict demands for the services and hence the cost of providing them. In fact, so fast did the costs of the FBI escalate that by 1920 it was running at a deficit and had to appeal for further funds via a membership drive. The principal reason for the need for extra funds was the development of commissioner system but this was deemed to be essential to the future of British business to enable it

44 A clear summary of this area of the work of the FBI is in *The Overseas Service of the Federation of British Industries*, London, FBI, 1919, pp. 1-19, 31-32.

45 See *Ibid.*, p. 5.

to meet the competition which would shortly arise. Even under favourable circumstances at least a year was required before the benefits of an overseas commissioner became apparent: "It is obvious, therefore, that as many Commissioner organisations as possible should be established in the immediate future while the markets of the world are denuded of goods and the intensity of demand makes it easy for any organisation which can assist supply to become widely known and appreciated, so that they shall be in a position to be of substantial assistance to members when intense international competition again sets in"[46].

The reorganisation of the consular service and its centralisation within the Foreign Office were seen as priorities from the earliest days of the FBI – and in this respect it echoed the views of another major commercial lobby group the Association of British Chambers of Commerce[47]. Expansion of the Foreign Office's remit was also seen as essential, with commercial attachés replaced by "officers of high rank, to be known as Commercial Counsellors". The FBI clearly envisaged high standards from an increased number of technical and commercial experts, with a promotion board as well as power to dismiss anyone who failed to do the job[48]. The need for a close relationship between the FBI and government explains why some of its key staff in the early years were drawn from the diplomatic service. Roland Nugent, for example, FBI director in 1916-1917 and again between 1919 and 1932 had an elite education at Eton and Trinity College Cambridge, followed by the diplomatic service 1910-1913 and then the Foreign Office[49]. His successor as Director between 1932 and 1945, Guy Locock, was similarly educated at an elite private school, Wellington College, and before joining the FBI as Assistant Director in 1918 had served in the Foreign Office from 1906. By 1918 was in charge of the foreign section of the Department of Overseas Trade[50]. Such a background as that of Nugent and Locock would have opened governmental doors to the FBI which might otherwise have remained closed.

The FBI had an annually elected President and a Grand Council. In addition to its headquarters in London, it had twelve provincial offices with a resident secretary. Of these provincial areas, Manchester became the most important. But, as was the case with the NCEO, there was a

---

46 See MRC, MSS 200/F/1/1/7, Report from the Finance Advisory Committee to the Executive Committee, 28 February 1920.

47 For further background see MacClintock, S., "The British Foreign Commercial Service", in *The University Journal of Business*, 1922, n. 1, pp. 69-80.

48 See *The Times*, 16 December 1916.

49 See "Obituary of Roland Nugent", in *Ibid.*, 20 August, 1962.

50 See "Obituary of Guy Locock", in *Ibid.*, 26 August 1958.

whole range of committees which met to consider particular aspects of business. Thus, by the early 1930s amongst others these included: the Production Department (dealing with, for example, fuel economy, pollution, industrial art, education, and trade organisation); the Empire and general overseas departments; the Foreign Trade Department (dealing with commercial treaties and agreements, the League of Nations and the International Chamber of Commerce); the Economics Department (tariffs, currency exchange questions); and others dealing with areas as diverse as films, insurance, shipping, trademarks and patents, and parliamentary procedure.

Further, the FBI sometimes organised surveys of particularly important markets with a view to promoting British manufacturing exports. One of these visited the USA in 1925 and it pointed to some significant differences between business organisations in the USA and the UK. The FBI survey considered that in 1925 the US economy would see "a prolonged period of prosperity", but added (with more accuracy) that new construction might become excessive and cause overproduction while speculative activity in real-estate and the development of hire purchase "contain elements of danger if carried much further"[51]. The report suggested that the extent of industrial organisation in the USA was greater than in any other country with the possible exception of Germany. It pointed to the existence of some 7000 trade associations (federal, state and municipal) and the efficiency of the leading associations such as the Chamber of Commerce of the USA, the National Manufacturers' Association and the National Industrial Conference Board. In the USA business leaders were "much more ready than with us to take an active part in the work of these Associations, even at great personal sacrifice", and the American business community provided support to them which was "out of all relation to what can be obtained for similar purposes in Great Britain"[52]. In the mid-1920s the FBI was represented in the USA by the Association of British Chambers of Commerce in New York. A serious problem which the FBI delegation identified in 1925 was the almost wholly negative image of Britain and of British industry in the American press –antiquated, uncompetitive, lacking in enterprise and "at the mercy of Communists". Such an image was catastrophic for British business and the FBI saw it as imperative that it take the initiative to put the "real facts" before the public in the USA and thus perform "a great service for British trade and British prestige in America"[53].

51 See Willey, F.V., Locock, G., *Report on a Visit to the United States of America*, London, FBI, 30 October 1925, p. 3.

52 See *Ibid.*, p. 9.

53 See *Ibid.*, pp. 11-12.

On the key question of free trade versus protection the FBI for several years did not have a publicly declared policy since to do so would have alienated important free trade cotton interests although it should be noted that even before the First World War there were protectionist elements in cotton textiles[54]. Protectionist sentiment was present from the earliest days of the FBI and during the course of the 1920s such sentiment became much more widespread. During the steep recession of 1921 business groups such as the National Union of Manufacturers lobbied hard and successfully for "safeguarding" of certain industries. Within particular industries pressure for protection came from groups such as the National Federation of Iron and Steel Manufacturers, formed in 1918. From 1924 the well-organised, well-funded and well-connected Empire Industries Association pushed for tariff protection[55]. All these pressures intensified after the downturn of 1929 and would culminate in the formal abandonment of free trade in 1932. By 1930 sentiment in the FBI had swung decisively towards protection with 96 per cent of its member bodies said to be in favour. The following year its publication "Industry and the Nation", the FBI set out in some detail how tariff reform should proceed[56]. During the 1930s it looked increasingly to imperial markets and for tariff protection. For the traditional manufacturing industries which made up most of the FBI membership, protection, rearmament and economic recovery eased their position from the mid-1930s. Links with European business organisations continued right up to 1939. One instance of this was the detailed discussions on co-operation which took place in the later 1930s between the FBI and Reichsgruppe Industrie- which itself had regular meetings with Confederazione Generale Fascista dell'Industria Italiana on prices and markets[57]. A meeting between the FBI and Reichsgruppe took place on the day Germany occupied Czechoslovakia in March 1939[58].

During the Second World War, peak employer organisations were immeasurably stronger and more effective than they had been twenty years earlier. Industrial unrest was on average much less in the Second World War than in the First, and the established existence of the FBI and NCEO meant that they found it much easier to liaise with

54 See Marrison, A., "Businessmen, Industries and Tariff Reform in Great Britain, 1903-30", in *Business History*, 1983, n. 25, pp. 168, 170.

55 See Capie, F., *Depression and Protectionism: Britain Between the Wars*, London, George Allen & Unwin, 1983, pp. 50, 64.

56 See *The Times*, 1 November 1932.

57 See MRC MSS200/f/1/1/83, Minutes of a meeting between the FBI and Reichsgruppe Industrie, 20 December 1938.

58 See Holland, R.F.,"Federation of British Industries", *op. cit.*., p. 298.

government. On all aspects of production and industrial relations constructive discussion took place between 1939 and 1945. However, one key area where employers' organisations found themselves fighting a rearguard action was reconstruction and the role of the state. Reconstruction planning started as early as 1940[59]. Employers expressed alarm at some of the content of the Atlantic Charter published in August 1941, especially the fifth clause which envisaged full economic co-operation between nations "with the object of securing for all improved labour standards, economic advancement and social security"[60]. The first meeting between the TUC, BEC, FBI and the government took place in November 1942[61]. Above all, many in the FBI opposed the comprehensive social welfare provision as envisaged in the 1942 Beveridge Report. For them, as for British Prime Minister Winston Churchill, winning the war had to come first[62]. Nevertheless, as the war turned in the Allies' favour there would be no escape from public discussion of reconstruction and from 1942 several employers' organisations and trade associations began to publish their preliminary reports on the postwar world and how the transition from war to peace should be handled. These included the FBI, the National Union of Manufacturers, the Association of British Chambers of Commerce, the London Chamber of Commerce and the Federation of Master Cotton Spinners' Associations. As ever the Economic League worked in the background emphasising to both the FBI and BEC in June 1942 the need to get Industry's message across to as many people as possible across by co-ordinated action to produce literature which was readily comprehensible. If this did not happen, "the minds of the male and female voter who can only think and read superficially will be made up by others than those responsible for Industry, Agriculture, Mining etc."[63]. Surveying the FBI report, economist H.W. Arndt declared that it "paints a dismal picture of Britain in decline – a debtor country, ousted from foreign markets, with dwindling assets, a declining ageing population, and war-damaged equipment"[64].

59 See *Daily Herald*, 28 October 1940; *Daily Telegraph*, 11 October 1940.

60 See MRC MSS 200/B/3/S/1/C940 Part 1, Copy of the Atlantic Charter, 15 August 1941.

61 See MRC MSS 200 B/3/2/C960, Reconstruction Advisory File, 1942-45.

62 See "Churchill's speech in Ottawa on 30 December 1941", in *The Times*, 31 December 1941.

63 See MRC MSS 200/B/3/S/1/C940 Part 1, Clive Cookson to Sir John Forbes Watson, 29 June 1942.

64 See Arndt, H.W. "British Businessmen on Reconstruction", in *International Affairs Review Supplement*, 1942, n. 19, p. 437.

If this was the picture in 1942, when the war ended employers' organisations had other challenges to face. The sweeping victory of the Labour Party in the election of 1945 brought with it a pledge to introduce a large scale social welfare programme which no employers' organisations wanted or welcomed, as well as Labour's commitment to nationalisation of industry and to maintaining high levels of employment. In the postwar years these and other major questions of economic policy would lead the FBI and other British employers' organisations into territory which none of them could have foreseen in 1939.

Business Interests in the Welfare State

The Strategies of Sweden's Business Associations during the Twentieth Century

Niklas STENLÅS

Uppsala University

1. Aims, purposes and previous research

The Swedish Employer's Association (hereafter SAF) and its role in Swedish twentieth century history is a relatively well researched area and a number of historical monographs have dealt with the SAF[1]. The Federation of Swedish Industries (hereafter IF), on the other hand, is severely under-researched and only a few minor academic works have dealt with the IF[2]. No attempts, however, have been made to analyse

1 See De Geer, H., *The Rise and Fall of the Swedish Model. The Swedish Employer's Confederation, SAF, and Industrial Relations over Ten Decades*, Chichester, Carden, 1992; *Id.*, *SAF I förhandlingar: Svenska Arbetsgivareföreningen och dess förhandlingsrelationer till LO och tjänstemannaorganisationerna 1930-1970*, Stockholm, SAF, 1986; *Id.*, *I vänstervind och högervåg: SAF under 1970-talet*, Stockholm, Allmänna förlaget, 1989; *Id. Arbetsgivarna. SAF i tio decennier*, Stockholm, Svenska Arbetsgivareföreningen, 1992; I *Från den Svenska modellen till Svenskt näringsliv: om SAF och den svenska arbetsmarknadens organisering under 1990-talet*, Stockholm, Ratio, 2007; Johansson, J., *SAF och den svenska modellen. En studie av uppbrottet från förvaltningskorporativismen 1982-1991*, Uppsala, Uppsala University, 2000; Swenson, P.A., *Capitalists against markets: the making of labor markets and welfare states in the United States and Sweden*, Oxford, OUP, 2002.

2 Only two short publications deal with the history of the IF: Ullenhag, K., "The Federation of Swedish Industries in Swedish Politics", in A.M. Kujilaars, K. Prudon, J. Visser (eds.), *Business and Society, Business and Society. Entrepreneurs, Politics and Networks in a Historical Perspective, Proceedings of the Third European Business History Association (EBHA) Conference*, Rotterdam, Centre for Business History, 2000; Matti, T., *Industriförbundet och den demokratiska utmaningen. Företagsledarnas professionaliseringsprocess 1900-1940*, Uppsala Papers in Financial and Business History, 2003, n. 18 (which deals with the role of the Federation in the professionalization of business leadership).

how the two associations related to each other, how they formulated their strategies vis-à-vis each other and their environment. Considering the fact that they to a large extent shared member companies as well as board directors make this question all the more interesting.

The overarching question for this chapter is how the two organisations defined their roles not only in relation to each other but also in relation to their historical environment. During the course of the twentieth century they have had to deal with the rise of the labour movement, the development of democracy, the corporatisation of society, the rise of the welfare state as well as the de-corporatisation, the internationalisation and the decline of the nation state following the end of the Cold War.

2. The formation of a national business interest

The SAF and the IF were founded in 1902 and 1910 respectively. The founding of the institutions coincided roughly with the foundation of labour unions and political parties on a national level. The Social Democratic party was founded in 1889 but did not achieve representation in parliament until 1896. The Liberal and the Conservative parties were founded in 1902 and 1904 respectively. The Agrarian party was founded in 1916 and the Communists split off from the Social Democrats in 1919. These five parties composed the political landscape of the twentieth century Sweden. The first unions on the national level were formed in 1886, eight years later there were seventeen. The first unions were formed by artisan laborers but towards the end of nineteenth century, the industry workers had taken the lead. There were 40 unions organising 70,000 workers and in 1898 the Trade Union Confederation (hereafter LO) was formed.

From the outset LO was a part of the Social Democratic movement and its purpose was to politicise the labour unions. Since 1894 the Social Democratic party had coordinated the labour unions but this was now to be done by LO. Only trade unions that affiliated their members as a body to the Social Democratic party were admitted into the LO[3].

The formation of business and industry organisations has been seen as a reaction to the organisation of the workers in labour unions. The general strike of 1902 has been regarded as the main event triggering the formation of the SAF[4]. However accurate that might be it is equally true to regard the years around the turn of the century 1900 as a period when local interest groups were forged into national ones. This was

3 See De Geer, H., *Arbetsgivarna, op. cit.*, pp. 28-29.

4 See *Ibid.*, p. 36.

especially true regarding politics where the newly founded non-socialist parties started out as elector-recruiting organisations with the purpose of securing the re-election of members of the parliament's second chamber already in office. While the parliamentarians represented local constituencies the formation of national parties began a process that would eventually lead to the subordination of the members of parliament under a national party program.

Up until 1921 (and especially before 1907) local interest groups dominated the elections to the parliament's first chamber where the number of votes were determined by wealth and where also organisations had the right to vote. This meant that Members of the parliament's first chamber typically were the heads of local business companies or at least were backed by businessmen.

A parallel to the political process can be found among business companies that were in the process of expanding from local markets to national ones. Sweden was still mainly an agricultural economy with a low degree of urbanisation. A significant part of the country's business companies were located in small communities in the countryside and most Swedish companies still had their main office located far from Stockholm. As local markets became national markets, and local companies became national ones also local business interests needed to reform on a national level.

When the SAF, was founded in 1902, three persons stood behind the initiative. Two of them were conservative Members of the parliament's first chamber and one of them was also one of the founders of the conservative party two years later[5]. SAF was thus closely knit to conservative politics from the outset. In the end of 1903 101 companies employing 24,000 workers were members of SAF. In 1907 the number of member companies was 997 employing 127,000 workers[6].

In a bold reinterpretation of the role of the employers in the making of twentieth century Sweden, Peter A. Swenson has argued that the employers did not just react to demands of the labour movement, as has previously been assumed, but rather forcefully pushed labour in the direction of centralism and solidarism – two traits that has characterised the labour market of the Swedish Welfare State. The weapon, employed by the newly founded Employer's association, was massive lockouts. This weapon was primarily effective against an organised opponent and hence, the SAF preferred organised unions as counterparts. The lockout

5 The founders were Robert Almström, Oscar Carlson and Gustaf Fredrik Östberg. Östberg was two years later instrumental in the founding of the Conservative party. See *Ibid.*, pp. 36-39.

6 See *Ibid.*, p. 41.

strategy was effective only if the unions were forced to reimburse their locked out members and only if all employers could be convinced to act in unison. According to Swenson militant lockouts "gave organised capital in Sweden the ability to hammer unions into a shape that made them useful as partners in centralised regulation of labor markets"[7].

Whereas many of the of Sweden's employers around the turn of the century 1900 were patriarchal in their outlook, building on a tradition of rural-industrial factory masters (*brukspatroner*), hostile to unions but benevolent towards their employees, sometimes with generous social benefit schemes within their companies, the new Employer's association took the opposite stance. The object was to bring wages down and to convince member companies to abolish selective benefits. The strategy has been labeled solidarism and in order to effectuate it, militant coordination was required. Lockouts were used both to bring employers into line and to intimidate the unions[8]. In 1905 the Swedish Metal Workers' Union (*Metallindustriarbetareförbundet*) had been supporting 4,000 workers on strike at 23 machine shops and shipyards. The Swedish Engineering Employer's Association (*Verkstadsföreningen*) responded by locking out 83 member firms employing roughly 13,800 workers[9]. The conflict was a huge success for the employers. Only two firms refused to obey the lockout order (which resulted in a loss of membership as well as the funds they had already paid to the association). The conflict funds of the labour unions involved was totally drained. Within the Engineering Employer's Association there were strongly divided opinions over the object of the conflict. Whereas industrial patriarchs such as the diary machinery producing Separator's chairman John Bernström wanted to crush the unions his younger predecessor Sigfrid Edström of ASEA, Sweden's General Electric, led the faction seeking centralised collective bargaining with a strong union. In 1916 Edström became the chairman of SAF, one of the architects of the Saltsjöbaden agreement in 1938 and perhaps the most prominent business leader of his time[10].

---

7 In the 1920's and 1930's Swedish workers acquired a reputation as the most militant in the world because of the number of working days lost to conflicts. Based on these statistics historians have argued that this militancy turned into a spirit of cooperation as a result of the Saltsjöbaden agreement in the late 1930's. Swenson points out that a substantial part of the labour disputes were actually a result of employer lockouts. See Swenson, P.A., *Capitalist against markets*, *op. cit.*, pp. 73-74.

8 See *Ibid.*, p. 72.

9 The Engineering Employer's Association was not a member of the Employers' Association until 1917 when it also became the most powerful of the Employer's Association's member associations.

10 See Swenson, P.A., *Capitalist against markets*, *op. cit.*, pp. 78-79.

In the following year SAF threatened a massive lockout as a repraisal for relatively minor incidents in only a few firms. The LO leadership, with the metalworker's conflict well in memory, agreed to settle matters in the so called 'December compromise' where the LO acknowledged total managerial rights in the work place. In exchange they were granted formal recognition from the employers. This deal has been regarded as a milestone on the labour movement's road to recognition and eventually to power but, according to Swenson, labours's gains were not really contested by the majority of the employers whereas the gains of the employers were central in their strategy of making unions cooperative. At the same time the SAF strengthened its internal control over its members through the passing of the paragraph 23 which required all members to submit all agreements to SAF's executive leadership for approval. Member companies that did not comply with SAF directives were threatened by expulsion which also meant that they would lose all fees and bonds invested in the organisation thus far. During the first decade of its existence, the SAF had thus been extraordinarily successful in introducing managerial absolutism, eliminating paternalistic company benefits, decompressing wages, strengthening internal control and getting the members into line[11].

The IF was founded in 1910. Behind the initiative were two of Sweden's most prominent industrialists and bankers. They had met aboard the Saltsjöbanan train almost daily for some time and so the plans for a new business organisation had ripened[12]. Just as SAF the IF grew rapidly. The organisation was, shortly after its foundation, composed by member companies employing 72,000 workers (20 per cent of the country's total workforce). Ten years later the figure had risen to 240,000 workers, more than 50 per cent of the workforce[13].

3. Corporatism, democratisation and politicisation

The IF and the SAF quickly adopted different strategies towards member companies, labour unions and the state. The IF sought to become a lobby organisation vis-à-vis the state or, perhaps the main channel for expressing the opinions of industry in dealings with the government, an increasingly important task as state regulations became more prominent as a consequence of the world wars as well as of the

11 See *Ibid.*, pp. 80-81, 98.

12 The industrialist was Erik Johan Ljungberg, managing director of Stora Kopparbergs Bergslags AB (today Stora-Enso) and the banker was Marcus Wallenberg, managing director of Stockholm's Enskilda bank (today SEB). See Gårdlund, T., *Marcus Wallenberg 1864-1943: hans liv och hans gärning*, Stockholm, Norstedt, 1976.

13 See Ullenhag, K., "The Federation of Swedish Industries", *op. cit.*., p. 373.

economic depression of the 1930s. The initial programme of 1910 stated that the purpose of the IF was "to represent Swedish industry in important matters of common interest"[14]. The board of the organisation during the 1910s has been described as patriarchal in its outlook. A prominent board member (Frans Kempe of the Mo & Domsjö), although somewhat extreme in his opinions, did not accept workers with union affiliation at his industries at all but rather chose to build a small welfare community around his own company.

The IF was able to influence state policy directly from the start because of the government's practice of circulating law proposals for review to important organised interests. Law proposals and government planning committees were reviewed regularly as a part of the political process. As the organisation grew it became more and more important as a spokesman for trade and industry vis-à-vis the state. Early in its history questions pertaining to trade policy, energy policy and the reformation of education were especially important to the IF but later on the IF reviewed policy proposals in virtually all policy areas. In 1960 the organisation estimated that it reviewed around 60 such proposals every year[15].

The organisation thus assumed an important formal role in the political system that it has retained during its entire existence. During both the First and the Second World War did the IF appoint representatives for trade and industry to the numerous crisis-management organisations that were created. The praxis of appointing representatives of trade and industry as experts in state commissions was retained also during peace which meant that the IF became an important semi-official part of the corporatist political system that was formed from the 1920s on[16].

The IF also played an important but essentially neglected role with respect to its member companies. Here the IF took on the task of informing, advising and educating its own members in matters important to industry. One such area was the rationalisation of industry. The IF was an important proponent for the 'rationalisation movement' in Sweden[17]. The members were reached through conferences, through the Federation's journal and through a substantial publication of books

---

14 See *Ibid.*, p. 372.

15 See *Sveriges Industri: Översikt utgiven år 1961 av Sveriges Industriförbund*, Stockholm, Sveriges Industriförbund, 1961, p. 156.

16 See Matti, F., *Industriförbundet och den demokratiska utmaningen*, *op. cit.*, pp. 40-41.

17 See De Geer, H., *Rationaliseringsrörelsen i Sverige*, Stockholm, SNS, 1978.

and leaflets. The IF also published annually "The Swedish Industrial Directory"[18].

Also important for the IF's ability to influence politics have been the informal relations between the Federation's board members and government and parliament. Between 1910 and 1920 the board continuously had at least one of its members in the Swedish government[19]. This practice was discontinued through the democratisation in 1922 which meant that business leaders' privileged access to parliament ceased and that conservative governments became scarce[20]. However, the practice of promoting leaders with political connections continued when Vilhelm Lundvik in 1926 was appointed managing director of the IF. As a former deputy state secretary Lundvik had connections in government. Subsequently Lundvik was appointed Minister of Trade in the conservative government in 1928 and the chairman of the Conservative Party, Arvid Lindman, tried to have Lundvik elected as Member of Parliament[21]. Also, when Sven E. Lundberg was elected vice chairman of the IF in 1943 his political connections as a conservative Member of Parliament was given as an explicit reason to prefer him over other candidates[22].

The IF retained strong bonds to the non-socialist political parties. From 1928 and onwards a fund-raising campaign among business companies was organised every election year. The campaign was coordinated from the managing director's office of the federation. Three trustees were chosen among the most prominent business leaders. The trustees collected funds from the biggest companies and negotiated the distribution with the leaders of the non-socialist parties. The campaign was named Unitas and went on from 1928 to 1938. Arvid Lindman, the leader of the conservative party, regarded Unitas with mixed feelings. On the one hand funds were more easily raised when businessmen themselves were leading the campaign. On the other hand the party lost some of its control over its own finances as the party's traditional

18 See *Sveriges Industri, op. cit.*, p. 156.

19 See Ullenhag, F., "The Federation of Swedish Industries", *op. cit..*, p. 377.

20 See Stenlås, N., "Kampen om högern. Uppbyggnaden av allmänna valmansförbundet 1904-1922", in T. Nilsson (ed.), *Anfall eller försvar?: högern i svensk politik under 1900-talet*, Stockholm, Santérus förlag, 2002.

21 See Johnson, A., *Brobyggare & Ifrågasättare – IUI från starten till namnbytet – 1939-2006*, Stockhom, Institutet för Näringslivsforskning, 2007, p. 17-19.

22 The selection of deputy managing director was crucial because of the practice of promoting the deputy to managing director after two years. See Stenlås, N., *Den inre kretsen. Den svenska ekonomiska elitens inflytande over partipolitik och opinionsbildning 1940-1949*, Lund, Arkiv förlag, 1998, p. 131.

sources of funding now handed their funds over to Unitas instead of directly to the party[23].

The SAF, on the other hand, had been created by ultra conservative parliamentarians and business owners with the purpose of being a 'fighting organisation' came to adopt a strategy of political neutrality in order not to compromise its ability to negotiate with the labour movement[24]. The neutral stance was probably not a strategy from the start but because relations between employers and unions developed so well it became increasingly more rational to settle labour market matters in negotiation and without political interference. It has been argued that employers and unions needed each other because fear for strong unions forced unorganised employers to into line while fear for being left without economic support in labour conflicts drove workers into unions. In the end of the 1920s and early 1930s Sweden was an exception to the downward international trend of unionisation with an organisation degree of 63 per cent. At the same time contemporaries judged the Swedish employers to be "one of the most powerful combinations of industrial employers the world over"[25].

However, a high degree of organisation is not the same thing as internal cohesion. Following its early success, the SAF had severe difficulties in the 1920s and 1930s in keeping its members into line. The problems resulted from the difficulties of upholding employer solidarism when different industry branches had different wage levels. In 1933 a Social Democratic government was formed and it became all the more important for the business organisations not to be associated with politics. The SAF succeeded in striking a deal with the LO that would keep state legislation out of the labour market. The state agreed not to interfere in any deal reached by the labour movement and employers. The informal deal, or perhaps it is better labeled "regime", was in effect up until the 1980s[26]. It effectively de-politicised the labour

23 See Stenlås, N., "The rise of Political Activism in Scandinavian Big Business 1900-1950", in H. Byrkjeflot, S. Myklebus, C. Myrvang, F. Sejersted (eds.), *The Democratic Challenge to Capitalism. Management and Democracy in the Nordic Countries*, Bergen, Fagbokforlaget, 2001, p. 271.

24 See Kugelberg, B., *Från en central utsikspunkt*, Stockolm, Norstedts, 1986, p. 43 [the memoirs of SAF's managing director between 1947 and 1966].

25 See Swenson, P.A., *Capitalist against markets*, *op. cit.*, p. 76.

26 The Agreement in itself does not seem to contain anything that would merit the enormous significance it has been attributed by the parties involved. The mythology around the agreement has puzzled historians who have speculated that it might rather have been the tacit understandings that evolved between the parties during the two years of negotiations that were important. See Åmark, K., *Facklig makt och fackligt medlemskap – De svenska fackförbundens medlemsutveckling 1890-1940*, Lund, Arkiv, 1986, p. 132.

market and made corporatism a central part of Swedish society and has been labeled the foundation of the "Swedish model".

But SAF's officially adopted political neutrality did not prevent it from becoming a powerful political actor. An important asset of the organisation was its conflict funds. Further assets could be drawn from the bonds issued by the member companies. The SAF thus controlled vast economic resources in order to protect its members in case of emergencies in the labour market. The Second World War among other things meant a stable peace in the labour market which, in turn, made it possible to free the resources in the conflict funds for other purposes. From 1942 and onwards SAF's conflict funds were used secretly to support non-socialist newspapers. The rationale behind this move was that the LO supported Social Democratic newspapers and the corporatist dualism of Swedish society thus required the employers to respond.

During the 1940s a series of initiatives were taken by the country's leading businessmen to support non-socialist political parties or to directly influence public opinion in a non-socialist direction. Decisions for these initiatives were taken informally within the business elite. Plans were agreed upon in informal meetings or directly in conjunction with board meetings of the SAF and IF. It has been argued that an informal "inner circle" of business leaders existed in the 1940s that were able to coordinate political actions through their networks and positions within different organisations. They sought to avoid drawing their respective organisations into politics where its corporatist role could be compromised but at the same time they exploited both the economic and the organisational resources of the business organisations[27].

4. The business associations in the Welfare State

The Social Democratic victory in the 1948 parliamentary election in conjunction with the economic upturn that became evident from the end of the 1940s put an end to the political controversies of the 1940s and it was very much a new landscape that faced the business organisations during the 1950s and 1960s. During the post-war period the two business associations assumed different roles in the emerging Swedish welfare society. At the same time they organised more or less the same members. The SAF solely dealt with labour market issues, emphasised a position of political neutrality and sought to cultivate good relations with the LO. Secret political support to the non-socialist parties

27 See Stenlås, N., *Den inre kretsen. Den svenska ekonomiska elitens inflytande över partipolitik och opinionsbildning 1940-1949*, Lund, Arkiv förlag, 1998; *Id.*, "The Rise of Political Activism", *op. cit.*.

continued up until the end of the 1960s (when public political funding was introduced) although at a much more relaxed pace than during the politically tense 1940s. The organisation also grew rapidly. In 1930 SAF represented 2,500 owners employing some 300,000 workers. Seventeen years later the number of member companies had increased to 10,700 employing 637,000 workers. At that point the organisation employed a staff of 80 persons. In 1978 it represented 36,000 owners employing a total of 1,335,000 workers. The staff had increased to 500[28]. As the organisation grew it gradually became more dominant and also tightened its grip over its members. During the 1950s central wage negotiations became the norm and the leading staff of the SAF assumed a pivotal role. The central leadership of SAF obtained the right to review all collective wage agreements in advance and it possessed the ultimate right to employ the lockout weapon.

SAF's leading staff became more important within the business elite than what had previously been the case. Dominant industrialists and bankers such as Marcus and Jacob Wallenberg were alarmed by the transfer of power from owners such as themselves to the employed staff in the SAF. However, the centralised wage negotiation system allowed no alternative[29]. The employed staff was given a very strong position in their capacity of wage negotiation experts. The organisation almost reached the position of sole spokesman for Swedish business which further added to the importance of the leading staff.

Bertil Kugelberg, the organisation's managing director between 1947 and 1966 was not a businessman but rather a lawyer who had worked his way up within the organisation. During the 1960s he became somewhat of a symbol of Swedish business and one of its foremost spokesmen. Kugelberg, and with him the entire SAF, were characterised by the association's role as negotiator[30]. He was regarded as a collaborator and he spoke very well of his counterparts within the unions. In his memoirs he wrote concerning the LO and its chairman Arne Geijer that "[t]he structure of our organisations and our work decided the outer forms, but within this framework we could develop a co-operation founded on equal respect [...] On my own part I tried to

---

28 See De Geer, H., *Arbetsgivarna, op. cit.*, p. 124; Giesecke, C.S., "SAF:s utveckling och ändrade roll under åren 1947-1977", in B. Kugelberg (ed.), *Fred eller fejd. Personliga minnen och anteckningar*, Stockolm, SAF, 1985, p. 105.

29 See "Minnesanteckningar från samtal med bankdirektören Marcus Wallenberg (telefon) den 13 oktober 1955" and "Minnesanteckningar från samtal med Jacob Wallenberg på Nobelfesten den 10 december 1955", memorandums drawn up by Bertil Kugelberg, vol. 2, F51 BF, SAF's archive, Föreningen Stockholms företagsminnen.

30 See Kugelberg, B. (ed.), *Från en central utkikspunk, op. cit.*, pp. 28-36.

develop a friendly, open and trustful relationship with him, and I dare believe that I succeeded fairly well"[31].

The corporative attitude within the business elite even if union friendly, however, expressed ambivalence towards the Social Democratic government. There was a certain fear that the labour movement would use its political power in an unduly way to affect labour market relations. According to Kugelberg, one of his predecessors Gustaf Söderlund expressed this concern by stating that relations in the labour market was 'as natural as those between the parties in any trade agreement [...] provided they were kept in the right spirit and that political infiltration was kept out"[32]. Kugelberg himself regarded (although in retrospect) the bonds between social democracy and unions with suspicion: "With time", he wrote, "a power conglomerate developed on the social democratic side which made it more and more difficult for SAF to gain attention. The position of the Association was weakened in this way".

The reluctance against political involvement was sometimes shared by the LO and both parts sought to keep government legislation away from the labour market. Ideally employers and unions would negotiate and if they agreed there were little need for the government to legislate. This labour market regime was developed from the end of the 1930s and became an integral part of the Swedish model where the corporative interests regulated the labour market without involvement of government legislation.

The commonly accepted picture of the labour market of the Swedish welfare society acknowledges the central role of the SAF as a well organised body of employers but would assign the chief agency to the labour movement rather than the employers. According to most literature, the well organised unions together with the social democratic government in government put the labour movement in a position where it could force a "historic compromise" where industrial peace and wage restraints were traded for a comprehensive set of welfare state programs[33].

31 See *Ibid.*, p. 72 [my translation].

32 See Kugelberg, B., *Upp i vind*, Stockolm, P.A. Norstedt & Söners förlag, 1985, p. 289.

33 See i.e. De Geer, H., *Arbetsgivarna...*, p. 99; Esping-Andersen, G., "Class Coalitions in the Making of West European Economies", in *Political Power and Social Theory*, 1982, n. 3, pp. 17, 19, 47; Rothstein, B., "State and Capital in Sweden: The Importance of Corporatist Arrangements", in *Scandinavian Political Studies II*, 1988, n. 3 pp. 255-56; Korpi W., "Den demokratiska klasskampen – Svensk politik i jämförande perspektiv", Stockholm, Tiden 1981, p. 27; *Id.*, *The Working Class and*

Labour market historian Peter A. Swenson has recently proposed a radical reinterpretation in which the employers rather than the labour movement is put in the lead. The employers, in Swenson's account, are not only credited as the primal agents of the great class compromise but also for other basic features of the Swedish welfare state that were institutionalised during the 1950s such as the solidaristic wage policy, the active labour market policy, compulsory health insurance and the public pension reforms. According to Swenson, the SAF had not only sought arrangements after these lines for a long time, but succeeded in interesting the labour union confederation for such policies long before they were accepted by the social democratic party. Thus, much of the welfare state policies, were invented by the employers, according to Swenson, and made possible only through the strong alliance between employers and unions that emerged after 1938[34].

The IF, on the other hand, sought to position itself as an expert organisation in business issues. Expert advice occupied a central position in the Swedish political system as did corporative interests. Both mechanisms provided the IF with good opportunities to influence politics. Its membership increased from 2,440 companies employing 373,000 workers in 1945 to 4,300 companies employing 720,000 workers in 1964. It is interesting to note, and in need of further analysis, that although the two business associations adopted different strategies and occupied different positions in Swedish society, they were to a large extent led by the same business leaders.

In its role as an expert advisory body the IF initiated or cooperated in the founding of several specialised expert organisations where the IF became one of the principal organisations. The most important one was The Institute for Industrial Research (IUI) which was founded in cooperation with SAF in the end of the 1930s with the purpose of

---

Welfare Capitalism: Work, Unions and Politics in Sweden, London, Routledge & Keegan Paul, 1978, pp. 47-48, 317-319.

34 Shortage of labour has characterised the Swedish labour market, goes Swenson's argument, and in order to avoid firms and branches to outbid each other, strict control of the members was needed on the part of the Employer's Association. The employers would agree to raise minimum wages and in return they would get the Trade Union Confederation's acceptance and even assistance for preventing companies and entire industrial branches from unduly wage increases and to eliminate selective company welfare benefits. These circumstances created a regime of depressed and relatively equal wages supported by both employers and unions as well as uniform needs for welfare programs on the national level. See Swenson, P.A., *Capitalist against markets*, *op. cit.*, pp. 71-141, 268-300. Swenson's book, although very thorough, is still alone about this interpretation. The book has been intensely criticised by Korpi, W., "Power Resources and Employer-Centered Approaches in Explanations of Welfare States and Varieties of Capitalism. Protagonists, Contenders, and Antagonists", in *World Politics*, 2006, n. 58, pp. 167-206.

providing the business organisations with statistics and authoritative research upon which it could base its dealings with government or unions. Other such specialised expert organisations jointly founded and funded by IF and SAF were The Production Board of Trade and Industry (*Industriens Produktionsråd*), The Media Service of Trade and Industry (*Industriens Presstjänst*), The Defence Board of Trade and Industry (*Industriens Försvarsbyrå*), the *Industriens Praktiknämnd* and the *Industriens Skattesakkunnige*. In the 1950s, 1960s and 1970s industrial and economic planning became increasingly important and the specialist expert organisations became an important planning tool for the SAF and the IF[35].

The IF also published a substantial body of literature. Between 1910 and 1984 the IF published more than 800 titles ranging from small brochures to monographs written by invited experts. This literature was aiming to educate the members of the organisation, to express its opinion in important areas or to illuminate important problems in the organisation's environment[36]. In this way it was possible to make authoritative statements, based on expert opinion, that affected expert and political opinion in the country.

The IF has not just functioned as an industrial bureaucracy. It has also provided big business leaders with a platform from which to act politically and from which to interpret the will and the views of industry. Although the IF has had strict formal rules concerning how the leadership has been elected it still seems to have been possible for factions within the business elite to dominate the organisation. One highly important such faction, both for Swedish economy and for the IF, has been the Wallenberg family. The Family's platform was originally the third biggest commercial bank, the Stockholms Enskilda Bank, but during the twentieth century a financial imperium gradually evolved around the family and the bank. The family controlled key ownership posts in several of the big export industries that grew rapidly after the Second World War. Between 1944 and 1969, the Wallenberg group increased its share of the number of employees in Swedish industry from 11 to 23 per cent[37]. The Wallenbergs dominated the IF throughout

---

35 See *Sveriges Industri*, *op. cit.*, p. 154.

36 See Eklund, M., *Publikationer från Sveriges industriförbund 1910-1984. En bibliografi sammanställd av Maria Eklund*, Stockholm, Sveriges Industriförbund, 1985.

37 See Lundin P., Stenlås, N., "Technology, State Initiative and National Myths in Cold War Sweden: An Introduction", in P. Lundin, N. Stenlås, J. Gribbe (eds.), *Science for Welfare and Warfare. Technology and State Initiative in Cold War Sweden*, Sagamore Beach, Science History Publications, 2010, p. 13; Olsson, U., *Furthering a Fortune. Marcus Wallenberg: Swedish Banker and Industrialist, 1899-1982*, Stockholm, Ekerlid, 2001, pp. 340-341.

its history. Marcus Wallenberg (the elder) was one of the two founders of the organisation and was the organisation's second chairman in 1912-1914. According to the statutes, a chairman was elected for two years and was then automatically succeeded by the vice chairman. Wallenberg's son, also named Marcus (the younger), chaired the organisation 1962-1964 and his son, Peter, 1987-1989. However, if we count also the chairmanships of the managing directors of the Wallenberg-owned companies as an indication of the family's influence within the organisation it becomes overwhelming[38]. According to one observer from the 1980's, the Federation was the Wallenberg family's "secretariat for political issues"[39].

5. Decorporatisation and the decline of the Swedish Model

During the 1980's the SAF once again lead the transformation of the Swedish labour market. This time, however, in the opposite direction, away from corporatism and in a market liberal direction. First, wage negotiations were decentralised. This was partly a process lead by the SAF itself or by its strongest branch organisation, the Engineering Employer's Association who pushed for decentralisation against the will of the majority of the member associations. Decentralisation of the wage negotiation process, however, meant a decline for the SAF both in terms of its dominance over its members and in terms of its position in the corporatist bargaining system central to the "Swedish model"[40].

During the 1980s and 1990s the SAF also gradually abandoned its proclaimed political neutrality and became an active opinion moulder in several political issues such as its opposition to the introduction of publicly controlled wage earner funds and its active support of Swedish membership in the EU. In 2001 the IF was merged with the SAF.

Conclusion

The first decades of the twentieth century can thus be characterised as a formation of a national business interest, a process that went hand in hand with the formation of a national labour interest and national political interests. Little has been published on the issue of business political activism in Scandinavia but was has been published seems to

---

38 See Karlsson, S., *I Sveriges och industrins tjänst*, Stockholm, Sellin & partner, 2001, pp. 154-157.

39 See Mayerson, P.M., *Sockerbagare i doktorshatt*, Stockholm, Fisher & Co, 1997, p. 84, quoted in Ullenhag, K., "European Institutions and Enterprises in Sweden. Aim and Scope", in H.G. Schröter (ed.), *The European Enterprise. Historical Investigation into a Future Species*, Berlin, Springer Verlag, 2008, p. 113.

40 See De Geer, H., *Arbetsgivarna*, *op. cit.*, pp. 158-175.

run counter to the dominant interpretation of Scandinavian political life, that of the big class compromise between capital and labour.

The official strategies of the dominant business associations SAF and IF were different from the outset. SAF were formed to combat unions and to handle the new situation that was emerging as a result of unionisation. IF on the other hand was formed to influence state policy. The organisations to a large extent organised the same member companies and the organisations also shared many board members. In their official capacities both organisations sought to adapt themselves to the emergent corporatism that dominated Sweden's political and social life during the twentieth century. The IF did so by becoming an industrial expert organisation while SAF, on the other hand, became the corporative counterpart of the LO. SAF was in this capacity so successful that it dwarfed any other industrial interests in the country, even the mighty Wallenberg family whose companies employed more than 10 per cent of the working force.

Unofficially and in secrecy, however, both organisations used their resources to support non-socialist politics. This was done from 1928 and escalated until 1948 and continued up until at least the end of the 1960s. The political strategies were formulated by the board members of the organisations and within the networks of the business elite rather than within the organisations themselves. An explanation for these dual strategies which seem to contradict each other and even to contra-productive to each other can be found if we assume that the organisations were governed in part by an organisation based logic and in part by a class based logic. It is interesting to note that the class based logic was so strong that it was actually possible to use SAF's resources for political purposes in the 1940s without the knowledge of most of its members. During the 1950s and 1960s the organisation-based logic took precedence and made SAF's employed staff the most powerful men in Swedish business.

When it comes to the question of the two associations' influence in Swedish politics this is a difficult problem to assess regarding the IF and regarding the SAF opinions differ between researchers. The main reason for the difficulty to discuss the extent of the IF's influence is the lack of research on the subject. The corporate political system, the organisation's expert role together with the high degree of organisation of member companies means that the IF was a central voice for Swedish industry.

Business Eurofederations and European Integration from the Second World War to the 1970s

Neil ROLLINGS

University of Glasgow

Introduction

In June 2012 there were 5,145 entries in the European Union's Transparency Register of Interest Representatives[1]. However, the register only opened in June 2008 (then called the Register of Interest Representatives) and registration is voluntary. While the register has been criticised for 'seemingly irrelevant registrations'[2], one recent estimate suggests that there are more like 15,000-20,000 interest groups operating in Brussels[3]. Political scientists now regard this system of interest representation as mature and sophisticated: it is the diversity and complexity of the relationships between interest groups and EU institutions which is stressed[4]. They contrast this position with the past by emphasising the co-evolution of interest group representation and European integration in three key respects: the types of organisation have diversified; the scope of the interests being represented has widened; and the number of interest groups has increased[5]. Thus with the growth in numbers of European interest groups so the largest

1 See data in https://webgate.ec.europa.eu/transparency/regrin/welcome.do?locale=en# [accessed 18 June 2012].

2 See Wonka, A., Baumgartner, F.R., Mahoney, C., Berkhout, J., "Measuring the size and scope of the EU interest group population", in *European Union Politics*, 2010, n. 3, p. 474.

3 See Coen, D., Richardson, J., "Learning to lobby the European Union: 20 years of change", in *Id.*, (eds.), *Lobbying the European Union: institutions, actors, and issues*, Oxford, OUP, 2009, p. 6.

4 See Coen, D., "Business lobbying in the European Union", in *Ibid.*, p. 145.

5 See Eising, R., *The political economy of state-business relations in Europe: interest mediation, capitalism and EU policy-making*, London, Routledge, 2009, p. 61.

category has recently become non-governmental organisations, replacing trade, business and professional associations, which had always previously been the largest grouping. However, when looking at interest groups at the outset of European integration political scientists highlight the dominance not just of business but of organised business, particularly so-called 'Eurofederations', federations of national trade associations. Indeed, some of the seminal early works on European integration from the 1950s and 1960s, particularly Haas' and Lindberg's books, highlighted the importance of such economic interest groups as motors of European integration[6].

While such neofunctionalist approaches have gone out of vogue among political scientists working on European integration, such political scientists have retained a close interest in the empirical study of the role of interest groups in the European polity and continue to recognise the central role played by organised business in the development of lobbying of European Union institutions. In this context, Berkhout and Lowery have recently begun to consider the ecology of these interest groups by trying to track the key developments since 1990[7]. However, to date, there has been no attempt to put these developments into a longer-term perspective. Indeed, the pre-Single Market Programme development of European interest groups has received little systematic study. Those that have addressed this issue all turn to the CONECCS database to map the historical development of European interest groups. This was a register of interest groups which ran from the early 1990s until 2008[8]. As part of the process of registering for the database organisations provided their founding date. It is these founding dates which have been used to demonstrate the historical development of European interest groups.

This paper shows that there are clear problems with using this database to present a history of the development of European interest groups and so tries to reconstruct a dataset of Eurofederations from contemporary sources. Analysing this data shows that research based on the CONECCS database has significantly underplayed the impact of the creation of the EEC on the creation and location of such Eurofederations. However, there is also a second issue highlighted

6 See Haas, E., *The uniting of Europe: political, social, and economic forces 1950-1957*, Stanford, Stanford University Press, 1958; Lindberg, L., *The political dynamics of European economic integration*, Stanford, Stanford University Press, 1963.

7 See Berkhout, J., Lowery, D., "The changing demography of the European Union interest system since 1990", in *European Union Politics*, 2010, n. 3, pp. 447-461.

8 Berkhout, J., Lowery, D., "Counting organized interests in the European Union: a comparison of data sources", in *Journal of European Public Policy*, 2008, 15(4), pp. 489-513.

which is more important, but perhaps not that surprising to economic historians given their knowledge of international trade associations in cartels[9]. Political scientists regard political representation, that is the logic of influence in the terms of Schmitter and Streeck[10], as the key activity of such organisations. Thus there is little interest in Eurofederations created before the Treaty of Rome (and certainly not before Marshall Aid)[11] since the concern of political scientists is with their relationship to the political dimensions of the development of the European Union and its predecessors: business associations are 'first and foremost political actors'[12]. Trade associations are regarded in this respect as interest groups[13]. As 'a superb weathervane of power' organised interests' location is seen as a good indicator of the shifting locus of political power[14]. In this sense organised business interests respond (either in anticipation of or in reaction to) the changing political environment. Accordingly, there is a tendency to relate the growth of European business organisations directly to the creation and development of European integration. Political scientists highlight the growth of such organisations after the Treaty of Rome[15]. Typical, in this respect, was the creation of UNICE (Union des Industries de la Communauté européenne), at which the national business federations of the six EEC member states came together, in 1958 in order to influence legislators[16]. Similarly, they point to an explosion in the number of

9 See Wurm, C., *Business, politics and international relations: steel, cotton and international cartels in British politics 1924-1939*, Cambridge, CUP, 1993. Kudō, A., Hara, T., (eds.), *International cartels in business history: proceedings of the Fuji conference*, Tokyo, University of Tokyo Press, 1991.

10 See Schmitter, P.C., Streeck, W., *The organization of business interests. A research design to study the associative action of business in the advanced industrial societies of Western Europe*, IIM Discussion Papers IIM/LMP, n. 31, Berlin, Wissenschaftszentrum, 1981.

11 See Sidjanski, D., "Pressure groups and the EEC", in C.A. Cosgrove, K. Twitchett (eds.), *The new institutional actors: the U.N. and the E.E.C.*, London, Macmillan, 1970, pp. 397-416.

12 See Lang, A., Schneider, V., Werle, R., "Between politics, economy, and technology: the changing environments of business associations", in J. Grote, A. Lang, V. Schneider (eds.), *Organized business interests in changing environments: the complexity of adaptation*, Basingstoke, Palgrave Macmillan, 2008, p. 44.

13 See Kirchner, E., Schwaiger, K., *The role of interest groups in the European Community*, Aldershot, Gower, 1981.

14 See Richardson, J., "Organised interests in the European Union", in K.E. Jørgensen, M. Pollack, B. Rosamund (eds.), *Handbook of European Union Politics*, London, Sage, 2006, p. 232.

15 See Lindberg, L., *The political dynamics*, *op. cit.*, p. 97. Greenwood, J., *Representing interests in the European Union*, Basingstoke, Macmillan, 1997, p. 245.

16 See Tyszkiewicz, Z., "UNICE: the voice of European business and industry in Brussels. A programmatic self-presentation", in D. Sadowski, O. Jacobi (eds.),

European business interest groups with the introduction of the single market programme[17].

This is problematic because it will be shown here that there were many Eurofederations in existence prior to the creation of the EEC in 1958 and that their membership was not restricted to the national associations of the Six. The final part of the paper, therefore, reflects on the factors that can explain the creation and continued existence of such Eurofederations, highlighting the uncertainty about the nature and path of European integration in the 1950s and 1960s, and thee internal economic functions of such organisations, the logic of membership, in particular in the exchange of information and the building of trust, both of which can be precursors of cartels but, it is argued here, cannot be assumed to represent cartelistic collusion. As Richard Tedlow has pointed out in the American case, US trade associations have continued to thrive over the course of the twentieth century despite the Sherman Act banning cartels[18]. Trade associations and, in the European case, European federations of national associations offer more to their members than just cartels or political representation.

1. Existing accounts of the activities of European interest groups 1945-1973

Existing accounts of the development of Eurofederations all come from political science. The most commonly used source now when trying to quantify the development of EU interest groups over time is the CONECCS database. This is the database that preceded the EU's Transparency Register and covered the period from the early 1990s to 2008. The database has been criticised for being overly focused on organised associations and, therefore, much more narrowly defined than other directories of interest groups and lobbyists[19]. However, from the perspective of tracking the development of European interest groups over time it is the only source which provides information on the date of

---

Employers' associations in Europe: policy and organizations, Baden Baden, Nomos Verlagsgesellschaft, 1991, p. 87.

17 See Mazey, S., Richardson, J., "Introduction: transference of power, decision rules, and rules of the game", in *Id.* (eds.), *Lobbying in the European Community*, Oxford, OUP, 1993, pp. 3-5; Woll, C., "Lobbying in the European Union: From *sui generis* to a comparative perspective", in *Journal of European Public Policy*, 2006, n. 3, p. 458.

18 See Tedlow, R., "Trade associations and price relations", in H. Yamazaki, M. Miyamoto (eds.), *Trade associations in business history*, Tokyo, University of Tokyo Press, 1988, p. 140; Galambos, L., "The American trade association movement revisited", in *Ibid.*, pp. 121-135.

19 See Berkhout, J., Lowery, D., "Counting organized interests", *op. cit..*, pp. 489-513.

creation of such groups[20]. Accordingly, it has become common to present the data shown in Figure 1, and drawn from the CONECCS database, as illustrating the growth of European interest groups over time, the spurts in growth associated with deeper integration (like the signing of the Treaty of Rome and the creation of the Single European Market), and the growing diversity of interest groups, in contrast to the early days of European integration when industrial federations of national trade associations were seen to predominate[21].

Drawing on the CONECCS database Eising uses this figure and depicts the development of European associations as follows[22]:

"Until the European Communities were set up, the number of European associations was relatively small. After small beginnings, the number of European interest groups increased substantially over time.... The CONECCS data indicate that their number more than quadrupled over the course of the next forty years. Clearly, the build-up of European institutions and the development of European policies led to a growing presence of EU level interest groups.

There are two major foundation waves. The first of them sets in with the foundation of the European Coal and Steel Community (ECSC) and loses pace in 1961/62, a few years after the foundation of the European Economic Community (EEC) and the European Atomic Energy Community (EURATOM). The second wave starts with the implementation of the Internal Market Programme (IMP) in the second half of the 1980s".

---

20 The new EU Transparency Register does not appear to require this information.

21 See Wessels, B., "Contestation potential of interest groups in the European Union: emergence, structure, and political alliances", in G. Marks, M. Steenbergen (eds.), *European integration and political conflict*, Cambridge, CUP, 2004; Beyers, J., Eising, R., Maloney, W., "Researching interest group politics in Europe and elsewhere: much we study, little we know?", in *West European Politics*, 2008, n. 6, pp. 1103-1128; Eising, R., *The political economy of state-business*, *op. cit.*

22 See Eising, R., *The political economy of state-business*, *op. cit.*, pp. 62-63.

Figure 1 – European Interest Groups according to domain and year of foundation fron 1843 to 2001 (Cumulated Frequencies)

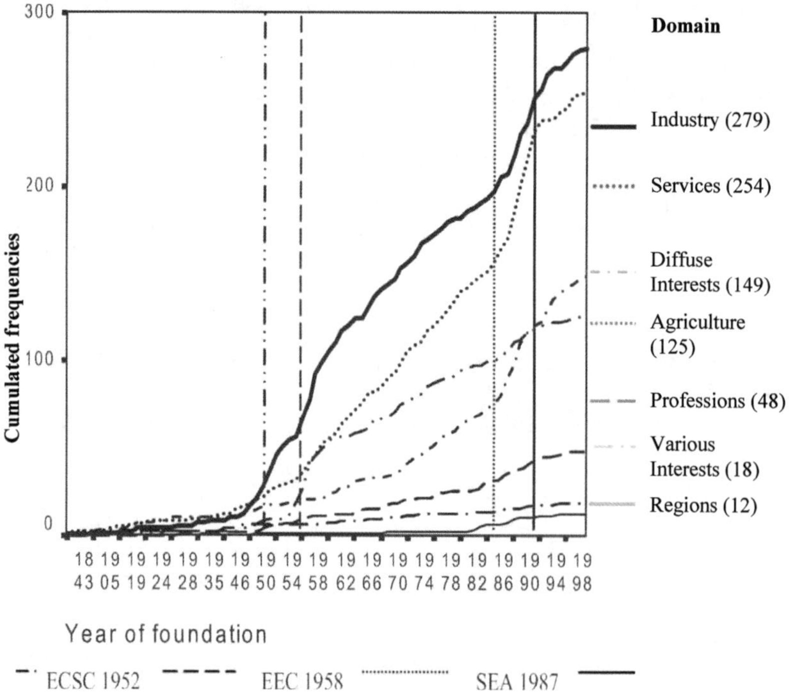

Source: General Secretariat of the European Commission. CONNECS data set, May 2002. Please note that vertical lines denote the implementation of different treaties or treaty changes.

However, using the CONECCS database for analysing the role and evolution of European interest groups during the formative years of European integration is problematic and flawed[23]. First, it ignores problems of interest group mergers and their winding up. Secondly, a number of interest groups included (8 in total) were created before 1945, 42 before 1955, in other words prior to the opening of the Messina discussions which led to the Treaty of Rome. A few were related to the European Coal and Steel Community but the majority had been created for different purposes.

This leads to the most fundamental problem: each interest group registered with the European Union sometime between the early 1990s and 2008 to appear in the CONECCS database. There is an enormous assumption being made here that these groups were active in lobbying

23 This uses Christine Mahoney's version of the 2003 database.

the European Commission prior to this date. The size of this leap of faith becomes clear if one looks at the particular groups listed in the CONECCS database which had relatively early dates of creation, say before the first enlargement in 1973. Many were international bodies rather than specifically European and it includes groups such as the Fédération Internationale des Acteurs (founded 1952), the International Association of Amusement Parks and Attractions (founded 1918), the International Federation of Camping and Caravanning (founded 1933) and the International Friends of Nature (founded 1895). It would be hard to see any of these as active in European integration in the 1950s and 1960s let alone as key players in its development, just that after 1990 they registered with the European Commission as a representative interest group. Nor is this a problem isolated to the pre-1958 period. International bodies continued to be formed which may have been active European interest groups before the 1990s but it is impossible to know, and certainly dangerous to assume, that they were lobbying at a European level from the date of their creation. In other words, the CONECCS database should not be used as political scientists have used it to track to development of European interest groups over the long term. What it does, however, show is that there were a significant number of private transnational organisations in existence at this time: the database names 278 organisations which were created by 1973 (out of a total of 687 organisations registered by 2003 which gave a date of creation), that is 40 per cent. It does provide some support for those that have argued that the extent of transnational governance in the post-war period has been downplayed[24]. This is particularly true when we also know that many European trade associations emerged or re-emerged after the Second World War.

Interesting as this is, it tells us little directly about the scale of European organised business in the post-war period. For this we need to turn back to the early seminal studies of European integration. Eising reminds us that Haas suggested that the creation of the European Coal and Steel Community only led to one peak association, two producers' groups, three consumers' groups and one organisation of dealers[25], while Lindberg referred to the European Commission having counted 222 European interest groups in 1961. This was by late 1961 and,

24 See Rollings, N., Kipping, M., "Private transnational governance in the heyday of the nation-state: the Council of European Industrial Federations (CEIF)", in *Economic History Review*, 2008, n. 2, pp. 409-431; Kaiser, W., "Bringing history back in to the study of transnational networks in European integration", in *Journal of Public Policy*, 2009, n. 2, pp. 223-39; Kaiser, W., Leucht, B., Geller, M., (eds.), *Transnational networks in regional integration: governing Europe 1945-1983*, Basingstoke, Palgrave Macmillan, 2010.

25 See Eising, R., *The political economy of state-business*, *op. cit.*, p. 63.

according to Lindberg, "all but a handful of which had been created since 1958". See in table 1 the breakdown of these groups by sector.

Table 1- European economic interest groups, late 1961

Sector	N.	Notes
Industry	89	Excluding industries dealing with food and drink
Commerce	42	Excluding trade in agricultural products
Handicafts	6	Including 2 groups related to industry and 2 related to trade
Agriculture	82	Including trade in agricultural products and organisations of agricultural workers
Trade unions	2	Excluding a large number of specialised groups
Banking	1	
Total	**222**	

Source: Lindberg, L., *The political dynamics, op. cit.*., p. 97.

Meynaud and Sidjanski's study of pressure groups in the European Community was the most thorough and considered change over time. It detailed 298 groups created between 1950 and 1968. Table 2 sets out the annual frequency of group creation.

Table 2 - Pressure groups created in the ECSC and the European Economic Community annually 1950-1968

Year	Groups created	Year	Groups created
1950	2	1960	42
1951	0	1961	28
1952	2	1962	24
1953	5	1963	18
1954	6	1964	11
1955	2	1965	8
1956	3	1966	3
1957	15	1967	8
1958	41	1968	3
1959	77	***Total***	***298***

Source: Meynaud J., Sidjanski D., *Les groupes de pression dans la Communauté européenne 1958-1968*, Brussels, ULB, 1971, p. 385.

As already mentioned, on the basis of these figures it has been concluded that associational development by interest groups tended to react to and follow European political integration.

These three works from the period provide some sense of developments in the early years of European integration but they cannot be compared very easily because they used different sources at different dates. Haas used the 1955 edition of the annual "Yearbook of

International Organisations" as the source for his analysis. It would appear that Lindberg's figures were from an October 1961 Agence Europe statement but that this was an updated summary of the EEC Commission's "Répertoire des organisme communs créés dans le cadre de la Communauté économique européenne par les associations industrielles, artisanales et commerciales des six pays" and a similar directory covering agriculture. The "Répertoire" was first published in 1960[26]. Meynaud and Sidjanski's study identified 323 interest groups in existence by 1968 of which they knew the date of establishment for 298, as shown in table 2. Their data came from two sources. Like Haas they used the "Yearbook of International Organisations", in their case the 11th edition published in 1967. However, while Haas just searched through the "Yearbook", recording 58 new international organisations emerging between 1949 and 1955, of which 29 were broadly Western European and "whose primary purpose is lobbying"[27], Meynaud and Sidjanski used a special section on 'Business and Professional Groups for the European Common Market Countries', which was only published between 1966 and 1969[28]. From this section 238 groups were pinpointed. The remaining 85 of the 323 came from information supplied by the EEC, quite probably (directly or indirectly) from the "Répertoire", but no further detail is provided[29].

Thus the two main contemporary sources available to consider the development of European interest groups in the 1950s and 1960s are the "Répertoire", a second edition of which was published in 1969 with regular updates thereafter, and the "Yearbook of International Organisations". Figure 2 compares Meynaud and Sidjanski's augmented data from the "Yearbook" with that from the 1969 "Répertoire"[30] and the CONECCS database. Figure 2 shows further evidence that the CONECCS database is at odds with the two contemporary sources. While the overall pattern is similar with a peak in 1959 like the two contemporary sources, the peak is far less pronounced and the whole profile is much flatter. The other two sources tell a much more consistent story with a much bigger peak around 1959. In other words, using the CONECCS database appears to understate the impact of the

26 See Commission of the European Communities (hereafter CEC), *Répertoire des organisme communs créés dans le cadre de la Communauté économique européenne par les associations industrielles, artisanales et commerciales des six pays*, Brussels, CEC, 1960.

27 See Haas, E., *The uniting of Europe*, *op. cit.*, p. 318.

28 This section was only published in the period 1966-1969: see http/www.uia.be/node/328064, accessed 20 February 2011.

29 See Meynaud, J., Sidjanski, D., *Les groupes de pression*, *op. cit.*, p. 383.

30 See CEC, *Répertoire des organisme communs créés*, *op. cit.*, 1969.

creation of the EEC in January 1958 on the creation of European interest groups. In other words, the contemporary sources illustrate that the creation of the EEC had a greater impact on the creation of Eurofederations than the existing political science literature would suggest, providing further evidence of the inadequacies of using the CONECCS database to reconstruct the historical development of European organised business interest groups.

Figure 2 - Comparison Numbers of European Interest Groups created (1950-1968)

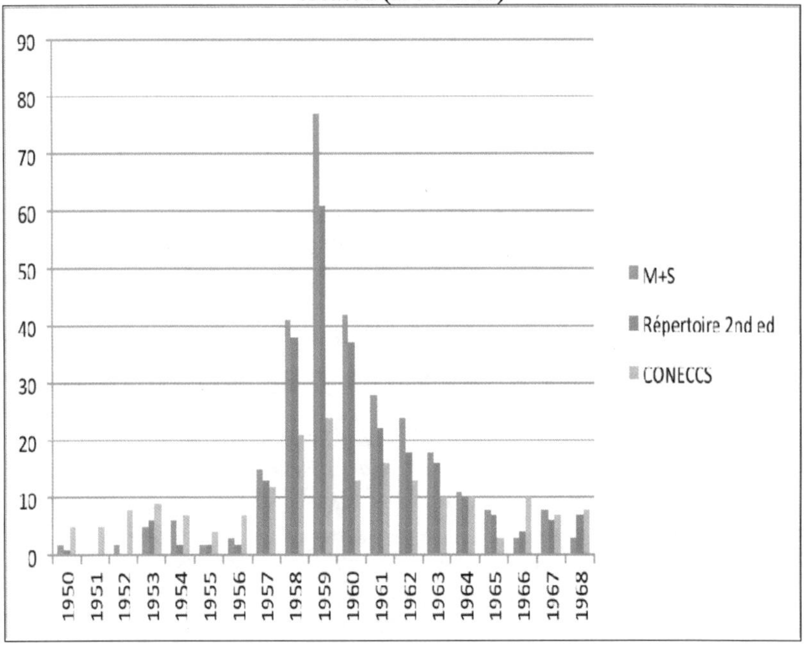

Sources: Meynaud, J., Sidjanski, D., *Les groupes de pression*, *op. cit.*, p. 383; CEC, *Répertoire des organisme communs créés*, *op. cit.*, 1969. Please note that the 2003 CONECCS database as used by Christine Mahoney [http://faculty.maxwell.syr.edu/chmahone/Mahoney_CONECCS_database.xls]

The data for the 1969 "Répertoire" is robust and is shown in Figure 3 which compares the creation dates listed in the 1969 edition with that for 1960 and 1973[31]. While the 1960 edition significantly underestimates the number of business organisations in existence the 1969 and 1973 editions are very similar apart from, as one might expect, the very end of the period.

---

[31] See *Ibid.*, 1973.

Figure 3 - Creation dates of Eurofederations from the 1960, 1969 and 1973 Répertoires

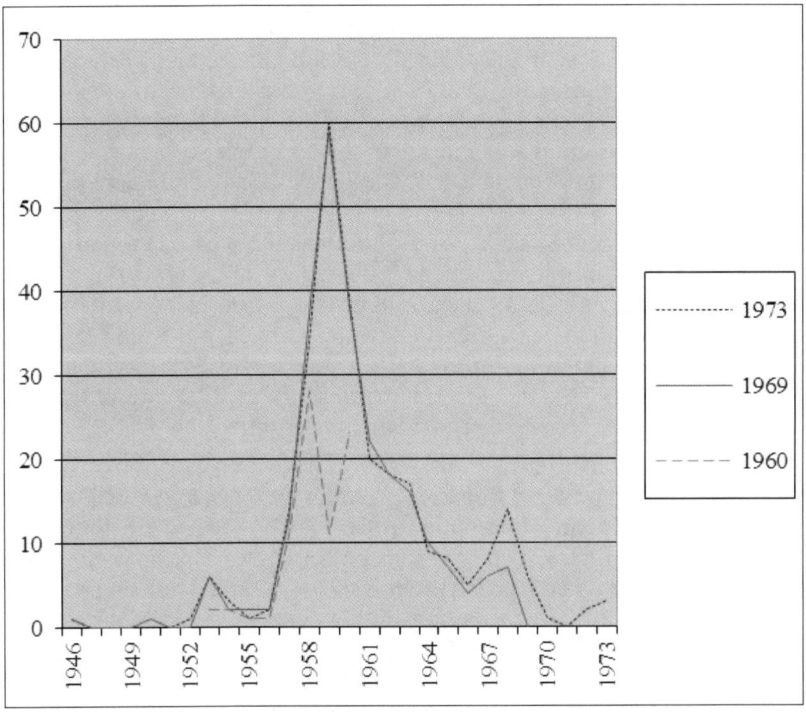

Source: CEC, *Répertoire des organisme communs créés*, *op. cit.*, various editions.

Further corroboration of the impact of the creation of the EEC comes from looking at the location of these Eurofederations. As early as 1960 the 136 Eurofederations listed in that year's Répertoire were predominately located in two cities – 48 in Paris and 52 in Brussels. Over time the dominance of Brussels increased: by 1969 125 of the 264 listed in the Répertoire were located in Brussels, with only 74 in Paris. The first enlargement in 1973 had little impact on this trend of locating close to the EEC's institutions (134 of 287 by now, with only 66 now based in Paris). In other words, the data presented in the Répertoire and in the special section of the Yearbook provide clear evidence that the creation of the EEC had a major impact on Eurofederations. This is true both in terms of their creation and their location.

However, there is an issue with these figures, which reflects an underlying problem with all the studies of the development of these Eurofederations. There is a danger of determinism in focusing exclusively on the European Economic Community. During the 1960s the "Répertoire" and the special section in the "Yearbook of International Organisations" both list only those Eurofederations which have membership limited to the nations of the Six. This is fine if one is only interested in the direct impact of the EEC but tells us little about the state of the development of Eurofederations more generally in Western Europe. This relates both to the issue of these Eurofederations acting as cartels rather than just as political lobbyists, but also to the uncertainty that surrounded the precise nature and path of European integration in the 1950s. In the 1950s it was by no means certain how European integration was going to develop or even if it would develop. As a result, concentrating on the ECSC and the EEC as forerunners of today's EU ignores this uncertainty and the varied responses that European business took to deal with that uncertainty.

Thus it is significant that while only member associations from the Six were listed in the "Répertoire", this was no longer so strictly adhered to after the first enlargement with sixteen of the listed Eurofederations listing members outside the Nine. This may not seem like many but hints at a problem with these sources for reconstructing the development of Eurofederations in the postwar years. In this respect a study by the Confederation of British Industry (CBI) is informative. In 1966 the CBI approached its trade association members for information on the extent to which "there was collaboration between organisations representing sectors of British industry and industries in other countries"[32]. Well over 100 organisations were listed (with others supplied confidentially) in response and there is enormous diversity in the nature of the geographical coverage of these organisations: international, West European, largely EEC, and EFTA were all listed. In other words, the sources which focus on the Six do not incorporate the whole population of Eurofederations.

This is illustrated more explicitly if one looks at the 1968-69 (12th) edition of the "Yearbook of International Organisations", published by the Union of International Associations (UIA)[33]. As already noted, Meynaud and Sidjanski used the special section on the "Business and Professional Groups for the European Common Market Countries". In

32 See Modern Records Centre (hereafter MRC), 1966, MSS200/C/3/S1/12/6, I.116.66. See also MRC 1962, MSS200/F/3/O5/2/23, "Trade association links with Europe", January 1962.

33 See Union of International Associations, *Yearbook of international organizations*, Brussels, UIA, 1969 (12th ed., 1968-69).

this edition there were 259 EC listed Eurofederations. However, although the majority were business Eurofederations, there were also a number of professional bodies (such as the Standing Committee of EEC Doctors), trade union groups, and agricultural interest groups. More importantly, within the general listing of the "Yearbook" there were nearly 130 further business organisations listed whose membership was restricted to Western Europe.

Of the 259 listed in the special section, 119 were located in Brussels and only 60 in Paris. However, a different picture emerges if we look at the other Western European group. Only 28 were based in Brussels with 52 in Paris. Much the same distinction emerges if we look at the creation dates of these organisations. This data is shown in Chart 4. Whereas there is a clear spike in the late 1950s and early 1960s from the special section, there is no such trend for the other Eurofederations, indeed, the highest rate of creation is in the early 1950s but is broadly consistent across the period. In other words, the creation of these organisations cannot be directly explained by the creation of the EEC since they were not created as a reaction to the developments of the late 1950s nor is there any clear aim to locate close to EEC institutions in Brussels. What other forces then can explain the creation of these other Eurofederations?

Figure 4 - Creation dates of Eurofederations comparing the special section of the "Yearbook of International Organisations" with its general listings of business Eurofederations 1945-1967

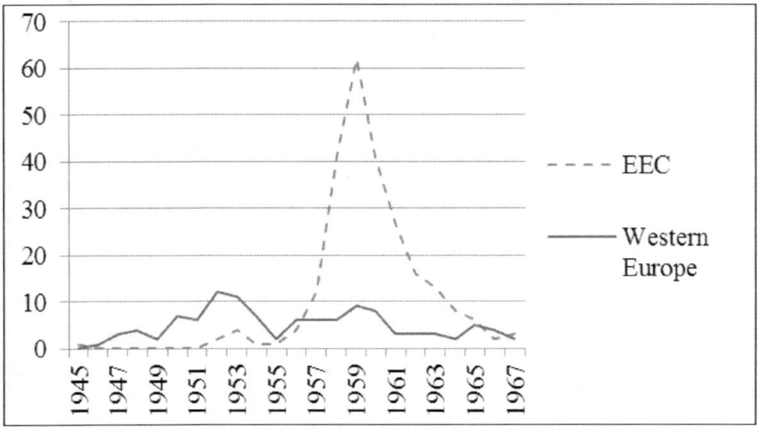

Source: Kipping M., Rollings N., "Europe from the bottom up: the role of business in the integration process", conference paper EBHA, Glasgow, August 2010.

As Haas noted at the time there were many other 'European' organisations also in existence or being created at this time. This reflected the uncertainty about the future of European integration that existed in the 1950s. This is important in a number of respects. First, it is clear that a significant number of the organisations listed were EEC member sub-associations of wider European or international bodies. Seventeen per cent of the organisations listed in the 1960 Répertoire had 'internation-al' in their title, often being 'working groups' or 'liaison committees' of wider organisations. Second, related to this, these international or wider European organisations were already in existence prior to the creation of the EEC. It was only the EEC working party, or equivalent, which was created, say, in 1959. For example, the 1960 "Répertoire" lists the Groupe de Travail "Integration Européenne de L'Union des Foires Internationales" as an organisation founded in 1958, while the Union des Foires Internationales was formed in 1925. Was the Groupe de Travail really an independent European business organisation as would be implied by taking the data from the Répertoire at face value?

Similarly, there were a significant number of Eurofederations with membership which extended beyond the Six at this time. Some were listed in the Répertoire but as only having membership from the Six while others did not feature. The mechanical engineering industries are illustrative here[34]. Various bilateral and multilateral meetings occurred after the Second World War. Then in 1954 the Organisme de Liaison des Industries Metalliques Européennes (herefater ORGALIME) was formed from trade associations from 11 European countries. It became the European representative organisation for the industry and it was listed by Meynaud and Sidjanski but is not included in the Répertoire until the 1974 edition. Following the 1973 enlargement there was now a willingness in that directory to list non-EEC members: trade associations from 13 European countries were given. However, it is even more significant that in previous editions of the Répertoire, all published after 1960, it was not ORGALIME that was listed but the Comité de Liaison des Industries Metalliques Européennes (hereafter COLIME), a subset of associations only from the Six. Indeed, in the 1960s its British members believed that the great value of ORGALIME was that it included both EEC and EFTA countries[35]. Again should one consider both organisations separately, only COLIME as the body representing associations in the Six, or ORGALIME as the key overarching European representative body of the industry? In addition, enlargement did not see the expansion of the interest groups of the Six

34 This section is drawn on Kipping M., Rollings N., "Europe from the bottom up: the role of business in the integration process", *op. cit.*

35 See MRC, 1966, MSS200/C/3/S1/12/6, I.116.66.

to accommodate new members but a shift back to recognising the wider European parent business organisation.

A final issue highlighted by this material relates to the false certainty of the date of creation of these organisations. ORGALIME was created in 1954 as 'an informal club' and the organisation celebrated its 50th anniversary early in 2005. However, in the 1974 Répertoire its date of creation was given as 1960, not 1954. In other words, although the directories concur in highlighting the late 1950s as the key period of growth of European interest groups, this was often a particular form of European interest group. In many respects this exaggerates the extent of change. Often, the formal date of creation was just part of a longer process of development which was more fluid and dynamic than the directories imply.

More generally, therefore, there are a range of issues highlighted here. The key underlying issue is the choice of appropriate parameters for the study of European interest groups. There is a danger that an overly narrow focus on formal political recognition, typified by the Répertoires, provides a misleading picture of the development of European interest groups in this period. Similarly, regarding these interest groups as a weathervane of power can also overstate the degree to which there was a shift towards lobbying European institutions from the late 1950s. Rather, many such business organisations were simply covering all bases, of which the EEC was just but one (if an important one). We need to appreciate the diversity of organisations in this period and with that the diversity of functions, economic as well as political, carried out by these organisations. In addition, the historical context is crucial, a point often overlooked by political scientists. The next section elaborates these points.

2. Understanding the historical context

There is a danger of exaggerating the degree of change that has occurred[36]. Just as federations of national associations still remain the most common form of European organised business interest, there is a danger of overstating the simplicity of arrangements in the past. If one looks at these federations of national associations in more detail one finds that membership varied considerably. Some were restricted to the member states while others, like ORGALIME, had wider European membership. Other business interest groups covered the whole of, or most of, Western Europe. Another geographical grouping of interest groups can be found around the EFTA countries. Thus, while political

[36] See Wallace, H., "Introduction", in *Id.*, A., Young (eds.), *Participation and policy-making in the European Union*, Oxford, OUP, 1997, p. 1.

scientists focus on UNICE (with its membership limited to EEC member states) this was by no means the only peak-level federation of national associations in Europe. There was the Council of European Industrial Federations (CEIF) which covered Western Europe and was created originally in the late 1940s as a representative body to the OEEC[37]. In addition, in 1958 CIFEFTA was created for the national industrial federations of EFTA countries and in 1961, with the transformation of the OEEC into the OECD a new body, BIAC (the Business and Industrial Advisory Committee) was established (though the CEIF continued in existence). Thus some European national industrial federations were members of three of these organisations, each with a different but overlapping membership. As a further complication, some countries were given observer status at those organisations of which they were not members. There was yet further overlap with other international and European business organisations. Most notable here are the chambers of commerce. Eurochambres was created in 1958 at the same time as UNICE to represent the interests of member states' national chambers of commerce[38]. In addition, the International Chamber of Commerce (ICC) was active in representing business opinion on European integration[39].

Nor was the Eurofederation of national associations the only model of organised business that existed at this time. For example, the Council of Directors of European Industrial Federations is a different type of body. It consisted of the director-generals of the peak-level national federations of various countries[40]. It was established in the late 1920s and in that period covered most of Europe, including Central Europe. After the Second World War it was quickly re-established but as a Western European body. It only met once a year but managed to build strong personal links between individuals, particularly as many of these director-generals remained in post into the 1960s.

A further variant was the Groupe des Présidents des Grandes Entreprises Européennes, formed in 1967, consisting of CEOs of leading European companies. Cowles may dismiss its significance as a

37 See Rollings, N., Kipping, M., "Private transnational governance", *op. cit.*.

38 See Greenwood, J., "Organized business and the European Union", in *Id.*, H. Jacek (eds.), *Organized business and the new global order*, Basingstoke, Macmillan, 2000, p. 84.

39 See Schneider, V., "Global economic governance by private actors: the International Chamber of Commerce", in *Ibid.*, pp. 223-240; Minoli, E., "Industry's views of trade regulation in the European Economic Community", in J.R. Crowley (ed.), *The antitrust structure of the European Common Market*, New York, Fordham University Press, 1963, pp. 46-58.

40 See Rollings, N., Kipping, M., 'Private transnational governance", *op. cit.*.

lobbying group compared to the ERT but its mere creation added to the types of European organised business in existence. Moreover, in 1970 the Groupe approached British business about the possible membership of three leading representatives given the prospect of UK membership of the European Community. There it was explained that the members had good links with their national governments and national federations and that the Industrial Commissioner of the EEC regularly attended their meetings. Also they had links with an American liberal trade group, the Emergency Committee on Atlantic Trade[41]. In this respect, it was significant that the Groupe directly approached the Industrial Policy Group, a group of about twenty leading British industrialists, trying to push a pro-business political agenda rather than going through the CBI.

The complex and varied forms of peak-level organised business was mirrored at the sectoral level too. ICI, the British chemicals producer, and one of its directors, provides a good example of the complex, overlapping and multilevel nature of business representation. In the early 1960s ICI belonged to about 80 trade associations (domestic as well as international)[42]. One of the company's directors from 1945 to 1960, Lincoln Steel, was active in many arenas in the role of a representative of business. He was a member of the Economic Planning Board and of the Consultative Committee for Industry, both tripartite national bodies, he was a director of the Economic League, Chairman of the British National Committee of the International Chamber of Commerce (ICC) 1951-63 and President of the ICC itself 1963-65. Most significant in relation to European integration he was also chairman of the Federation of British Industries Overseas Trade Policy Committee from 1950 to 1965 (when the Federation of British Industries merged with two other business representatives to form the Confederation of the British Industry) and of its European Integration Panel from its creation in the mid-1950s. It is not only the number of organisations on which Steel sat which is relevant but also the mix of national and international bodies. Individuals like Steel and those on the Groupe de Présidents were often at the heart of a complex and diverse web of business representative organisations, not simply reliant on one form of representation, a distant federation of national associations as Cowles has suggested, and provided a direct link between European large companies and the institutions of European integration.

41 See MRC, 1970, MSS200/C/3/DG2/67-8, John Jewkes to Industrial Policy Group members, 16 February 1970.

42 See Grove, J.W., *Government and industry in Britain*, London, Longman, 1962, p. 128.

Conclusion

Accounts of the development of Eurofederations in the early years of European integration have been dominated by political scientists, both those writing at the time and those more recently who have cast their eye back from the present day. As a result, the focus has been on the political role of these organisations and on their direct relationship to the development of the EEC and its successors. More than this the current conventional wisdom is based on a misuse of a source. This paper has turned to the sources used in the contemporary studies to reconstruct a picture of the development of these Eurofederations. This has shown that, in relation to the EEC, the conventional political science position underplays the impact of the Treaty of Rome and the pull of Brussels. However, a more fundamental finding relates to the overly narrow depiction of Eurofederations as only those tied to the EEC. It has been shown that a significant number of these organisations were created in the early 1950s, had a wider range of national members than that associated with the Six, and did not feel such a strong compulsion to be based in Brussels close to the institutions of the EEC.

It is suggested that the explanation for this latter group of Eurofederations was due to two related factors. First, the nature of European integration was far less certain in the 1950s than it appears today looking back. Thus there was a need for a range of bodies reflecting different possible forms of European political integration – Western Europe, the EEC and EFTA. However, this is still an insufficient explanation. A second factor is the non-representative functions of these Eurofederations, relating to the logic of membership. For some this may have meant the re-establishment of European cartels after the Second World War but for others it represented the need for information pooling and exchange given the fundamental uncertainties of the postwar world, with the aim of helping business to see through the fog that lay across Europe at this time[43].

---

[43] See Genovese, D., Mullin, W., "The Sugar Institute learns to organise information exchange", in N. Lamoreaux, D. Raff, P. Temin (eds.), *Learning by doing in markets, firms, and countries*, Chicago, University of Chicago Press, 1999, pp. 103-38; Vives, X., "Information sharing: economics and antitrust", in *The pros and cons of information sharing*, Stockholm, Swedish Competition Authority, 2006, pp. 83-100.

CONCLUSION

New Outlooks on the History of European Business Interest Associations

1. The European BIAs' history and Business History

The aim of this volume is to allow scholars to improve their knowledge about the genesis and development of European BIAs and also to make some comparison between different organisations models[1]. These models were related to entrepreneurs' goals and the scale of enterprises. They also depended on the relationships existing between BIAs, trade unions and public authorities, as well as, obviously, on the prevailing economic climate. It is clear that good relations with workers and public authorities were an important part of the structure which allowed European BIAs' to orient themselves towards more effectively solving bureaucratic problems, improving the quality of members' managers and workers, and advertising members' products in foreign markets. It is also clear that BIAs, representing nationally significant enterprises and particularly multinational enterprises, pursued aims and strategies quite dissimilar to those followed by BIAs representing SMEs. Different laws allowed BIAs' members to enact different policies and this becomes clearly evident when analysing alternative approaches to the creation and support of what might be considered as cartels rather than just support networks. As with the majority of studies of BIAs, the research in this volume registered differences between horizontal and vertical BIAS. Also reconfirmed is the fact that the interconnection between the interests of a geographical territory and its productive sectors obviously modified the goals and results of BIAs' activities, whether in a specific region or industrial district, or indeed nationally. Furthermore, it is clear that the services offered by BIAs to their members expanded from the nineteenth century into the twentieth century, whereas there was little change in their lobbying activities.

1 Please note that we use the definition "Business Interest Associations (BIAs)" as synonymous with "Employers' Organizations", "Employers' Associations", "Business Associations" (the other terms used in the articles of this volume as well as in the bibliography) even if the most recent and up-dated studies in economic history and in business indicate that there are some minor semantic differences between these four definitions, which may attribute to them four different meanings.

Finally, it has been demonstrated that European BIAs' structures were strongly modified because of: a) the birth of trade unions and related changes in relations with the workforce; b) the end of the Second World War and the subsequent distribution of ERP aid during post-war reconstruction, the related importation of the US model of business organisation and the consequent improvement in the productivity of industrial plants, as well as the beginning of the project of European integration (and the possibility for European companies to access wider markets and to modernise plants and machinery).

On top of these findings, it should be noted that this volume is only one of the results of some recent research programs analyzing the European BIAs' history, and in particular their structures and their impact on European social and economic development: all of these programs have tried to recover the "lost time" after the 1980s and to take advantage of the huge changes in the political landscape which accompanied the demise of the USSR and allowed for greater comparative analysis of Eastern Europe (evident in this volume in the Russian case). New studies have also implemented alternative approaches to what went before. Most of the studies undertaken in the 1970s and in 1980s focused almost exclusively on national BIAs[2]: there were few studies about regional or local BIAs and their influenced on the local economy[3]. So the new analysis has concerned itself with local BIAs also, in particular where they assumed significant regional or national relevance. Moreover, during the 1990s and at the beginning of the new millennium, BIAs were somewhat neglected, and while there were some important exceptions[4], most of the writing on the history of BIAs took

2 See, for example, Feldman, G.D., Nocken, U., "Trade Associations and Economic Power: Interest Group Development in the Iron and Steel and Machines Building Industries. 1900-1933", in *Business History Review*, 1975, n. 4, pp. 413-445; Miyamoto, M., "The Development of Business Associations in Prewar Japan", in H. Yamazaki, M. Miyamoto (eds.) *Trade Associations in Business History*, Tokio, University of Tokio, 1988, pp. 9-52; Kikkawa T., "Functions of Japanese Trade Associations before World War II: the case of cartel organizations", in *Ibid.*, pp. 53-86; Rodgers, T., "Employers Organisations, Unemployment and Social Politics in Britain during the Inter-War Period", in *Social History*, 1988, n. 13, pp. 315-342.

3 See Coleman, W.D. Jacek H. (eds.), *Regionalism, Business Interests and Public Policy*, London, Sage, 1989, pp. 201-230; Schmitter, P.C., Lanzalaco, L., "L'organizzazione degli interessi imprenditoriali a livello regionale", in *Stato e mercato*, 1988, n. 22, pp. 68-98.

4 Among the studies conducted during the 1990s and at the beginning of the new millennium (besides those quoted in the articles of this volume) see, for example, Scranton, P., "Webs of Productive Association in American Industrialization: Patterns of Institution-Formation and Their Limits, Philadelpia, 1880-1930", in *Journal of Industrial History*, 1998, n. 1, pp. 9-37; Nyssens, M., *Raison d'être des associations et théorie économique*, Louvain la Neuve, IRES-UCL Louvain, 1998; Doner, R.F., Schneider, B.R., "Business Associations and Economic Development:

the form of celebratory commemorative books by former BIA leaders or their ghost authors, which displayed bias and were uncritical. There was little of much benefit to scholars. So recent programs on BIAs' history had to refocus on both local (district or regional level) and national BIAs, on the motivation and rationale of entrepreneurs in creating BIAs, on the different circumstances of the genesis and development of the structures of the new organisations and the services they provided, on the benefits to members and stakeholders, and on the general contribution of BIAs to European industrialisation[5].

In particular, new studies are confirming that BIAs often had an important role in European industrialisation and this justifies the increased volume of research on the history of BIAs. However, even if it is evident that studies about European BIAs are important for Business History, there remains scope for much further research[6]. Business

Why Some Associations Contribute More Than Other", in *Business and Politics*, 2000, n. 3, pp. 261-288; Calvo Caballero, P., *Asociacionismo y cultura patronale en Castilla y León durante la Restauración (1874-1923)*, Salamanca, Junta de Castilla y León, 2003; Dumoulin, M. (eds.), *Economics Networks and European Integration / Les réseaux économiques dans le processus de construction européenne*, Bruxelles, PIE Peter Lang, 2004; Brion, R., Hatry, P., Moreau, J.L., Peeters, T., *100 ans pour l'entreprise. Fédération des Entreprises de Belgique*, Bruxelles, Racine, 1995; Bassignana, P.L., Berta, G. (eds.), *La metalmeccanica torinese tra le due guerre nelle carte dell'AMMA (1921-33)*, Turin, Samma, 1995; *Id.* (eds.), *La metalmeccanica torinese nel secondo dopoguerra 1945-1972*, Turin, Samma, 1997.

5 It is not possible to list here all the recent studies about BIAs' history, particularly on their role in social and economic development. Among those which were not quoted in the articles of this volume, see Reveley, J., Ville, S., "Enhancing Industry Association Theory: A Comparative Business History Contribution", in *Journal of Management Studies*, 2010, n. 5, pp. 837-858; Schroeder, W., Weßels, B. (eds.), *Handbuch Arbeitgeber- und Wirtschaftsverbände in Deutschland*, Wiesbaden, Verlag fur Sozialwissenschaften, 2010; McKinlay, A., "The Paradoxes of British Employer Organizations, 1897-2007", in *Historical Studies in Industrial Relations*, 2011, n. 31-32, pp. 89-113; Carnevali, F., "Social Capital and Trade Associations in America, c. 1860-1914: a microhistory approach", in *Economic History Review*, 2011, n. 3, pp. 905-928; Rollings, N., Moguen-Toursel, M., "European Organised Business and European Integration in the Post-Second World War Period", in *Economic History Yearbook*, 2012, n. 1, pp. 103-123. As well as the research projects referred to in this volume, it is also important to remember the session entitled "Self-Seeking or Developmental: the Role of Industry Associations" which was held at the 15th WEHC (Utrecht, August 2009), the proceedings of which have never been published unfortunately, and, finally, some EBHA sessions partially dedicated to BIAs' activities (such as in Bergen 2008 and Glasgow 2010).

6 On new perspectives in Business History studies see Scranton, P., Fridenson, P., *Reimagining Business History*; Baltimore, JHUP, 2013; "Tendances de l'histoire des entreprises", in *Entreprise et Histoire*, 2009, n. 2 (in particular Amatori, F., "Business History: State of the Art and Controversies", pp. 11-23; Rowlinson, M., Delahaye, A., "The Cultural Turn in Business History", pp. 90-110). See also the

History studies actually continue to undervalue the role of BIAs' bureaucratic support for enterprises and also the BIAs' lobbying activity in defence of entrepreneurs' interests. European BIAs facilitated the development of their member enterprises and also increased their contractual power in their dealings with public authorities and trade unions. BIAs regularly collaborated with both public authorities and trade unions on the establishment of new rules concerning taxes and tariffs, commercial trade, labour contracts (wages and workplace safety), strikes (and lock-outs), patents, infrastructure priorities, public utilities (in particular on the system of distribution and price setting). Generally, European BIAs helped enterprises to increase their productivity and sales, to arrange agreements with trade unions, and to improve their managers and workers' professional skills. Furthermore, as indicated by many European Integration History studies (which started during the 1990s), BIAs (and then the union of European BIAs and the Eurofederation) strongly influenced the integration process and the life of European institutions and policies[7]. Finally, when BIAs achieved their goals, both producers and stakeholders often profitted, although in other cases only the enterprises gained while most of stakeholders lost out. All this means that European BIAs influenced (whether in a positive or negative manner) the history of European enterprises and the history of European societies. This implies that the study of the history of European BIAs allows for a deeper understanding of the real social and economic impact of all productive sectors where entrepreneurs created national or local BIAs. It also facilitates an interesting comparison with the history and experiences of BIAs in the rest of the world and in particular with American and Japanese BIAs. All these considerations *de facto* explain why Business History studies can not be considered "complete" if they do not give more importance to the history of BIAs. The main problem remains how to correctly estimate the impact of BIAs' activity, that is

programs and debates of the sixteen annual congresses of the European Business History Association (EBHA).

7 Besides articles published in the *Journal of European Integration History*, see Dumoulin, M., Girault, R., Trausch, G. (eds.), *L'Europe du Patronat. De la guerre froide aux années soixante*, Bern, Peter Lang, 1993; Fauri, F., "La fine dell'autarchia: i negoziati commerciali dell'Italia dal 1947 al 1953", in *Rivista di storia economica*, 1995, n. 3, pp. 329-365; *Id.*, "La costruzione del MEC negli anni '50: atteggiamento e posizioni della Confindustria", in *Rivista di Politica Economica*, 1996, n. 2, pp. 89-134; Bussière, E., Dumoulin, M. (eds.), *Milieux économiques et intégration européenne en Europe occidentale au XXe siècle*, Arras, Artois Presses universitaires, 1998; Moguen-Toursel, M., *L'ouverture des frontières européennes dans les années '50. Fruit d'une concertation avec les industriels?*, Bruxelles, PIE Peter Lang, 2002; Bussière, E., Dumoulin, M., Schirman, S. (eds.), *Europe organisée, Europe du libre-échange? Fin XIXe siècle – années 1960*, Bruxelles, PIE Peter Lang, 2006.

how to calculate the improvement of the quality of life in Europe linked to: BIAs lobbying of, and relationship with, public authorites; BIAs bargaining with trade unions; and the (variable) equilibrium achieved between vertical, horizontal, local and national BIAs.

2. Notes on studies about European BIAs' genesis

All studies about the process of the foundation of BIAs in European countries, including the articles in this volume, show that it began, depending of the degree of industrialisation in each country, between the second part of nineteenth century and the first decades of the twentieth century. The genesis of BIAs was linked to the reaction of businessmen to the first worker-organisations and/or to state pressure or the rigours of the free market. Many BIAs were initially created as voluntary associations for the development of industry and commerce. In the following years there was a diversification of voluntary associations and, at the start of the twentieth century, a tendency among the entrepreneurial class towards self-organisation[8]. For example, Valeriy Kerov affirms that in Russia merchants' self-management bodies in cities were class organs with a philantropic identity and that "manufactory councils" were no more that state institutions with poor entrepreneurs' assistance. However, BIAs arose and these organisations carried out the specific functions defined by the religious character of the links between their members (Old Believers Communities).

This reading highlights the density and dynamism of business organisations. Furthermore, the new historiographical vision, in comparison to the traditional view, as Pierre Vernus rightly pointed, is based on a local-level approach. As Cedric Humair argued, "on the eve of the First World War the Swiss economy was criss-crossed by a dense network of business interest associations which were deployed at the local, cantonal and national level" and the cantonal system of BIAs was extremely heterogeneous. Vernus identified that in France "before the end of the nineteenth century each main activity of the sector had its own syndicate and sometimes several. Consequently, a trend to a higher level of organisation could be observed before 1914"[9].

8 See Lanzalaco, L., "Business Interest Associations", in G. Jones, J. Zeitlin (eds.), *The Oxford Handbook of Business History*, Oxford, OUP, 2007, pp. 293-296.

9 Besides the contributions in this volume see Vernus, P. (ed.)., *Les organisations patronales. Une approche locale (XIXe-XXe siècles)*, Cahiers du Centre PIerre Léon d'histoire économique 1, Lyon, Centre Pierre Léon d'histoire économique et sociale, 2002; Humair, C., "Du libéralisme manchestérien au capitalisme organisé: genèse, structuration et spécificités de l'organisation patronale suisse (1860-1914)", in D. Fraboulet, P. Vernus (dir.), *Genèse des organisations patronales en Europe (19e–20e siècles)*, Rennes, PUR, 2012, pp. 133-142.

From the end of the nineteenth century BIAs started as societies across Europe, promoting common values and offering a network and platform for discussion. Following different models, they aggregated into regional and national organisations and in same cases (in Switzerland and the Netherlands) became powerful actors in their societies and a characteristic feature of the business system. BIAs then evolved into organisations lobbyng in the interest of their membership and, in several cases, the function of the BIAs as a guild developed logically from their social function: mutual agreements in the interests of all members contributed to the creation of a closed professional group[10]. In that case the BIAs became cartel organisations. Finally, the BIAs had an important role in providing information and services for their members. In Russia, as in Switzerland and France, the function of representation of interests to legislative, governmental and public institutions was prioritised. In the Netherlands and in Italy, however, the social function was an important one and was implemented in parallel with the negotiating function.

Moreover, the foundation of BIAs, as for example in the Dutch case, was related to the political and socio-economic context so that wider historical legacies determined the characteristics of these organisations. At the end of the nineteenth century the increase in the number of BIAs was a direct consequence of agrarian crises. In Switzerland, after the market crash of 1873 and during the Long Depression, the free competition advocated by "Manchester capitalism" was set aside to allow for the organisation of capitalism according to the logic of professional and national solidarity. The inadequacy of the collaboration between business circles and the federal state was denounced and, at the same time, the representatives of finance capital, large-scale industry and the big banks emerged as the main protagonists of the adoption of organised capitalism wherein the BIAs should be within the state field. The solution was to turn the Union Suisse du Commerce et de l'Industrie into a state-recognised chamber of commerce while preserving its private character. In France, from 1884 to 1914 the legalisation of *syndicats professionnels* as associations of small and medium entreprises oriented the way both employers and workers organised. The members of these *syndicats* had to pratice the same activity and this fact hampered the formation of inter-branch organisations that were created as associations after the passing of the 1901 Act on associations. This process of historical inquiry can also evaluate the effectiveness of employer associations in respect of their associates. Some authors have stressed the explanatory power of structural factors such as legislation on associations or trade

10 See Lazonick, W., *Business organizations and the myth of the market economy*, Cambridge, CUP, 1991, pp. 14-15.

policy[11]. In other cases, such as the Italian or Swiss, the position on the international markets, the role of managers and the relationship with the Trade Unions had a structural influence.

With reference to the interpretative framework of Eliassen and Svaasand[12], the essays highlight how the BIAs grew at national level through a spontaneous spreading of small organisations that gradually integrated, as in the Italian and Swiss cases, from a previous federation consolidating its national role while also establishing new associations in the area. The same historical reconstructions confirm another important element: the exogenuos actors are determinants in every process of consolidation towards the peak associations and political formations (as in France and, as indicated in the second chapter of this volume, Sweden) or cultural and religious movements (the Netherlands and Russia) affected these organisations. The concentration and stabilisation of the emergence of BIAs in the early twentieth century was the effect of the centralisation process that strengthened the position of workers' trade unions. The Dutch case, where BIAs played a key role in the organisation of social relations (as suggested by the "poldermodel" which was relevant for Dutch social and economic development) is illustrative of a general trend: the number of collective bargains increased in the 1920s and 1930s as did government influence on socio-economic affairs during the First World War and especially during the 1930s. Moreover, most agreements between employees and employers still had a strong local or regional nature. At the same time, the emergence of BIAs reflects the economic development of the first decades of the twentieth century: associations had to eliminate risks, to promote exiting business interests and to control increasing competition. In Russia, the new wave of foundation activity coincided with the revolution of 1905-1907. From Moscow to St. Petersburg the Russian Convention of Representatives of Industry and Trade was established with a strong federative character, unifying large firms and companies as well as entrepreneurial associations. The Russian political and social system greatly influenced the creation of a new type of business organisation. The birth of BIAs normally coincided with the foundation of labour unions and, above all, of political parties on a national level. Local interests were reforged into national ones and the non-socialist parties recruited BIAs to support

---

11 See Martinelli, A., Schmitter, P.C., Streeck W., "L'organizzazione degli interessi imprenditoriali", in *Stato e Mercato*, 1981, n. 3, pp. 423-445; Schmitter, P.C., Streeck W., *The Organizaton of Business Interests; Studying the Associative Action of Business in Advanced Industrial Societies*, Max-Planck-Institut für Gesellschaftsforschung Discussion Papers, n. 1, Köln, Max-Planch-Institut, 1999.

12 See Eliassen, K.A., Svaasand, L., "The Formation of Mass Political Organizations: An Analytical Framework", in *Scandinavian Political Studies*, 1975, pp. 95-121.

members of the parliament: even the heads of local business companies were members. In Sweden, the Federation of Swedish Industries and the Swedish Employer's Association were founded in 1902 and 1910 respectively. The founding of the institutions coincided with the foundation of labour unions (from 1886) and, above all, of political parties on a national level (that is the Social Democratic party in 1896, the Liberal party in 1902, the Conservative party in 1904, the Agrarian party in 1916 and the Communist party in 1919).

From the Italian experience to the Swedish one, the process of concentration of various associations, as with the consolidation of functions in the regulation of the market, was tied to the relationship between the expectations held by entrepreneurs of the political system and, on the other side, to the political attitude of institutions toward the business world. A major question concerned the ways in which industry associations were recognised as performing a public function[13]. In most cases, the assignment of a role on the public stage was accompanied, especially in Switzerland and Italy, by the delegation from the state of some aspects of regulation of the market, both in terms of improved forms of production (technological innovation, research and training) and the labour market (employment and contracts). Another characterisitc of the relationship between the state and industrial associations, and one that emerged in different ways and at different times, was the involvement of BIAs in the definition and realisation of specific policies for employment: compulsory insurance, industrial relations and, finally, social security protection. This set of issues was often played out at national level and this was regularly the case in the period between the last decade of the nineteenth century and the years between the two world wars. Also in this context, essays allow us to understand the substantive content of strategies pursued by BIAs. Several points emerge from these contributions. Firstly, there was often disagreement among entrepreneurs in different sectors when a new economic and social policy has to be introduced. Then, there often occurred the emergence in different countries of cross-class strategic alliances in response to social legislation. The effects of these relationships depended on interactions between employers and workers and also on BIAs capabilities in negotiations with the trade unions and the public authorities.

---

[13] See Windmuller, J.P., Gladstone, A., *Employers Associations and Industrial Relations: a comparative study*, Oxford, Clarendon Press, 1984; Windmuller, J.P., *Collective Bargaining in Industrialized Market Economies: a reappraisal*, Geneva, ILO, 1987.

3. Notes on studies about European BIAs' attitudes and activities during the twentieth century

In this volume there are few studies concerning European BIAs' evolution over a large part of twentieth century: scholars can analyze only the Dutch and Swedish cases in full, while for the French, English and Italian BIAs the contribution are chronologically limited and concern only some vertical BIAs or some horizontal BIAs with their headquarters in a limited area (despite its importance for industrialisation). However, the case studies present very useful findings which help us to understand the process of integration of BIAs into European society and by which to make interesting comparisons with the existing literature. Most of them concern the peak associations and there is also the contribution about the Eurofederations, that is BIAs operating on international markets.

All recent contributions about European BIAs' activity during the twentieth century showed that they progressively enlarged their services for their members and also their social and economic role, in particular those organising business at the international level. BIAs continued to coordinate all practices useful for controlling the market mechanism, that is agreements and cartels (where they were allowed) or mergers and acquisitions[14]. European BIAs continually expanded their lobbying activity for supporting their members' interests and, at the same time, dealt with public authorities and in particular with trade unions whose relevance increased substantially after the Second World War. Furthermore, BIAs improved their methods for providing information and services to members, for promoting the values and image of entrepreneurship, and for creating a network for debates on the relevance of private enterprises for European development. They also promoted and favoured agreements between members on prices, production, markets and qualities. Their main aims remained constant: to maintain and improve members' efficiency, quality and technical progress, and to increase members' profitability by the elimination of risks and the control of prices and production. However, as European institutions progressively limited agreements reducing the level of competition, BIAs' goals were adjusted somewhat to promote quality and a better

---

[14] About the role of BIAs in the European cartels see, for example, Barjot, D. (ed.), *International cartels revisited / Vues nouvelles sur les cartels internationaux. 1880-1960*, Caen, Editions du Lys, 1994; Müller, M., Schmidt, H.R., Tissot, L. (eds.), *Regulierte Märkte: Zünfte und Kartelle / Marchés régulés: corporations et cartels*, Zurich, Cronos Verlag, 2011.

knowledge of products for consumers and of the markets for producers[15].

BIAs also aggregated into regional and national organisations and this allowed them to progressively increase their contractual power, to make agreements with public authorities and trade unions and to become one of major socio-economic actors. This happened, in different periods, in the case of the French UIMM, the Italian Assolombarda and the Swedish SAF: all three helped their members to improve their productive skills, participated in the regulation of the labour market and contributed to the formulation of laws favouring entrepreneurship (and which very nearly removed all limits to the free activity of enterprises). They also assumed leading roles in peak associations and even had some representatives in parliamentary institutions.

On the question of their relations with the public authorities it is interesting to note that during the twentieth century the BIAs' position regarding political parties changed. Initially, links with the conservative parties were strong: for example, some of leaders of the IF and SAF, also founded the Swedish conservative party; in Italy, BIAs were linked to the liberal party and in the period after the First World War, as well as playing a part in the development of popular parties (catholic or socialist), BIAs' members were among those who sponsored the fascist movement. In the following years, even if BIAs always supported parties which helped the entrepreneurs' interests, the need to have good relations with social democratic or labour parties encouraged BIA leaders to be more pragmatic. Most BIAs had no further direct relations with conservative parties and so they assumed a particular political position: the protection of their members' interest became the protection of all society's interests because the safeguarding of industrial activities represented the safeguarding of workplaces and of the national economy. This had a number of implications: conflicts with trade unions and public authorities were only based on economical arguments, that is BIAs became politically neutral (even if they clearly looked unfavourably on socialist parties) and increased their likelihood of negotiating satisfactorily with the representatives of labour movement (trade unions

[15] On the lobbies including BIAs in the European institutions see, for example, Coen, D., Richardson, J., *Lobbying the European Union. Institution, Actors, and Issues,* Oxford, OUP, 2009; Greenwood, J., *Interest Representation in the European Union*, Basingstoke-New York, Palgrave McMillian, 2009; Bouwen, P., "Corporate Lobbying in the European Union: the logic of access", in *Journal of European Public Policy*, 2002, n. 3, pp. 365-390; *Id.*, "Exchanging access goods for access: A comparative study of business lobbying in the European Union institutions"; in *European Journal of Political Research*, 2004, n. 3, pp. 337-369; Klüver, H., "The Contextual Nature of Lobbying: Explaining Lobbying Success in the European Union", in *European Union Politics*, 2011, n. 4, pp. 483-506.

and parties); enterprises had to agree, in particular from the 1960s, to pay higher real wages, that was to be compete by the quality of their products more so than their prices.

Relations with public autorities and trade unions occasionally presented major difficulties. So while BIAs tried to minimise divisions among their internal membership, they concentrated their activity on the control of government expenditure and taxation (as in the case of the FBI, formed in UK in 1916). They also used their newspapers to underline how public institutions and, in the Italian case, public enterprises lost money because of their inefficiency and to explain to people that all this obliged private producers and their workers to pay more taxes which curbed social and economic development. In other cases (or periods) positive relations were based on collaboration: this happened in particular during the economic crises of the 1930s and 1970s and involved BIAs and other parties prioritizing the survival of enterprises. Workers and capitalists had to reduce their earnings and the contribution of the public authorities consisted of the reduction of taxation and the distribution of subsidies, that is increasing the public debt and transferring of debt to future generations (whose quality of life would depend on the the positive or negative results of these new industrial policies and agreements).

A further crucial issue concerning European BIAs' attitudes is linked to the initiation and development of peak associations, that is national BIAs grouping all horizontal and vertical BIAs and coordinating their different interests. These BIAs were normally founded between the end of the nineteenth and the early twentieth centruy and they strongly influenced national economies: furthermore, from the 1950s, their lobbying activity also impacted on the process of European integration[16]. In this volume the relations between BIAs and governments about the laws regulating the birth of the ECSC and EEC are not the main focus of the contributions: however, there are indications that some leaders of the Assolombarda supported the government during the treathies of Paris and Rome. The case of the Assolombarda is a clear example of the significant role assumed by European BIAs in the period of post-war reconstruction and in the 1950s: it in fact illustrates how

16 On the European BIAs and their relation with the European institutions see, besides the contributes listed in notes 7, and 14, and 15: Michel, H. (ed.), *Représenter le patronat européen. Formes d'organisation patronale et modes d'action européenne*, Bruxelles, PIE Peter Lang, 2013; Morguen-Toursel, M. (ed.), *Firm Strategies and Public Policy in Integrated Europe (1950-1980) Confrontation and Learning Economic Actors*, Bruxelles, PIE Peter Lang, 2007; Arcq, E., Dufresne, A., Pochet, P., "The Employers: the Hidden Face of European Industrial Relations", in *European Review of Labour and Research*, 2003, n. 2, pp. 302-321.

European BIAs assisted public institutions and how they opposed decisions which threatened the BIAs' interests.

There is also an innovative perspective and analysis of European integration: it is dedicated to the relationship between the evolution of business interest representation at the European level and the history of European integration and it presents some sense of the motives and forces behind the creation of these Eurofederations. By criticising the methods of analysis previoulsy used, the article shows that, in relation to the EEC, the conventional political science position underplays the impact of European integration. It also underlines that most Eurofederations created in the early 1950s had a greater interest in the evolution of the EEC even if, at the start, they did not know and understand all the real effects of integration. Eurofederations had a very relevant role because they allowed their members to have more information about the decisions of the European institutions and, moreover, they permitted continued lobbying activity on the new directives and laws of the EEC.

The contributions in this volume can not give scholars a definitive history of European BIAs. This volume only desires to encourage scholars to pursue further analysis of BIAs, even if this line of inquiry is not a priority in Business History. Studies focusing on the relationship between BIAs and European integration, or new BIAs' attitudes and lobbying activities concerning national industrial policies, can inspire future researchers and set the goals of future scholarship. In any case, as is clearly indicated in the introduction, there is much work to be done on new topics: there is also a real challenge for cliometrics concerning the correct evalutaion of the impact of BIAs on European social and economic development. Even if the archives of some BIAs (especially the local ones) are not easily analyzed (or they do not exist), it is always possible to undertake studies based on documents about BIAs which are held by public institutions or other BIAs: it is also possible to use their newspapers, while acknowledging that their articles were designed to defend the BIAs' interests and thus require external verification. All this implies that there remain further possibilities for scholars to create new knowledge about European BIAs, that is to put in evidence some new outlooks about them.

Andrea M. Locatelli & Paolo Tedeschi

Notes on contributors

Bram Bouwens works at the Department of History of the University of Utrecht. His research focuses on business history. He wrote or jointly authored several books and articles, including histories of the Dutch paper and board industry, alcohol industry and dredging industry. He participates in the Dutch research program BINT (www.bintproject.nl). In 2012 he published with J. Dankers a volume on business interest associations, cartels and mergers and acquisitions in the Netherlands. Currently he is involved in the BEAT project (www.uu.nl/business-history) and works in close cooperation with K. Sluyterman on the history of the Dutch brewer Heineken. He is also manager of commissioned research at the Research Institute for History and Culture of the University of Utrecht.

Aldo Carera is Chair Professor of Economic History at the Catholic University of Milan. He is also the Director of the Archivio per la storia del movimento sociale cattolico in Italia "Mario Romani" (Archives of the Italian catholic movement), the President of the Fondazione Giulio Pastore (Foundation for studies concerning the labour problems), and the President of the Association Bibliolavoro (a research centre on the labour history). His researches and publications focus mainly on the Italian economic history, in particular the social and economic development of the Lombardy (19th-20th centuries), and the labour history, in particular the history of Italian catholic trade unions.

Joost Dankers is Associate Professor and manager commissioned research at the Faculty of Humanities of the University of Utrecht. He co-authored several studies on Dutch companies like the Iron and Steel Company Hoogovens, de United Glass Producers, Rabobank Nederland and the saving banks. Together with B. Bouwens he wrote a volume on coordination and competition in the BINT-series on Dutch business in the twentieth century. This research was also presented in papers and articles on cartels, mergers and acquisitions and business interest organisations.

Danièle Fraboulet is Chair Professor of Contemporary Economic History at the University of Paris 13 - Sorbonne Paris Cité. She manages a 5 year research program concerning the Business Organisations in Europe (19th-20th centuries), punctuated by an annual scientific meeting of which the results are published. She has extensively published on the history of French enterprises and business interest associations (*Les* *entreprises sous l'Occupation*, Paris, CNRS-Editions, 1998; *Quand les patrons s'organisent. Stratégies et pratiques de l'Union des industries métallurgiques et minières 1901-1950*, Villeneuve d'Ascq, Septentrion, 2007) and she was one of editors of the *Dictionnaire historique des patrons français*, Paris, Flammarion, 2010. Her other main research field is the risk management of industrial hazards and accidents (late nineteenth century – twentieth century).

Cédric Humair is Senior Lecturer ("maître d'enseignement et de recherché") of Contemporary History at the University of Lausanne and at Ecole Polytechnique Fédérale of Lausanne. His main fields of research are: the Swiss economic and political history, the tourism and transport history and the social history of technology. His most recent publication is (with L. Tissot, eds.), *Le tourisme suisse et son rayonnement international. "Switzerland, the playground of the world"*, Lausanne, Antipodes, 2011.

Valeriy Kerov is Chair Professor of Contemporary Economic History at the Peoples' Friendship University of Russia (Moscow). He is Academic Secretary of the Inter-College Academic Center of Comparative Historical and Anthropological Studies. He is also member of the Economic History Center of the Lomonosov Moscow State University. He is in the editorial board of directors of a number of historical journals in Russia and Ukraine. Its main publications include: *"Behold the Man and His Cause...": Confessional and Ethical Factors of Old Believers' Entrepreneurship in Russia*, Moscow, Econ-inform Publ., 2004; *Private Entrepreneurship in Pre-Revolutionary Russia: Ethnic Confessional Structure and Regional Development, 19th-early 20th Centuries* (co-authored), Moscow, ROSSPEN, 2010.

Andrea M. Locatelli is Assistant Professor in Economic History at the Catholic University in Milan where he teaches Economic History and Business History. He has published on the economic development of the Lombardy (18th-20th centuries) and on the evolution of the banking system in Italy. His recent research topics concern the history of Lombard business organisations and the Italian fiscal and administrative system from the 1860s to the 1970s.

Philip Ollerenshaw is Associate Professor of Economic and Business History at the University of the West of England, Bristol. His main research interests are British, Irish and European economic history (19th-20th centuries). His recent publications include: *Northern Ireland in the Second World War: Politics, Economic Mobilisation and Society, 1939-45*, Manchester, Manchester University Press, 2013; (with L. Kennedy, eds.), *Ulster Since 1600*, Oxford, OUP, 2012.

Irina Potkina is Professor of History and deputy director for the international scientific links at the Institute of Russian History, RAS, Moscow. Her main fields of research are the Russian economic history and the Russian business history (nineteenth century - early twentieth century). Her last publications include: "Property Rights in Imperial Russia: Achievements, Deficiencies, Miscalculations", in *Economicheskaya Istoria*, 2010/1, n. 8, pp. 26-31; *Legal Regulation of Entrepreneurial Activities in Russia, the 19th - the first quarter of the 20th century*, Moscow, Izdatelstvo Norma, 2009.

Neil Rollings is Professor of Economic and Business History at the University of Glasgow. He has written widely on post-1945 business-government relations in the UK and in relation to European integration. He is the author of *British business in the formative years of European integration 1945-1973*, Cambridge, CUP, 2007.

Niklas Stenlås is Associate Professor in Economic History at the University of Uppsala. He has written about the business associations, the business elite and their relations to the non-socialist political parties in Sweden. He has also written about the Swedish defence industry and Sweden's military-industrial complex. Presently he is researching the role of experts in the formation of the Swedish Welfare State.

Paolo Tedeschi is Assistant Professor in Economic History at the University of Milan-Bicocca DEMS where he teaches Economic History and European Integration History. He is also Assistant Professor Associé at the University of Luxembourg where he teaches European Integration History. His recent research and publications concern in particular: the history of European integration, the economic history of the Lombardy (18th-20th centuries), and the history of Lombard business organisations, trade unions and friendly societies.

Pierre Vernus is Assistant Professor ("maître de conférences") in Contemporary History at the Université Lumière Lyon 2. His main research interests are: the business and economic history (in particular about silk processing industries), the history of business interest organisations and the digital history. He collaborates to a 5-year research program concerning the Business Organisations in Europe (19th-20th Centuries). His main publications include: (with D. Fraboulet, eds.), *Genèse et morphologies originelles des organisations patronales en Europe (XIXe-XXe siècles)*, Rennes, PUR, 2012; *Art, luxe et industrie. Bianchini Férier, un siècle de soieries lyonnaises, 1888-1992*, Grenoble, Presses universitaires de Grenoble, 2006.

Index

« Enjeux internationaux »

Studies in international relations, particularly historical, stem from the changing face of diplomacy over time, where the deeper forces at play, such as those once defined by Pierre Renouvin, are taken into account. Individual states, and those who define and implement their policies, are placed at the heart of global life. According to this concept, countries pursue a course of action by taking advantage of the most diverse range of tools they can rely on, such as economic or cultural resources, which act alone or interact with others.

The study of international relations grew into different fields of analysis during the twentieth century, but it is now subject to a new scrutiny in this era of globalisation. This concept, which coincides with the development of neo-liberal analysis since the 1980s, reveals a new awareness about the increased number of actors – NGOs and multinational companies, for example – but also the large autonomy they enjoy when it comes to action.

This series aims to portray these new perspectives and their impact on current research. Without casting aside studies in international relations that focus on states, it tries to better understand the diverse range of factors that play out on the world stage and how they relate to each other – from the high stakes in sport to the use of colonial memory. This series targets academics and analysts who wish to apply twentieth century history to contemporary thought.

Published Books

N° 1 – Catherine LANNEAU, *L'inconnue française. La France et les Belges francophones (1944-1945)*, 2008, ISBN 978-90-5201-397-8

N° 2 – Frédéric DESSBERG, *Le triangle impossible. Les relations franco-soviétiques et le facteur polonais dans les questions de sécurité en Europe (1924-1935)*, 2009, ISBN 978-90-5201-466-1

N° 3 – Agnès TACHIN, *Amie et rivale. La Grande-Bretagne dans l'imaginaire français à l'époque gaullienne*, 2009, ISBN 978-90-5201-495-1

N° 4 – Isabelle DAVION, *Mon voisin, cet ennemi. La politique de sécurité française face aux relations polono-tchécoslovaques entre 1919 et 1939*, 2009, ISBN 978-90-5201-496-8

N° 5 – Claire LAUX, François-Joseph RUGGIU & Pierre SINGARAVÉLOU (dir./eds.), *Au sommet de l'Empire. Les élites européennes dans les colonies (XVIe-XXe siècle) / At the Top of the Empire. European Elites in the Colonies (16th-20th Century)*, 2009, ISBN 978-90-5201-536-1

N° 6 – Frédéric CLAVERT, *Hjalmar Schacht, financier et diplomate (1930-1950)*, 2009, ISBN 978-90-5201-542-2

N° 7 – Robert JABLON, Laure QUENNOUËLLE-CORRE et André STRAUS, *Politique et finance à travers l'Europe du XXe siècle. Entretiens avec Robert Jablon*, 2009, ISBN 978-90-5201-543-9

N° 8 – Alain BELTRAN (ed.), *A Comparative History of National Oil Company*, 2010, ISBN 978-90-5201-575-0

N° 9 – Sarah MOHAMED-GAILLARD, *L'Archipel de la puissance ? La politique de la France dans le Pacifique Sud de 1946 à 1998*, 2010, ISBN 978-90-5201-589-7

N° 10 – Marie-Anne Matard-BONUCCI, Anne DULPHY, Robert FRANK et Pascal ORY (dir.), *Les relations culturelles internationales au vingtième siècle. De la diplomatie culturelle à l'acculturation*, 2010, ISBN 978-90-5201-661-0

N° 11 – Yves-Marie PÉRÉON, *L'image de la France dans la presse américaine, 1936-1947*, 2011, ISBN 978-90-5201-664-1

N° 12 – Léonard LABORIE, *L'Europe mise en réseaux. La France et la coopération internationale dans les postes et les télécommunications (années 1850-années 1950)*, 2010, ISBN 978-90-5201-679-5

N° 13 – Catherine HOREL (dir.), *1908, la crise de Bosnie cent ans après*, 2011, ISBN 978-90-5201-700-6

N° 14 – Alain BELTRAN (ed.), *Oil Producing Countries and Oil Companies. From the Nineteenth Century to the Twenty-First Century*, 2011, ISBN 978-90-5201-711-2

N° 15 – Frédéric DESSBERG et Éric SCHNAKENBOURG (dir), *Les horizons de la politique extérieure française. Régions périphériques et espaces seconds dans la stratégie diplomatique et militaire de la France (XVIe-XXe siécles)*, 2011, ISBN 978-90-5201-717-4

N° 16 – Alya AGLAN, Olivier FEIERTAG et Dzovinar KÉVONIAN (dir.), *Humaniser le travail. Régimes économiques, régimes politiques et Organisations internationale du travail (1929-1969)*, 2011, ISBN 978-90-5201-740-2

N° 17 – Pierre JOURNOUD & Cécile MENÉTREY-MONCHAU (dir./eds.), *Vietnam, 1968-1976. La sortie de guerre / Vietnam, 1968-1976. Exiting a War*, 2011, ISBN 978-90-5201-744-0

N° 18 – Louis CLERC, *La Finlande et l'Europe du Nord dans la diplomatie française. Relations bilatérales et intérêt national dans les considérations finlandaises et nordiques des diplomates et militaires français, 1917-1940*, 2011, ISBN 978-90-5201-750-1

N° 19 – Yann DECORZANT, *La Société des Nations et la naissance d'une conception de la régulation économique internationale*, 2011, ISBN 978-90-5201-751-8

N° 20 – Lorenz PLASSMANN, *Comme dans une nuit de Pâques ? Les relations franco-grecques 1944-1981*, 2012, ISBN 978-90-5201-769-3

N° 21 – Alain BELTRAN (dir./ed.), *Le pétrole et la guerre / Oil and War*, 2012, ISBN 978-90-5201-770-9

N° 22 – Valentine LOMELLINI, Les relations dangereuses. *French Socialists, Communists and the Human Rights Issue in the Soviet Bloc*, 2012, ISBN 978-90-5201-843-0

N° 23 – Martial LIBERA, *Un rêve de puissance. La France et le contrôle de l'économie allemande (1942-1949)*, 2012, ISBN 978-90-5201-859-1

N° 24 – Séverine Antigone MARIN, *L'apprentissage de la mondialisation. Les milieux économiques allemands face à la réussite américaine (1876-1914)*, 2012, ISBN 978-90-5201-853-9

N° 25 – Claire SANDERSON & Mélanie TORRENT (dir./eds.), *La puissance britannique en question. Diplomatie et politique étrangère au 20e siècle/ Challenges to British Power Status. Foreign Policy and Diplomacy in the 20th Century*, 2012, ISBN 978-90-5201-892-8

N° 26 – Elena GRETCHANAIA, *« Je vous parlerai la langue de l'Europe... ». La francophonie en Russie (XVIIIe-XIXe siècles)*, 2012, ISBN 978-90-5201-885-0

N° 27 – Alfred WAHL, *Histoire de la Coupe du monde de football. Une mondialisation réussie*, 2013, ISBN 978-2-87574-046-5

N° 28 – Catherine FRAIXE, Lucia PICCIONI et Christophe POUPAULT (dir.), *Vers une Europe latine. Acteurs et enjeux des échanges culturels entre la France et l'Italie fasciste*, 2013, ISBN 978-2-87574-047-2

N° 29 – Danièle FRABOULET, Andrea M. LOCATELLI & Paolo TEDESCHI (eds.), *Historical and International Comparison of Business Interest Associations. 19th-20th Centuries*, 2013, ISBN 978-2-87574-079-3.